MANIFEST DESTINY

CHRIS DINGESS — WRITER

MATTHEW ROBERTS — PENCILER

TONY AKINS & — INKERS
STEFANO GAUDIANO

OWEN GIENI — COLORIST

PAT BROSSEAU — LETTERER

ARIELLE BASICH — ASSISTANT EDITOR

SEAN MACKIEWICZ — EDITOR

MATTHEW ROBERTS & OWEN GIENI
COVER ART

IMAGE COMICS, INC.
Robert Kirkman – Chief Operating Officer
Erik Larsen – Chief Financial Officer
Todd McFarlane – President
Marc Silvestri – Chief Executive Officer
Jim Valentino – Vice-President

Eric Stephenson – Publisher
Corey Murphy – Director of Sales
Jeff Boison – Director of Publishing Planning & Book Trade Sales
Jeremy Sullivan – Director of Digital Sales
Kat Salazar – Director of PR & Marketing
Branwyn Bigglestone – Controller
Drew Gill – Art Director
Jonathan Chan – Production Manager
Meredith Wallace – Print Manager
Brian Skelly – Publicist
Sasha Head – Sales & Marketing Production Designer
Randy Okamura – Digital Production Designer
David Brothers – Branding Manager
Olivia Ngai – Content Manager
Addison Duke – Production Artist
Vincent Kukua – Production Artist
Tricia Ramos – Production Artist
Jeff Stang – Direct Market Sales Representative
Emilio Bautista – Digital Sales Associate
Leanna Caunter – Accounting Assistant
Chloe Ramos-Peterson – Library Market Sales Representative
IMAGECOMICS.COM

Robert Kirkman – Chairman
David Alpert – CEO
Sean Mackiewicz – Editorial Director
Shawn Kirkham – Director of Business Development
Brian Huntington – Online Editorial Director
June Alian – Publicity Director
Jon Moisan – Editor
Arielle Basich – Assistant Editor
Andres Juarez – Graphic Designer
Paul Shin – Business Development Assistant
Johnny O'Dell – Online Editorial Assistant
Dan Petersen – Operations Manager
Nick Palmer – Operations Coordinator

International inquiries: ag@sequentialrights.com
Licensing inquiries: contact@skybound.com

www.skybound.com

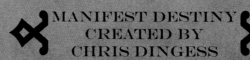 MANIFEST DESTINY
CREATED BY
CHRIS DINGESS

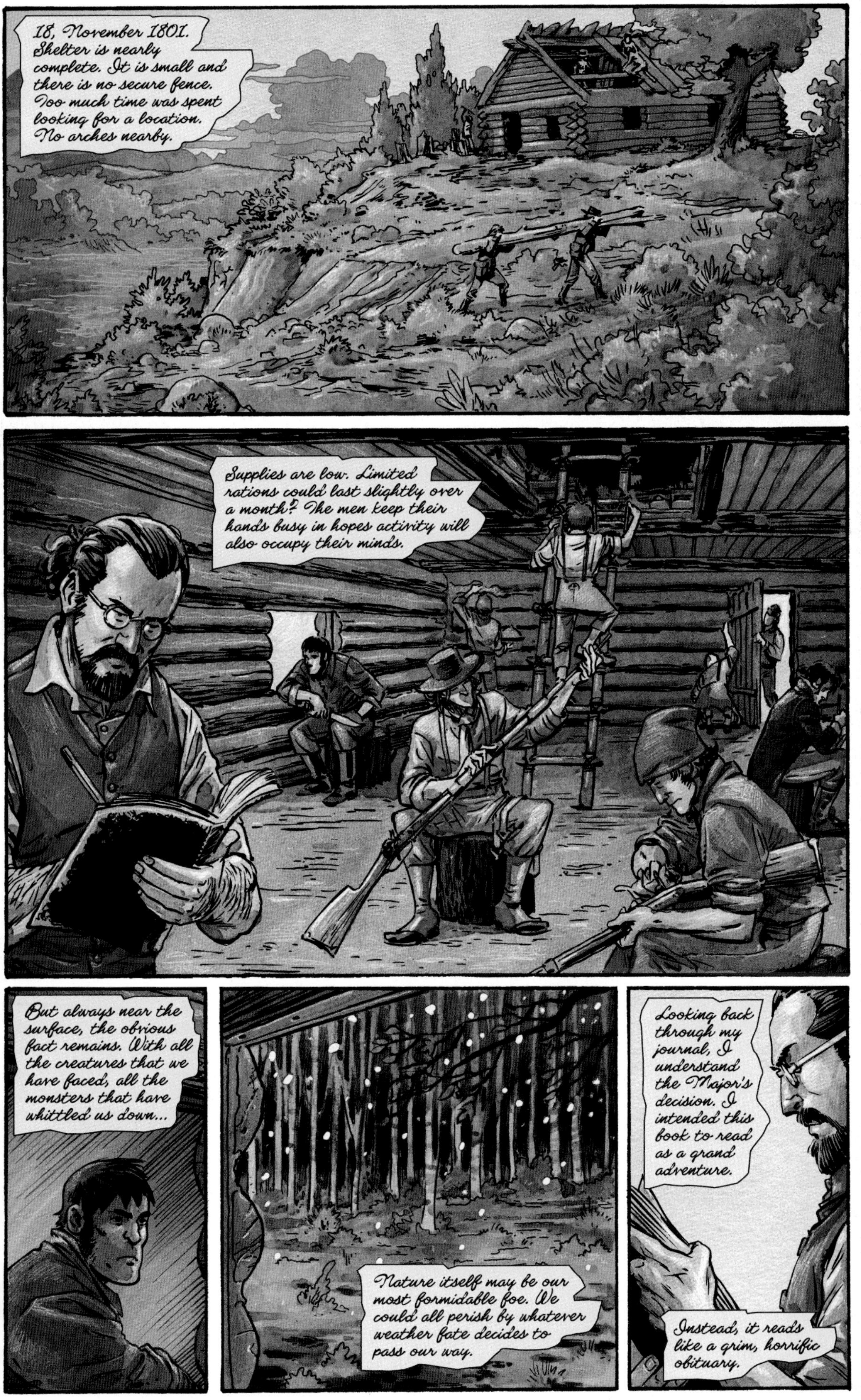
18, November 1801. Shelter is nearly complete. It is small and there is no secure fence. Too much time was spent looking for a location. No arches nearby.
Supplies are low. Limited rations could last slightly over a month? The men keep their hands busy in hopes activity will also occupy their minds.
But always near the surface, the obvious fact remains. With all the creatures that we have faced, all the monsters that have whittled us down...
Nature itself may be our most formidable foe. We could all perish by whatever weather fate decides to pass our way.
Looking back through my journal, I understand the Major's decision. I intended this book to read as a grand adventure.
Instead, it reads like a grim, horrific obituary.

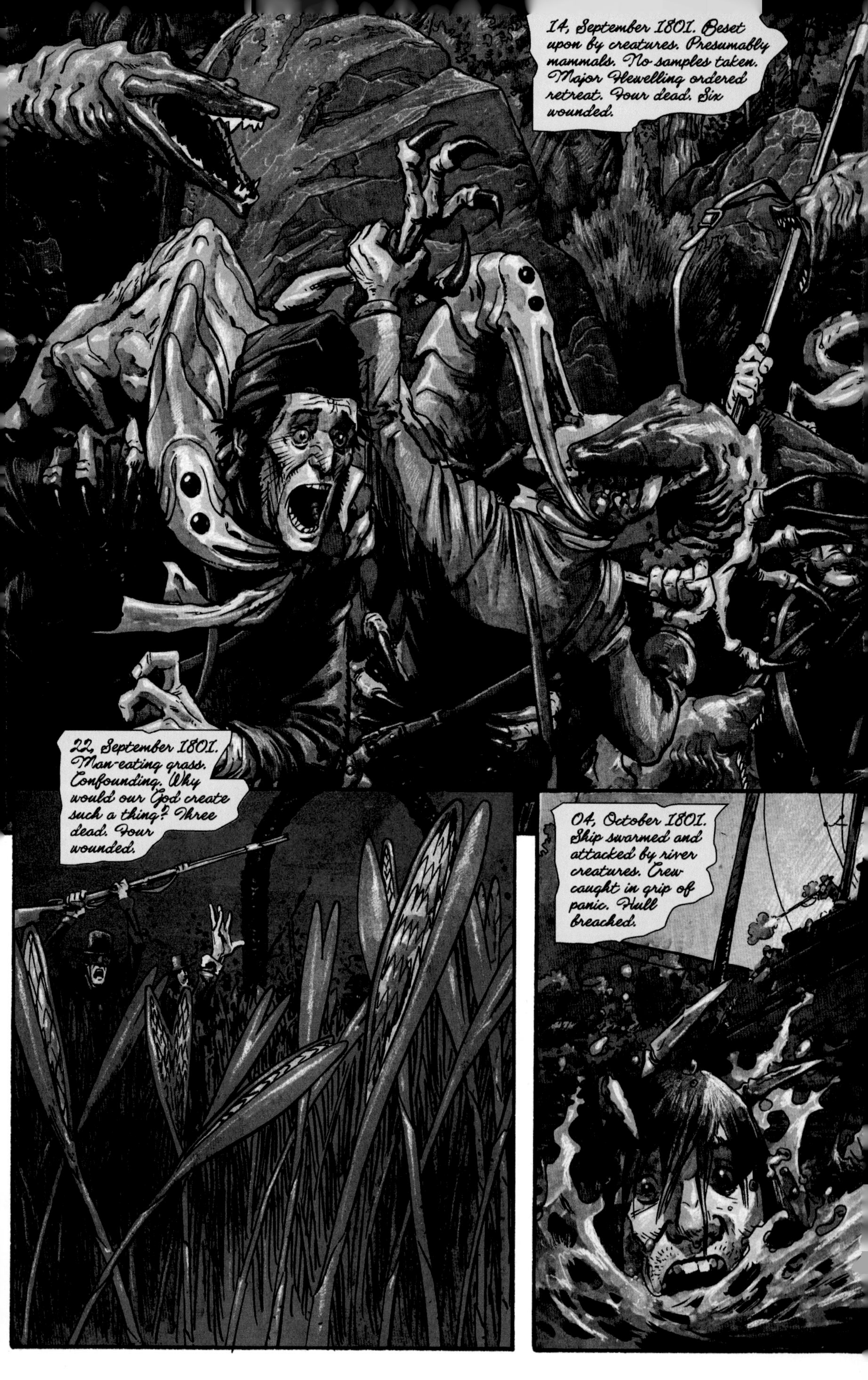
14, September 1801. Beset upon by creatures. Presumably mammals. No samples taken. Major Flewelling ordered retreat. Four dead. Six wounded.
22, September 1801. Man-eating grass. Confounding. Why would our God create such a thing? Three dead. Four wounded.
04, October 1801. Ship swarmed and attacked by river creatures. Crew caught in grip of panic. Hull breached.

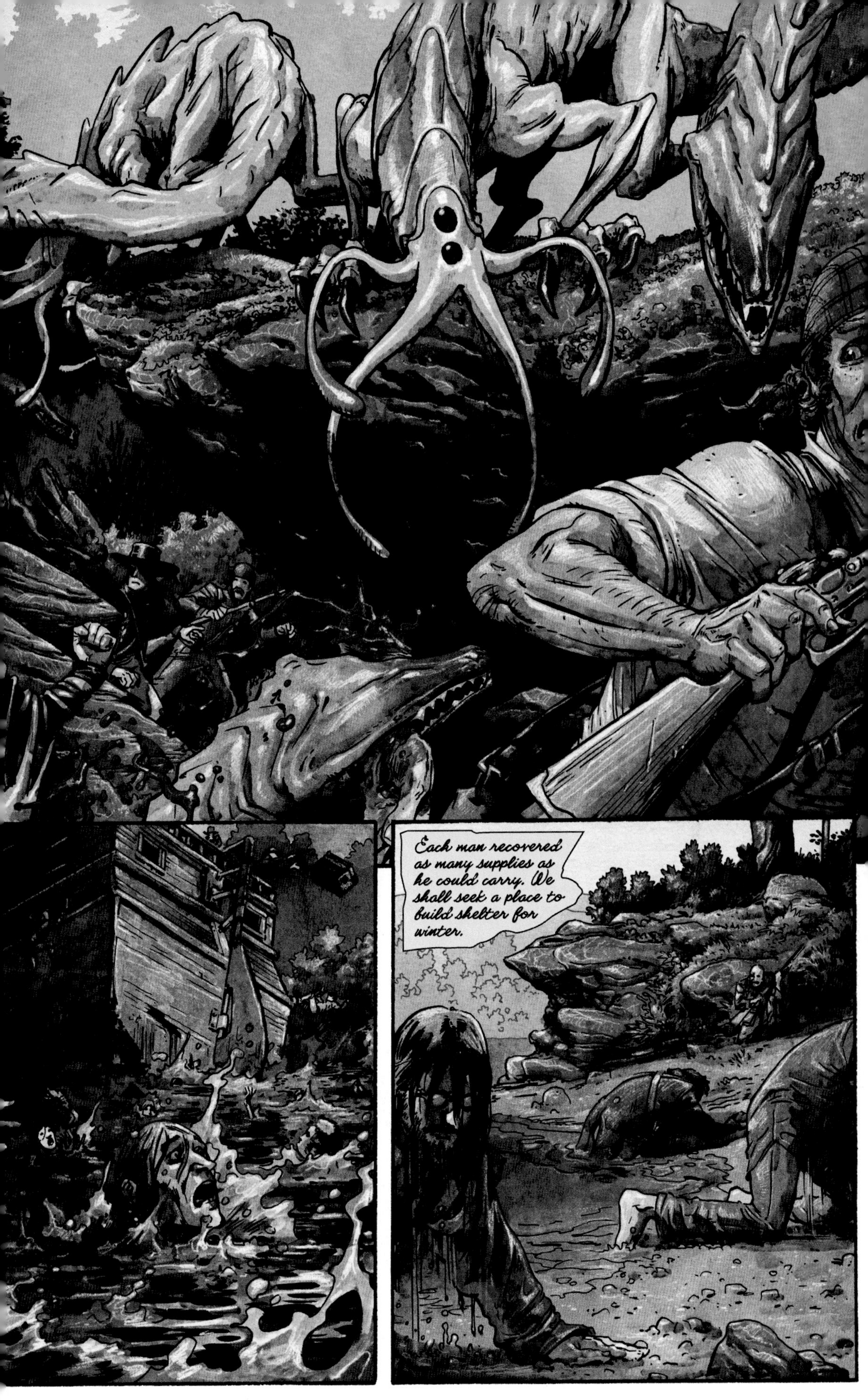
Each man recovered as many supplies as he could carry. We shall seek a place to build shelter for winter.

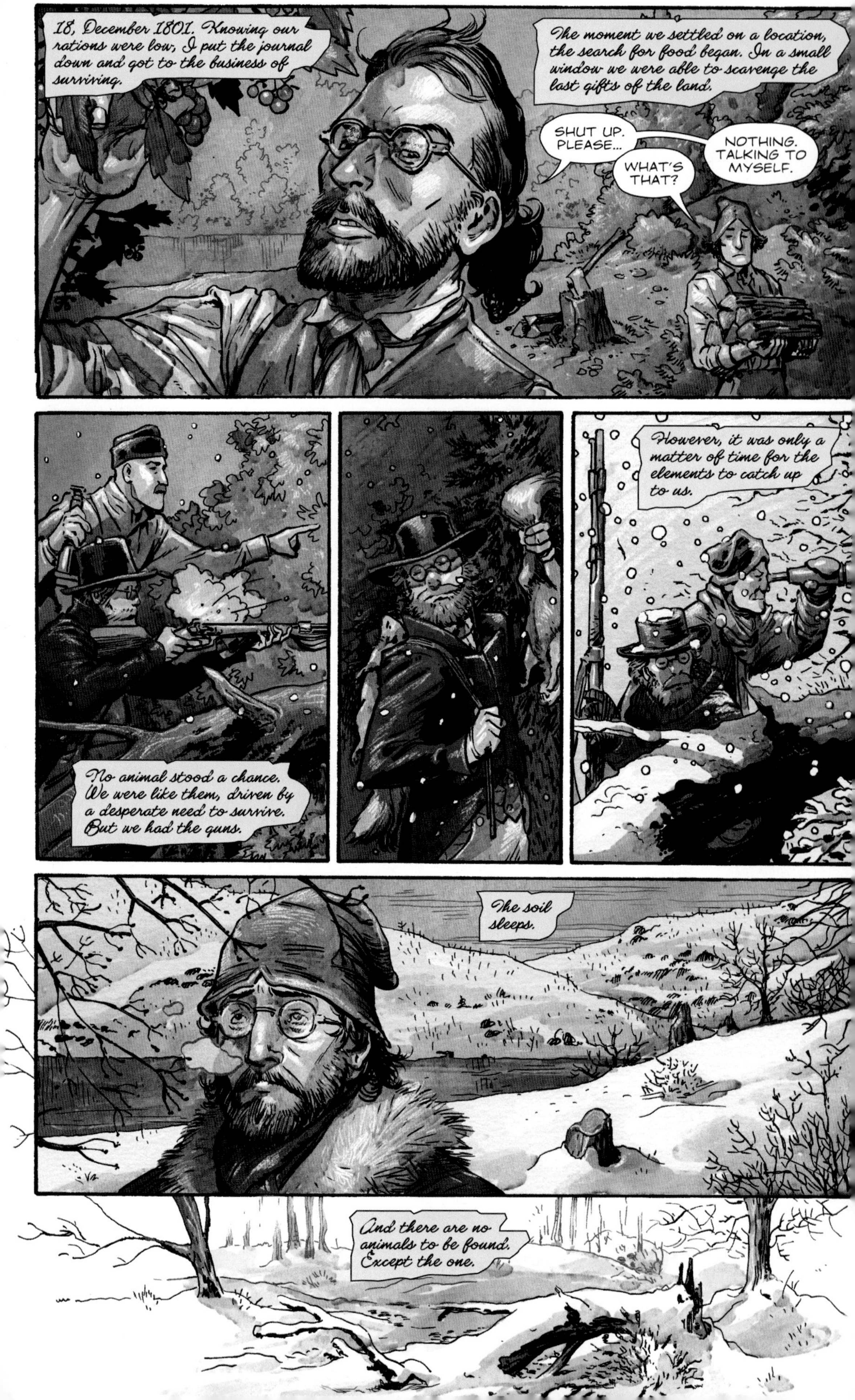
18, December 1801. Knowing our rations were low, I put the journal down and got to the business of surviving.
The moment we settled on a location, the search for food began. In a small window we were able to scavenge the last gifts of the land.
SHUT UP. PLEASE...
WHAT'S THAT?
NOTHING. TALKING TO MYSELF.
No animal stood a chance. We were like them, driven by a desperate need to survive. But we had the guns.
However, it was only a matter of time for the elements to catch up to us.
The soil sleeps.
And there are no animals to be found. Except the one.

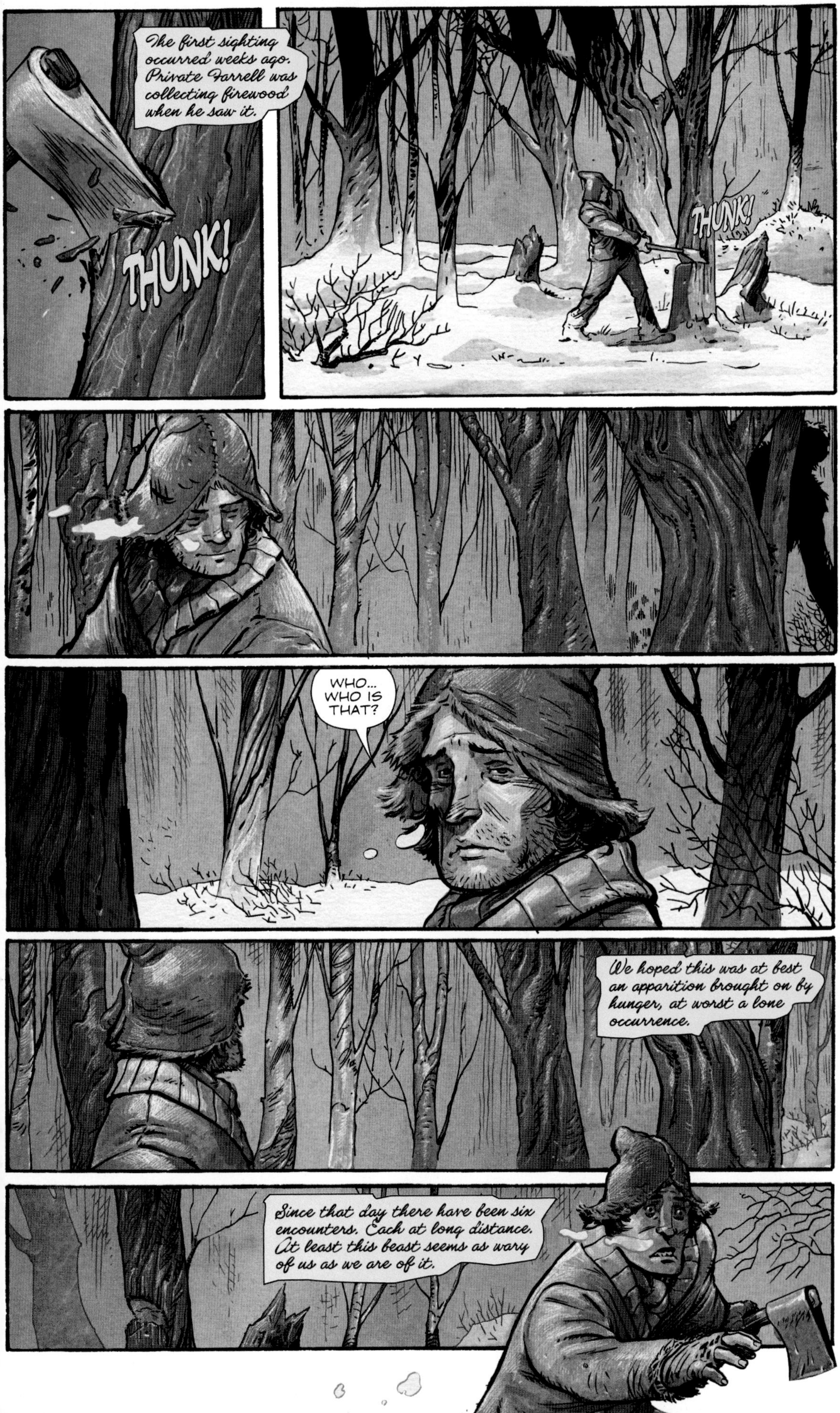
The first sighting occurred weeks ago. Private Farrell was collecting firewood when he saw it.
THUNK!
THUNK!
WHO... WHO IS THAT?
We hoped this was at best an apparition brought on by hunger, at worst a lone occurrence.
Since that day there have been six encounters. Each at long distance. At least this beast seems as wary of us as we are of it.

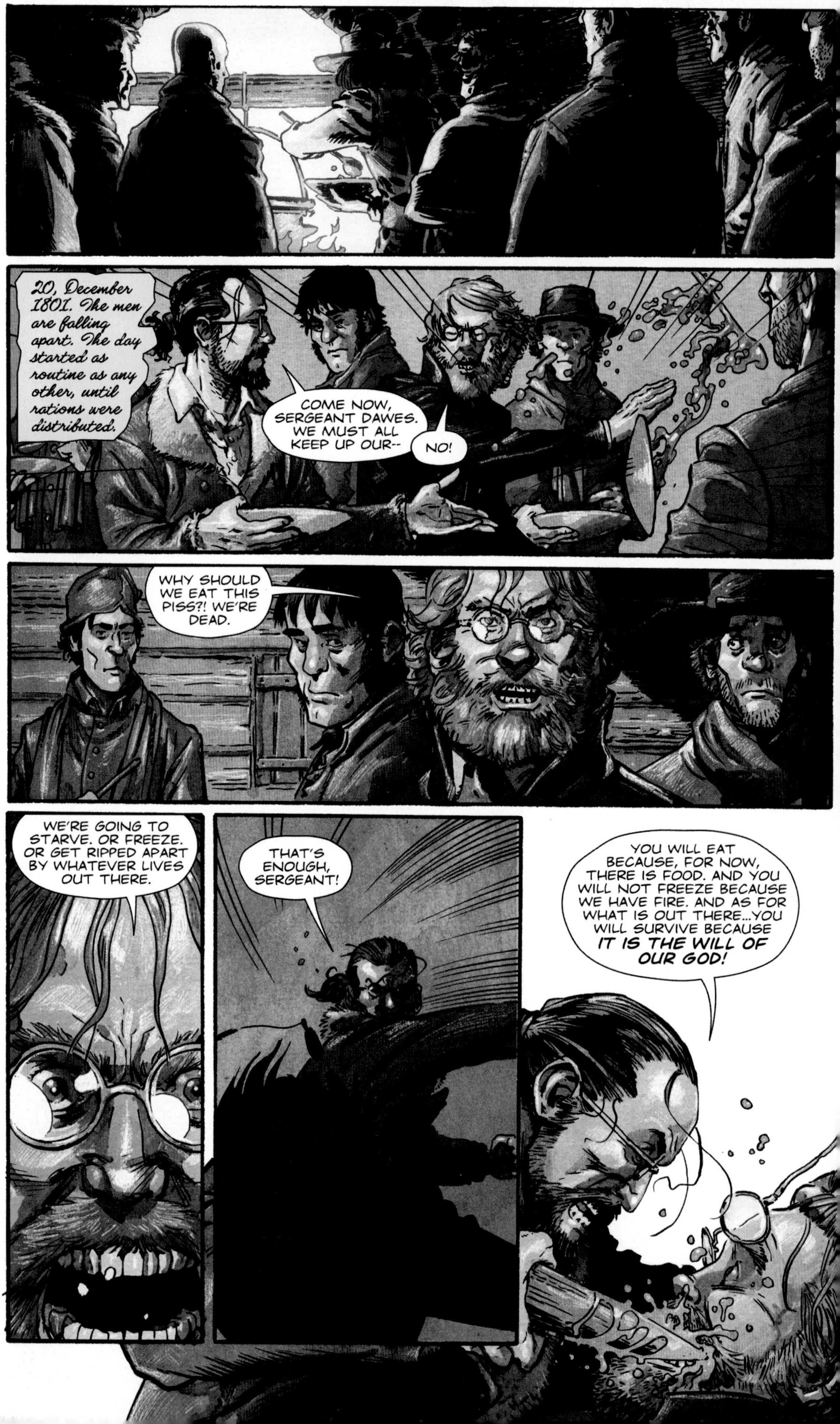
20, December 1801. The men are falling apart. The day started as routine as any other, until rations were distributed.
COME NOW, SERGEANT DAWES. WE MUST ALL KEEP UP OUR--
NO!
WHY SHOULD WE EAT THIS PISS?! WE'RE DEAD.
WE'RE GOING TO STARVE. OR FREEZE. OR GET RIPPED APART BY WHATEVER LIVES OUT THERE.
THAT'S ENOUGH, SERGEANT!
YOU WILL EAT BECAUSE, FOR NOW, THERE IS FOOD. AND YOU WILL NOT FREEZE BECAUSE WE HAVE FIRE. AND AS FOR WHAT IS OUT THERE...YOU WILL SURVIVE BECAUSE ***IT IS THE WILL OF OUR GOD!***

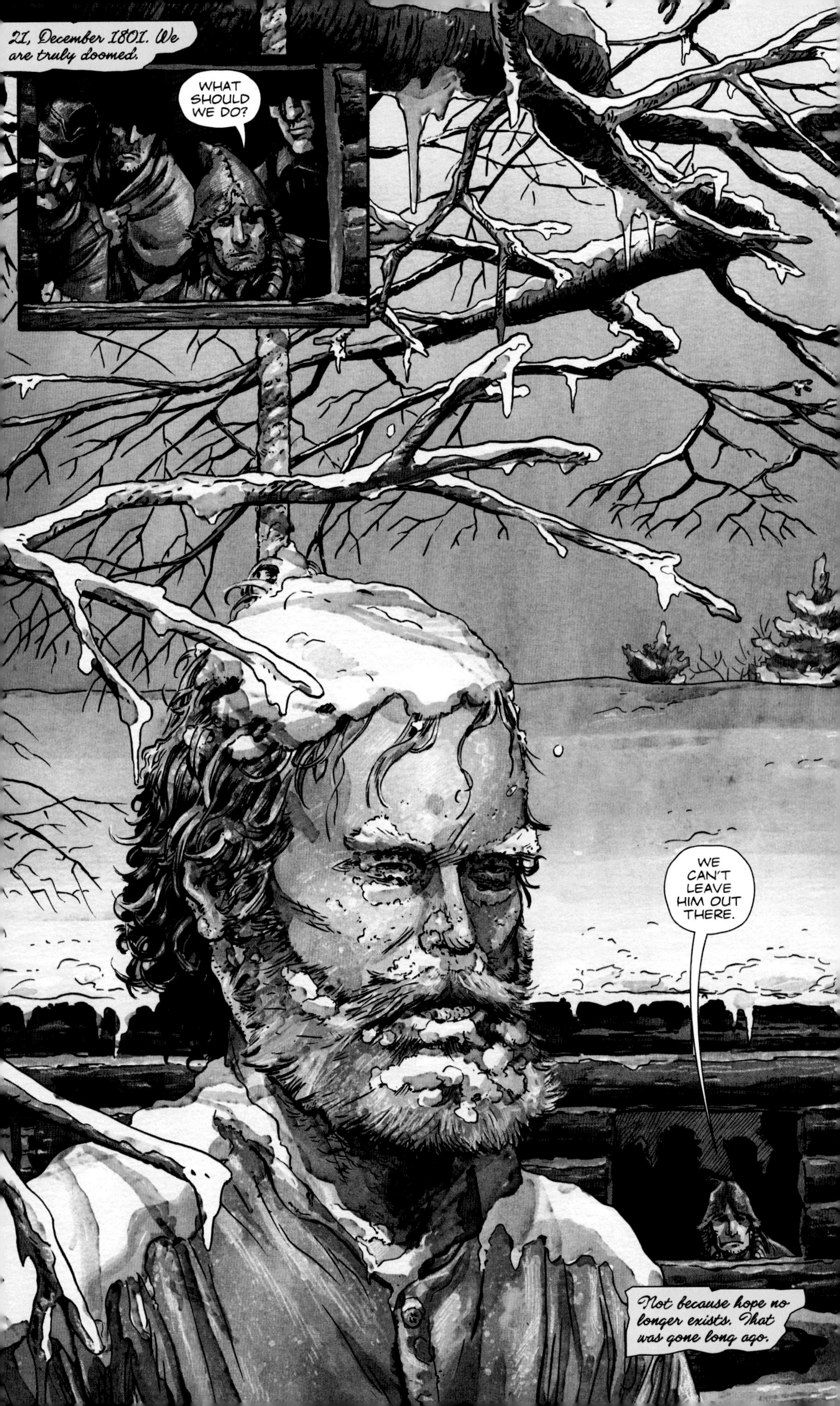
21, December 1801. We are truly doomed.
WHAT SHOULD WE DO?
WE CAN'T LEAVE HIM OUT THERE.
Not because hope no longer exists. That was gone long ago.

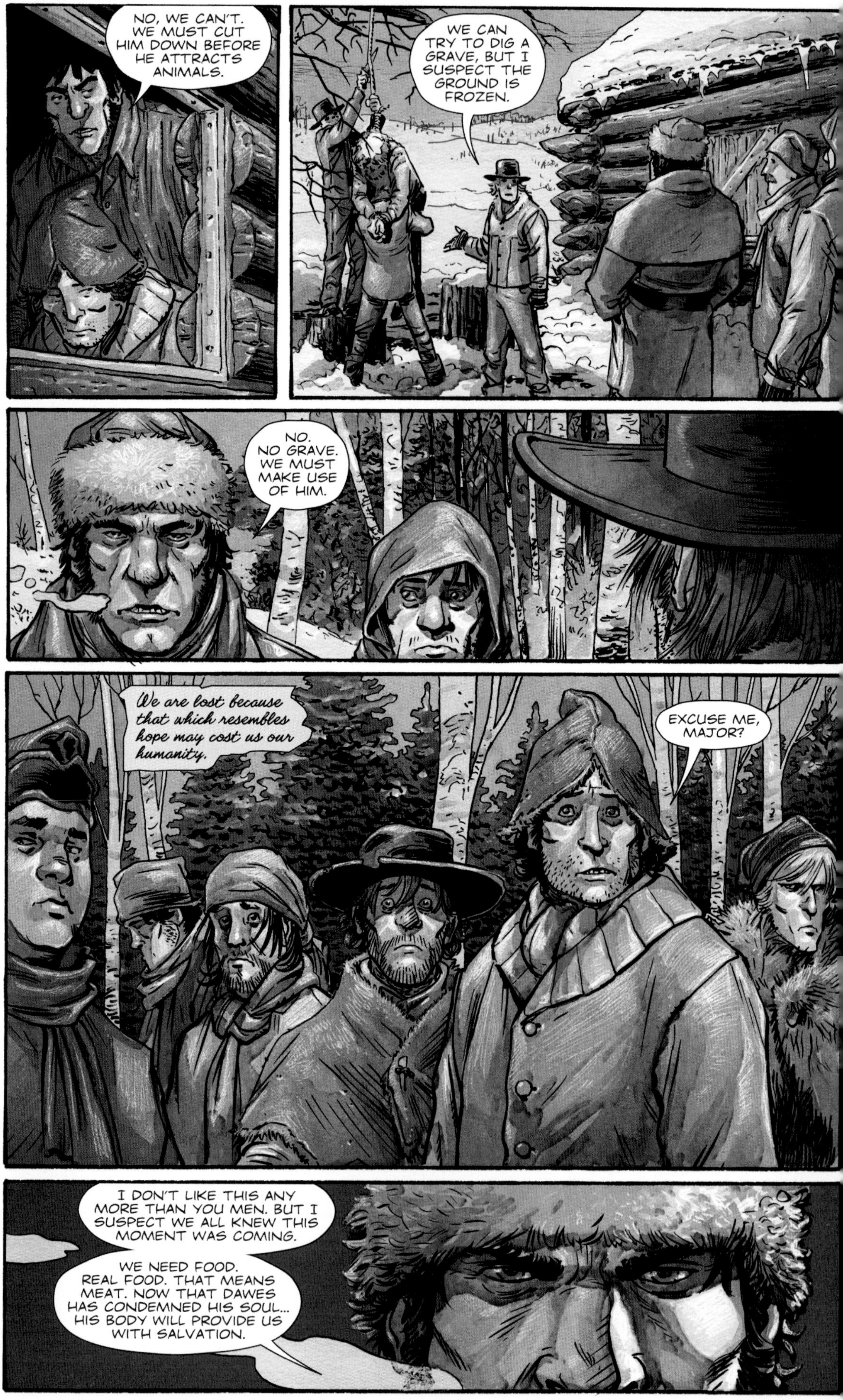
NO, WE CAN'T. WE MUST CUT HIM DOWN BEFORE HE ATTRACTS ANIMALS.
WE CAN TRY TO DIG A GRAVE, BUT I SUSPECT THE GROUND IS FROZEN.
NO. NO GRAVE. WE MUST MAKE USE OF HIM.
We are lost because that which resembles hope may cost us our humanity.
EXCUSE ME, MAJOR?
I DON'T LIKE THIS ANY MORE THAN YOU MEN. BUT I SUSPECT WE ALL KNEW THIS MOMENT WAS COMING.
WE NEED FOOD. REAL FOOD. THAT MEANS MEAT. NOW THAT DAWES HAS CONDEMNED HIS SOUL... HIS BODY WILL PROVIDE US WITH SALVATION.

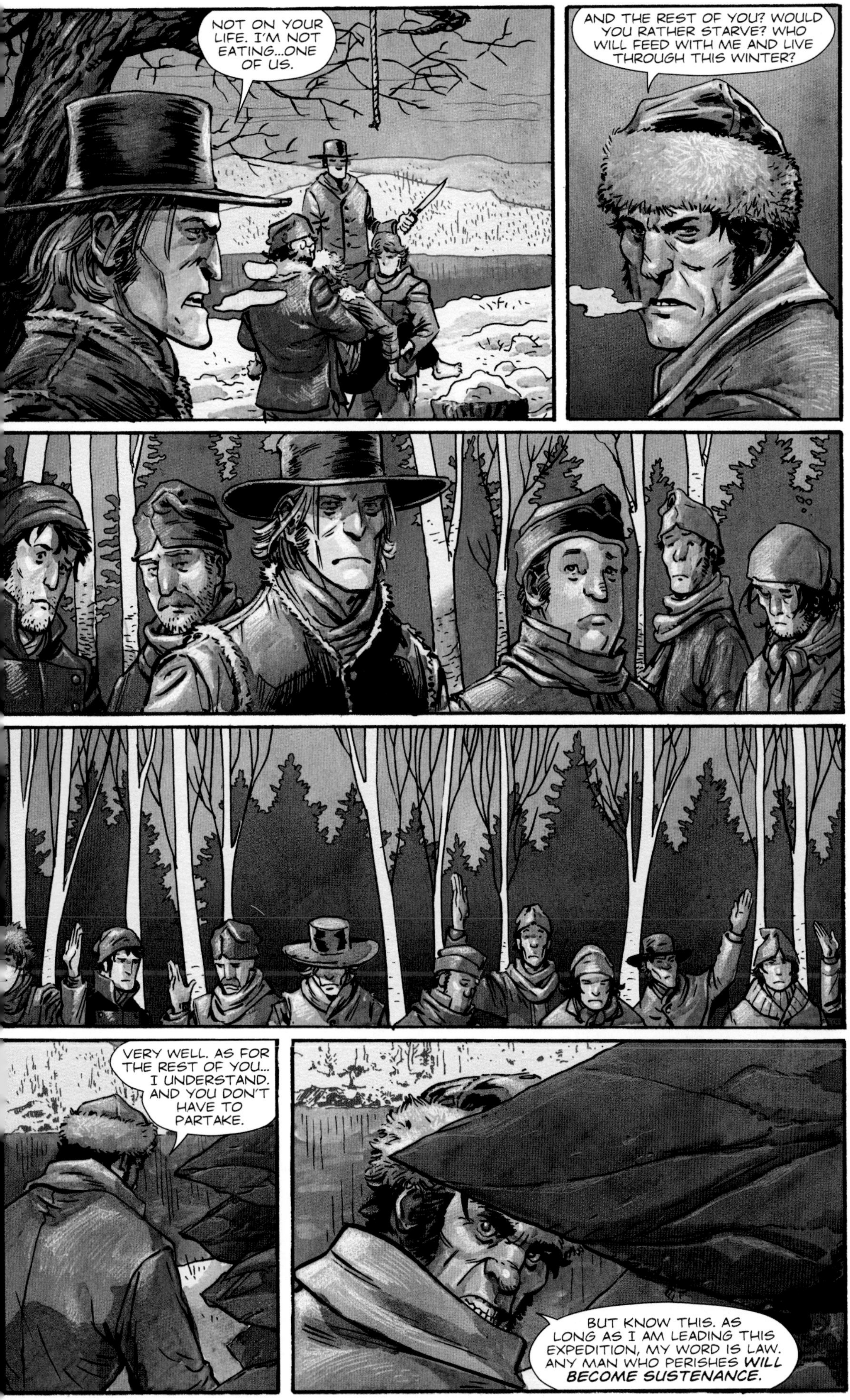
NOT ON YOUR LIFE. I'M NOT EATING...ONE OF US.
AND THE REST OF YOU? WOULD YOU RATHER STARVE? WHO WILL FEED WITH ME AND LIVE THROUGH THIS WINTER?
VERY WELL. AS FOR THE REST OF YOU... I UNDERSTAND. AND YOU DON'T HAVE TO PARTAKE.
BUT KNOW THIS. AS LONG AS I AM LEADING THIS EXPEDITION, MY WORD IS LAW. ANY MAN WHO PERISHES WILL BECOME SUSTENANCE.

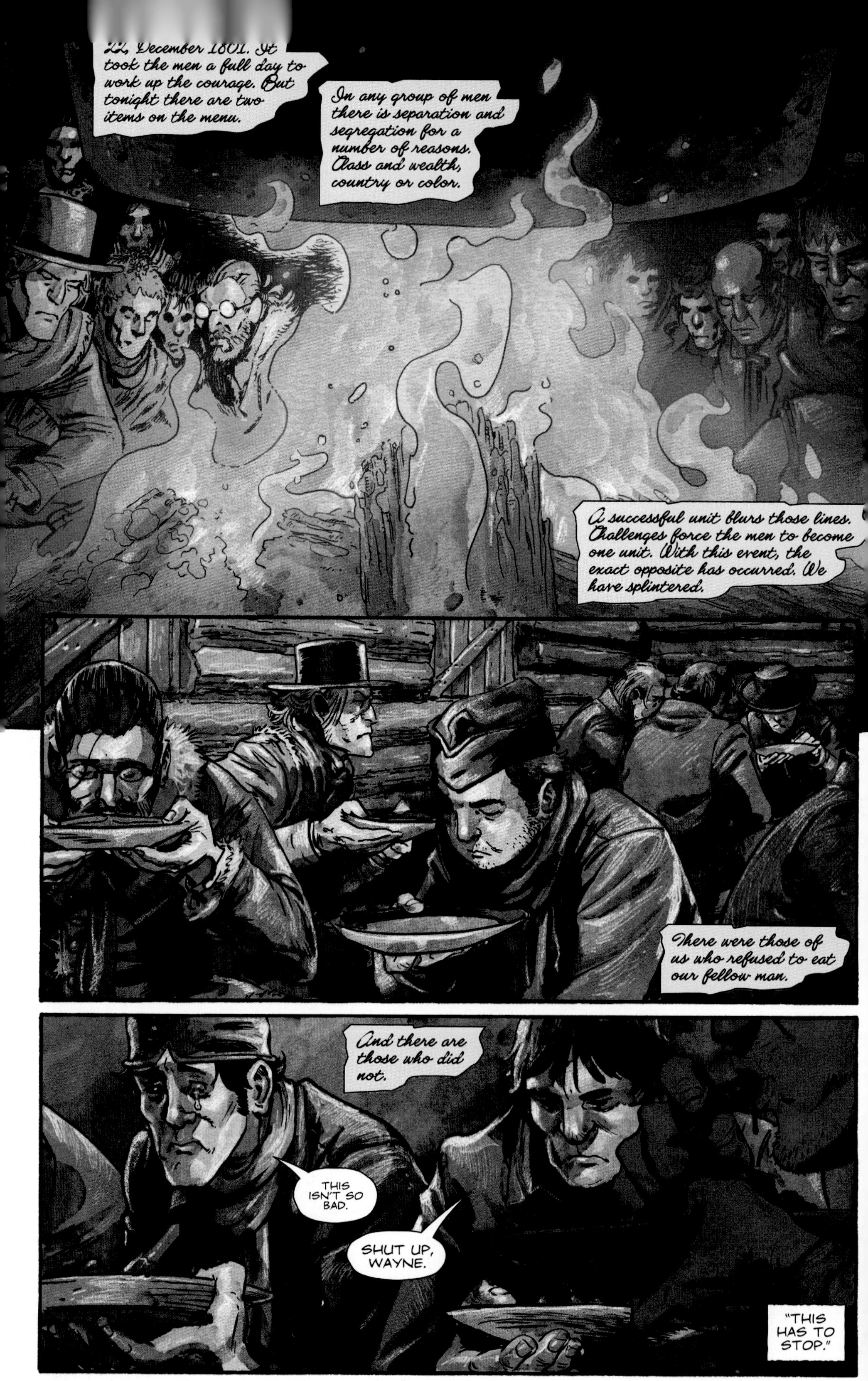
22, December 1801. It took the men a full day to work up the courage. But tonight there are two items on the menu.
In any group of men there is separation and segregation for a number of reasons. Class and wealth, country or color.
A successful unit blurs those lines. Challenges force the men to become one unit. With this event, the exact opposite has occurred. We have splintered.
There were those of us who refused to eat our fellow man.
And there are those who did not.
THIS ISN'T SO BAD.
SHUT UP, WAYNE.
"THIS HAS TO STOP."

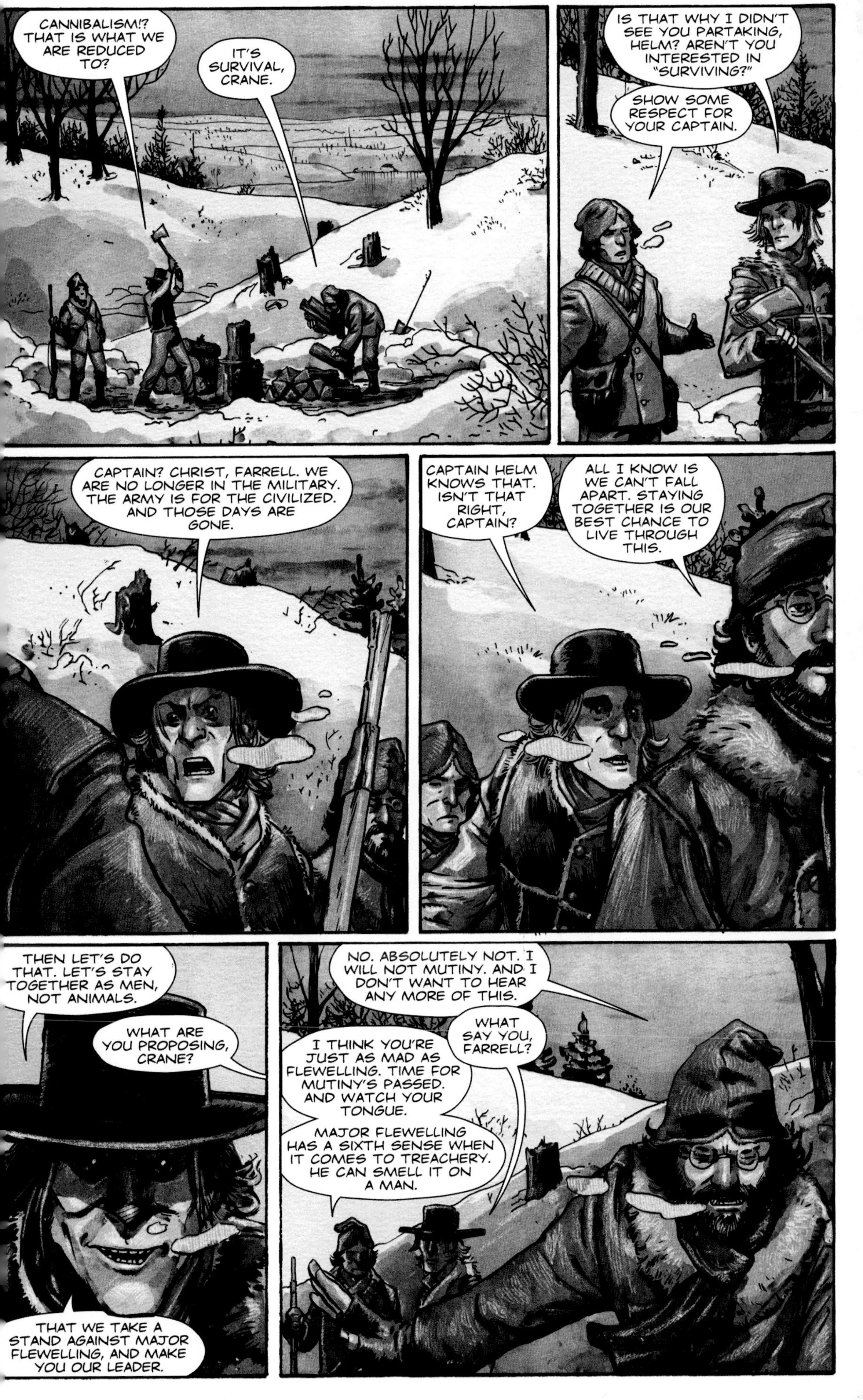
CANNIBALISM!? THAT IS WHAT WE ARE REDUCED TO?
IT'S SURVIVAL, CRANE.
IS THAT WHY I DIDN'T SEE YOU PARTAKING, HELM? AREN'T YOU INTERESTED IN "SURVIVING?"
SHOW SOME RESPECT FOR YOUR CAPTAIN.
CAPTAIN? CHRIST, FARRELL. WE ARE NO LONGER IN THE MILITARY. THE ARMY IS FOR THE CIVILIZED. AND THOSE DAYS ARE GONE.
CAPTAIN HELM KNOWS THAT. ISN'T THAT RIGHT, CAPTAIN?
ALL I KNOW IS WE CAN'T FALL APART. STAYING TOGETHER IS OUR BEST CHANCE TO LIVE THROUGH THIS.
THEN LET'S DO THAT. LET'S STAY TOGETHER AS MEN, NOT ANIMALS.
WHAT ARE YOU PROPOSING, CRANE?
THAT WE TAKE A STAND AGAINST MAJOR FLEWELLING, AND MAKE YOU OUR LEADER.
NO. ABSOLUTELY NOT. I WILL NOT MUTINY. AND I DON'T WANT TO HEAR ANY MORE OF THIS.
WHAT SAY YOU, FARRELL?
I THINK YOU'RE JUST AS MAD AS FLEWELLING. TIME FOR MUTINY'S PASSED. AND WATCH YOUR TONGUE.
MAJOR FLEWELLING HAS A SIXTH SENSE WHEN IT COMES TO TREACHERY. HE CAN SMELL IT ON A MAN.

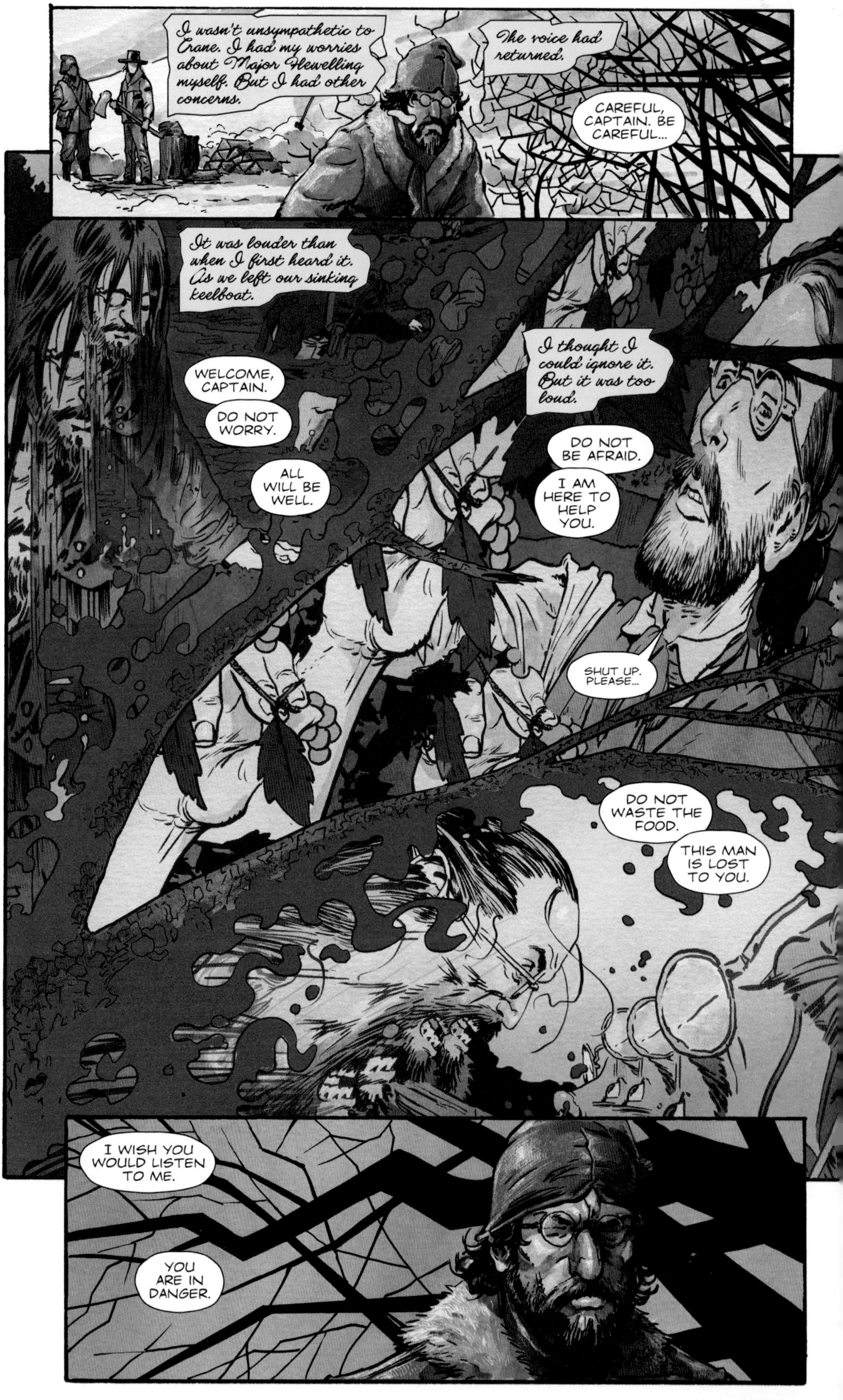
I wasn't unsympathetic to Crane. I had my worries about Major Flewelling myself. But I had other concerns.
The voice had returned.
CAREFUL, CAPTAIN. BE CAREFUL...
It was louder than when I first heard it. As we left our sinking keelboat.
WELCOME, CAPTAIN.
DO NOT WORRY.
ALL WILL BE WELL.
I thought I could ignore it. But it was too loud.
DO NOT BE AFRAID.
I AM HERE TO HELP YOU.
SHUT UP. PLEASE...
DO NOT WASTE THE FOOD.
THIS MAN IS LOST TO YOU.
I WISH YOU WOULD LISTEN TO ME.
YOU ARE IN DANGER.

23, December 1801. We are all in danger.

STUPID GODDAMN SNOW.

CRANE?

YES, MAJOR?

HOW GOES IT WITH THE ROOF?

ALMOST DONE.

CAN I HAVE A WORD?

I'LL FINISH UP.

What Farrell said about Major Hewelling's clairvoyance in regards to mutiny?

It's true.

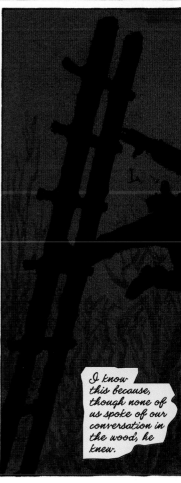

I know this because, though none of us spoke of our conversation in the wood, he knew.

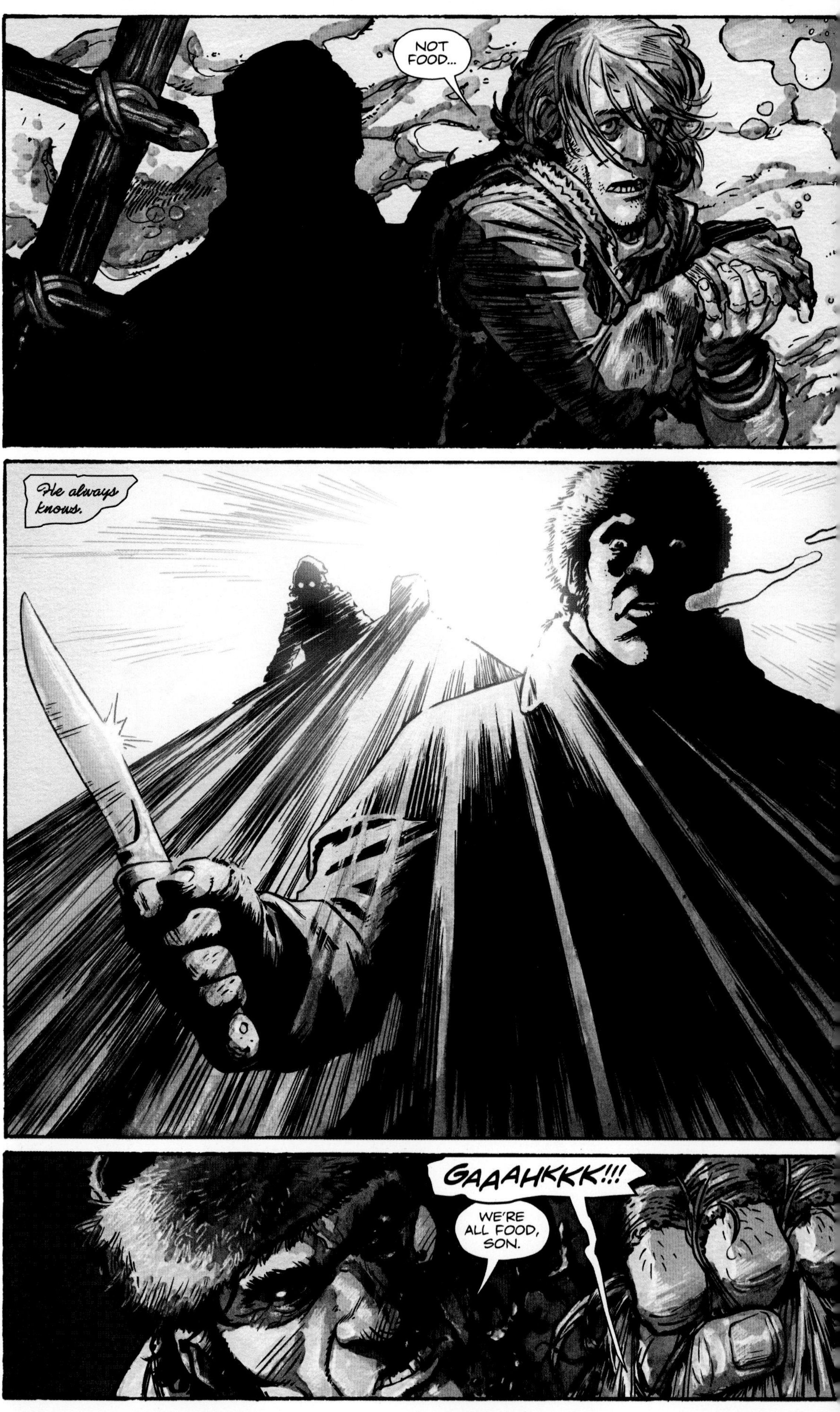
NOT FOOD...
He always knows.
GAAAHKKK!!!
WE'RE ALL FOOD, SON.

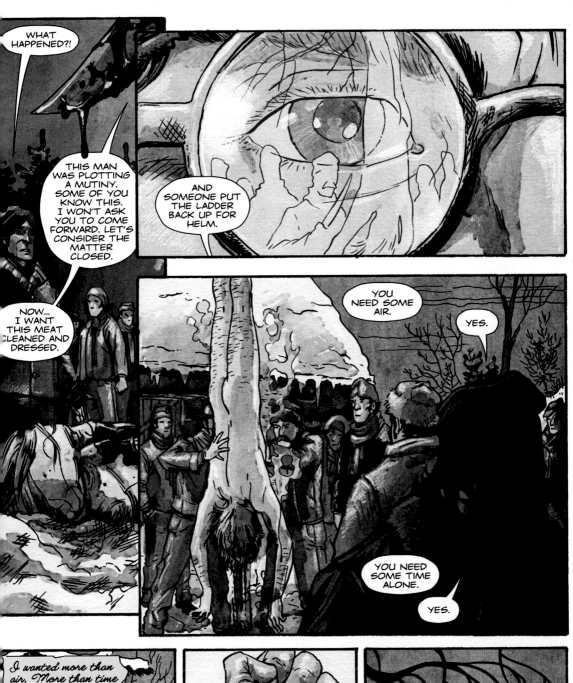

WHAT HAPPENED?!

THIS MAN WAS PLOTTING A MUTINY. SOME OF YOU KNOW THIS. I WON'T ASK YOU TO COME FORWARD. LET'S CONSIDER THE MATTER CLOSED.

AND SOMEONE PUT THE LADDER BACK UP FOR HELM.

NOW... I WANT THIS MEAT CLEANED AND DRESSED.

YOU NEED SOME AIR.

YES.

YOU NEED SOME TIME ALONE.

YES.

I wanted more than air. More than time alone.

I KNOW WHAT YOU ARE THINKING. DO NOT DO IT.

I DON'T HAVE TO LISTEN TO YOU ANYMORE.

DON'T DO IT!

WHO--?

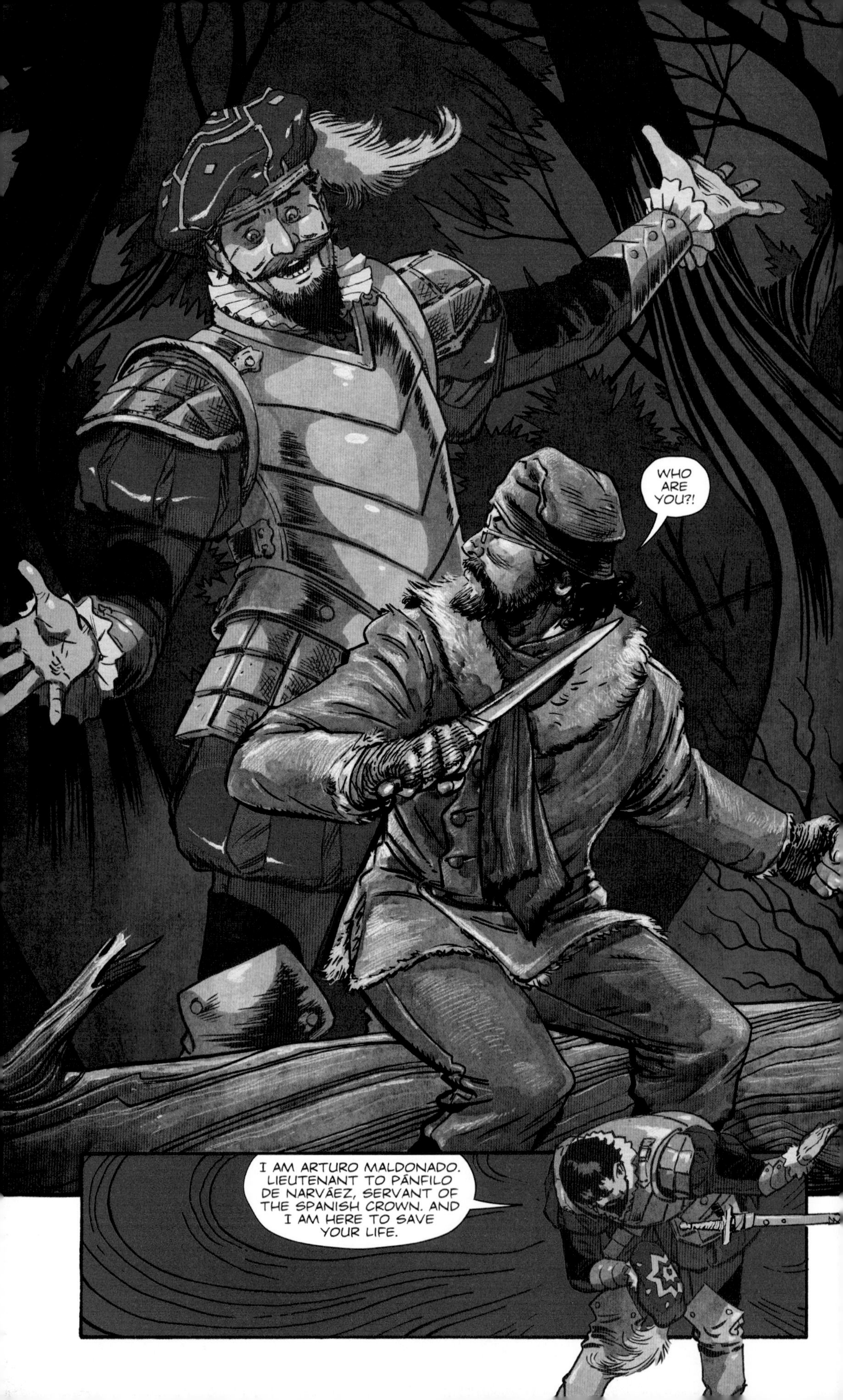
WHO ARE YOU?!
I AM ARTURO MALDONADO. LIEUTENANT TO PÁNFILO DE NARVÁEZ, SERVANT OF THE SPANISH CROWN. AND I AM HERE TO SAVE YOUR LIFE.

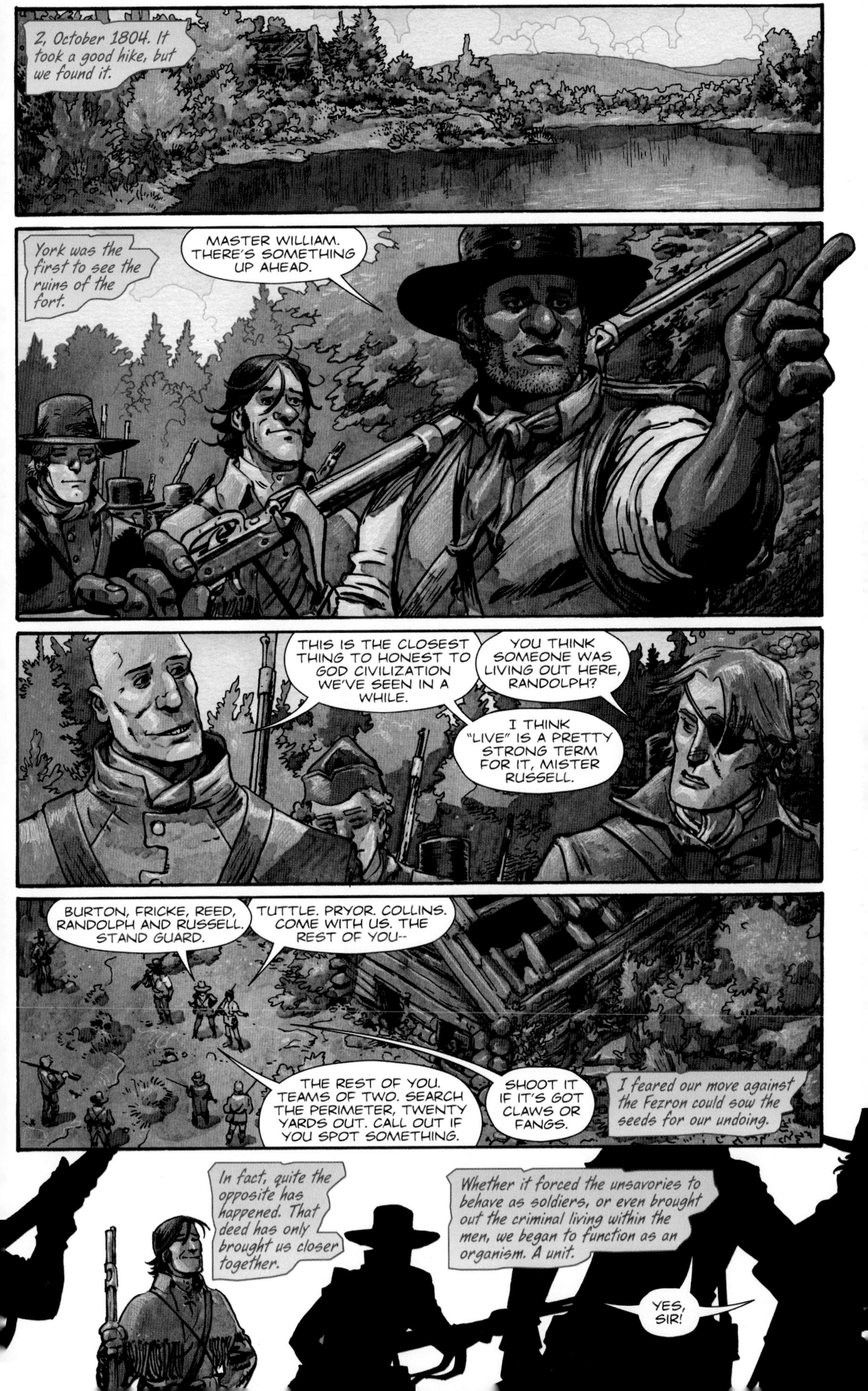
2, October 1804. It took a good hike, but we found it.
York was the first to see the ruins of the fort.
MASTER WILLIAM. THERE'S SOMETHING UP AHEAD.
THIS IS THE CLOSEST THING TO HONEST TO GOD CIVILIZATION WE'VE SEEN IN A WHILE.
YOU THINK SOMEONE WAS LIVING OUT HERE, RANDOLPH?
I THINK "LIVE" IS A PRETTY STRONG TERM FOR IT, MISTER RUSSELL.
BURTON, FRICKE, REED, RANDOLPH AND RUSSELL. STAND GUARD.
TUTTLE. PRYOR. COLLINS. COME WITH US. THE REST OF YOU--
THE REST OF YOU. TEAMS OF TWO. SEARCH THE PERIMETER, TWENTY YARDS OUT. CALL OUT IF YOU SPOT SOMETHING.
SHOOT IT IF IT'S GOT CLAWS OR FANGS.
I feared our move against the Fezron could sow the seeds for our undoing.
In fact, quite the opposite has happened. That deed has only brought us closer together.
Whether it forced the unsavories to behave as soldiers, or even brought out the criminal living within the men, we began to function as an organism. A unit.
YES, SIR!

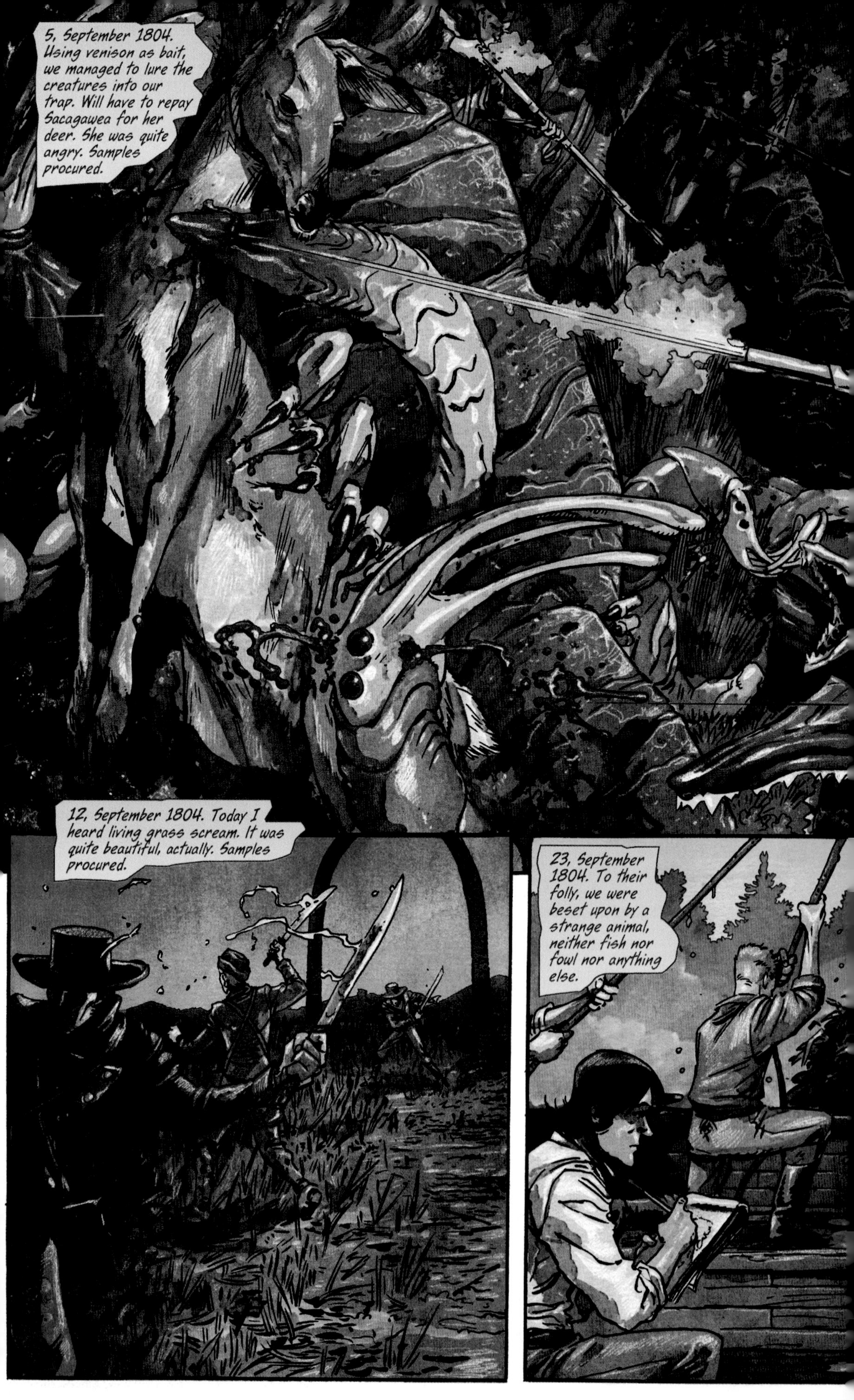
5, September 1804. Using venison as bait, we managed to lure the creatures into our trap. Will have to repay Sacagawea for her deer. She was quite angry. Samples procured.
12, September 1804. Today I heard living grass scream. It was quite beautiful, actually. Samples procured.
23, September 1804. To their folly, we were beset upon by a strange animal, neither fish nor fowl nor anything else.

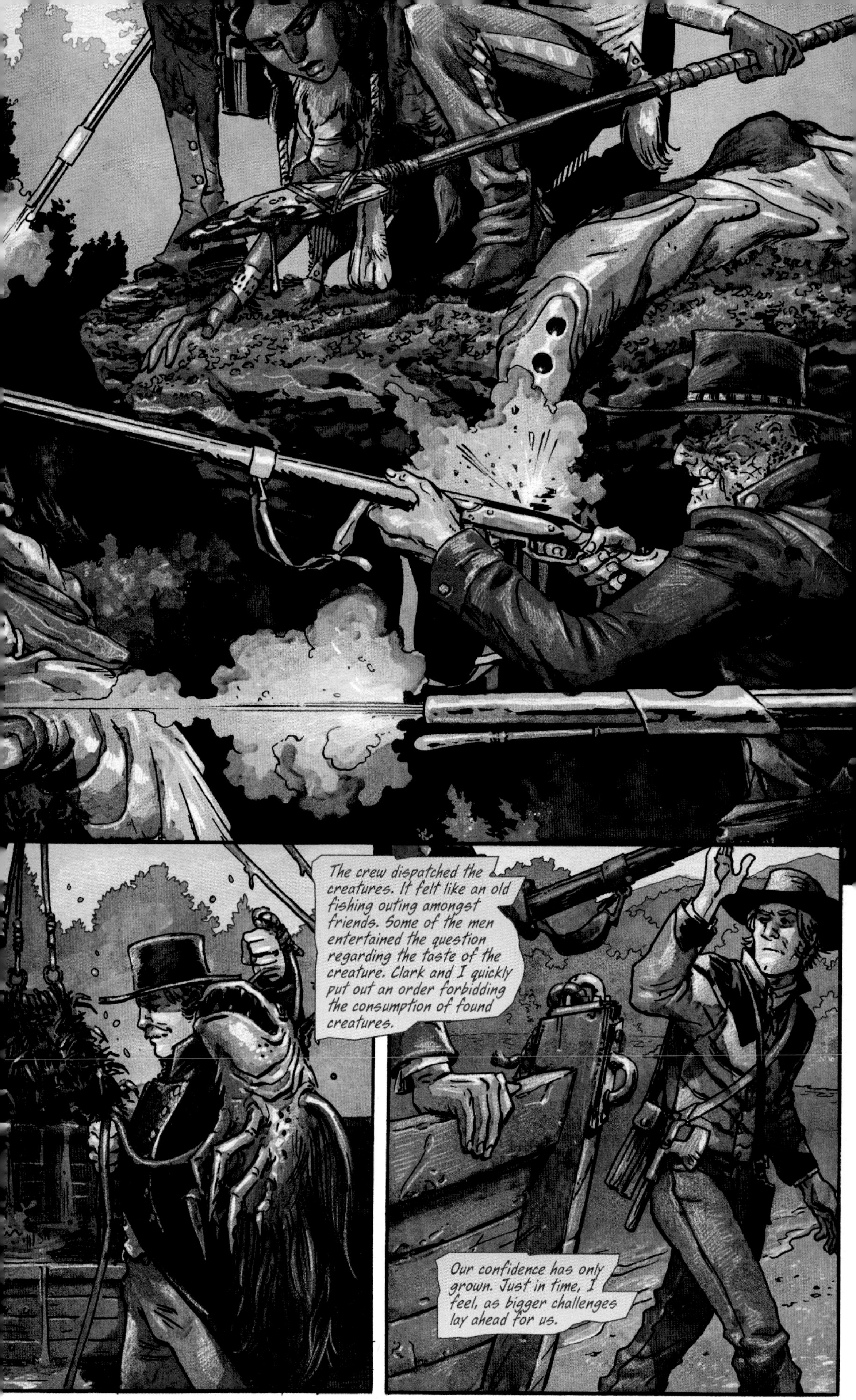
The crew dispatched the creatures. It felt like an old fishing outing amongst friends. Some of the men entertained the question regarding the taste of the creature. Clark and I quickly put out an order forbidding the consumption of found creatures.
Our confidence has only grown. Just in time, I feel, as bigger challenges lay ahead for us.

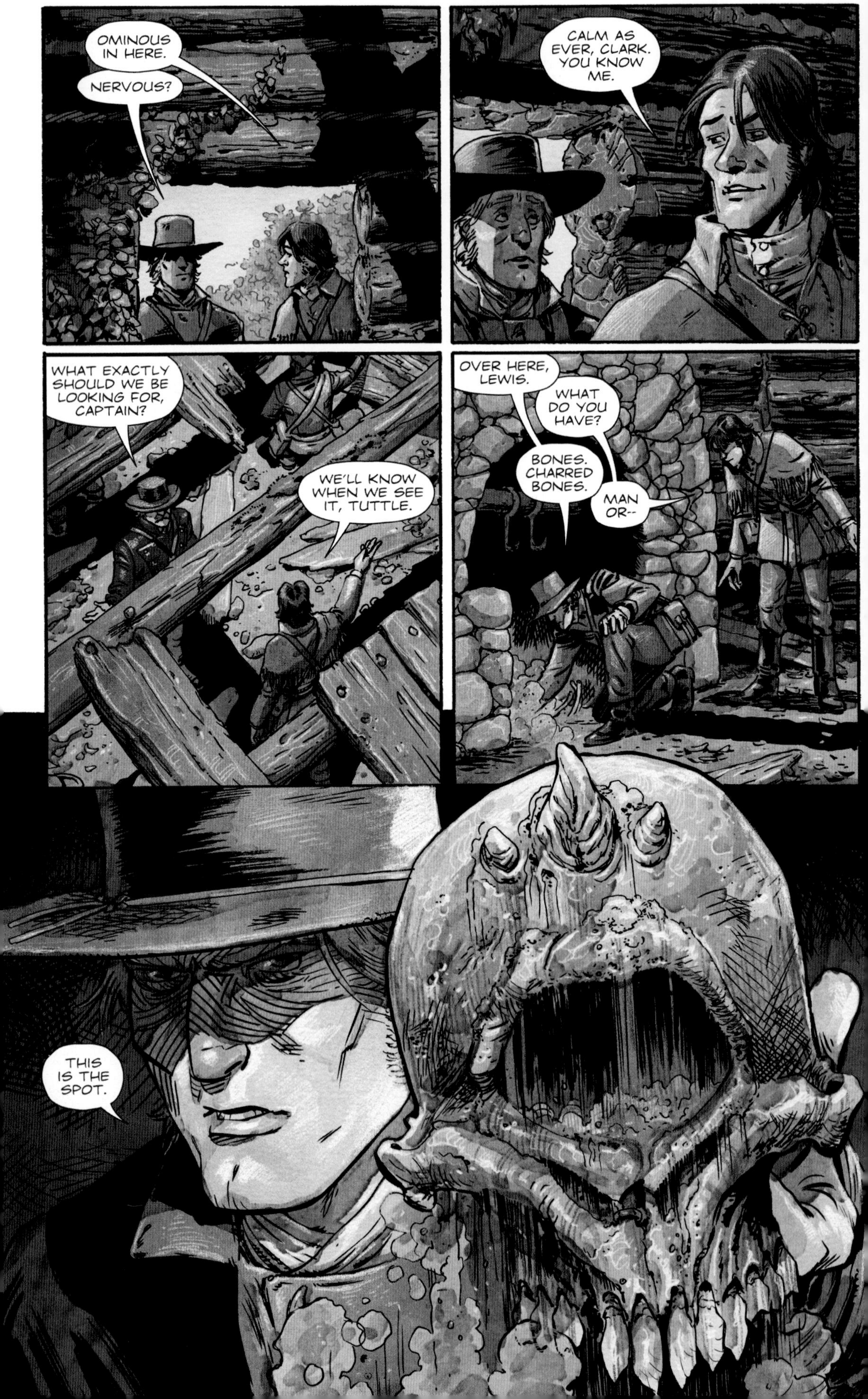

OMINOUS IN HERE.
NERVOUS?
CALM AS EVER, CLARK. YOU KNOW ME.
WHAT EXACTLY SHOULD WE BE LOOKING FOR, CAPTAIN?
WE'LL KNOW WHEN WE SEE IT, TUTTLE.
OVER HERE, LEWIS.
WHAT DO YOU HAVE?
BONES. CHARRED BONES.
MAN OR--
THIS IS THE SPOT.

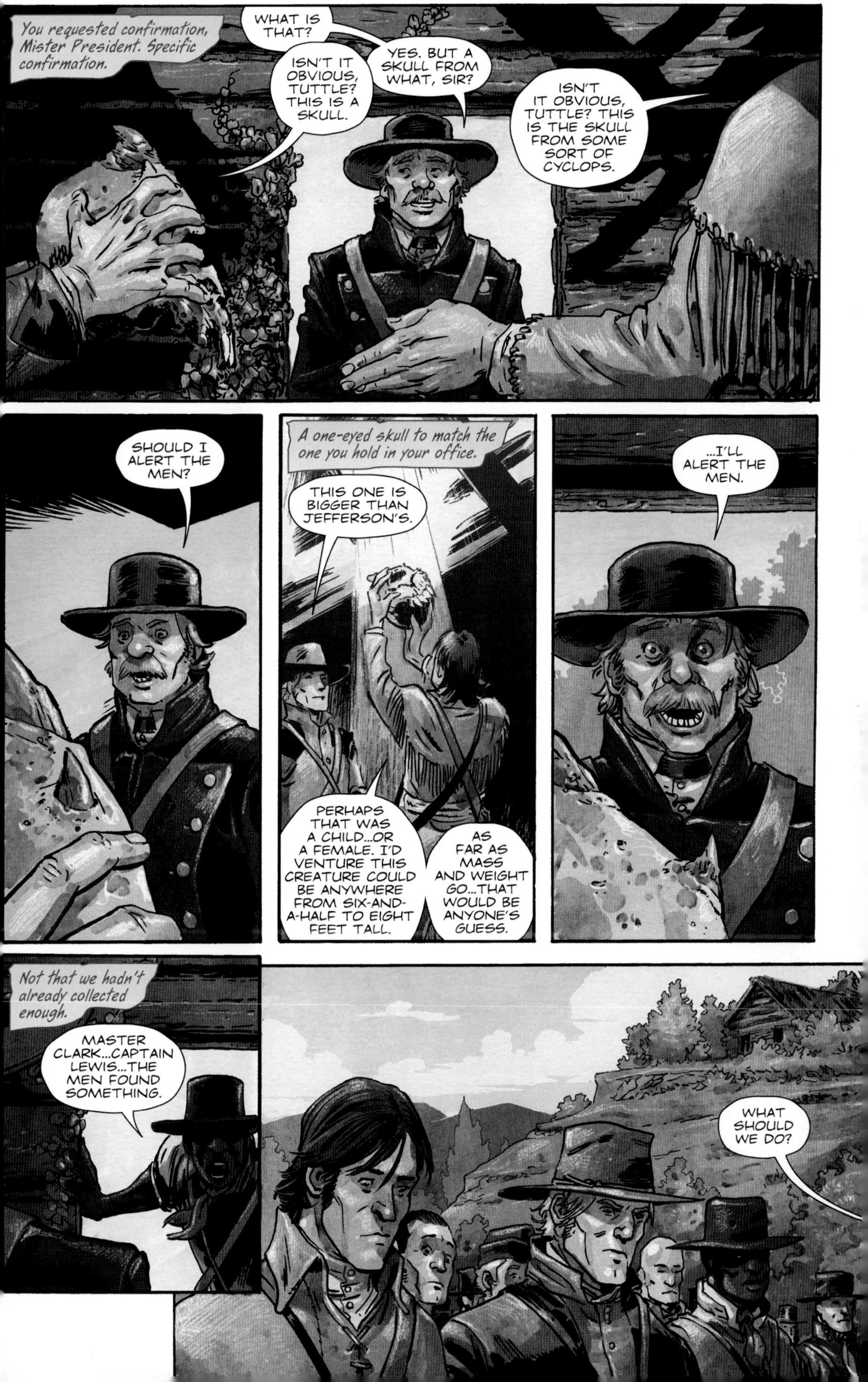

You requested confirmation, Mister President. Specific confirmation.
WHAT IS THAT?
ISN'T IT OBVIOUS, TUTTLE? THIS IS A SKULL.
YES. BUT A SKULL FROM WHAT, SIR?
ISN'T IT OBVIOUS, TUTTLE? THIS IS THE SKULL FROM SOME SORT OF CYCLOPS.
SHOULD I ALERT THE MEN?
A one-eyed skull to match the one you hold in your office.
THIS ONE IS BIGGER THAN JEFFERSON'S.
PERHAPS THAT WAS A CHILD...OR A FEMALE. I'D VENTURE THIS CREATURE COULD BE ANYWHERE FROM SIX-AND-A-HALF TO EIGHT FEET TALL.
AS FAR AS MASS AND WEIGHT GO...THAT WOULD BE ANYONE'S GUESS.
...I'LL ALERT THE MEN.
Not that we hadn't already collected enough.
MASTER CLARK...CAPTAIN LEWIS...THE MEN FOUND SOMETHING.
WHAT SHOULD WE DO?

1 Minotaur hide (with autopsy notes and samples).
1 sample of parasitic flora.
1 Ranidea/Giant Frog corpse.
6 jars of Fezron intestines & fluids.

WE LET THEM REST IN PEACE.

NO.

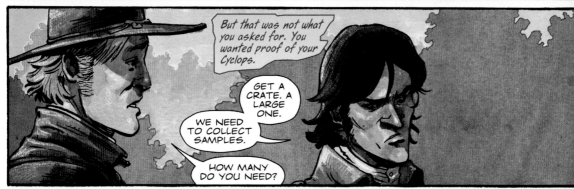

But that was not what you asked for. You wanted proof of your Cyclops.

GET A CRATE. A LARGE ONE.

WE NEED TO COLLECT SAMPLES.

HOW MANY DO YOU NEED?

Today, Mister President, we found it in spades.

IF IT HAS ONE EYE, IT GOES IN THE BOX.

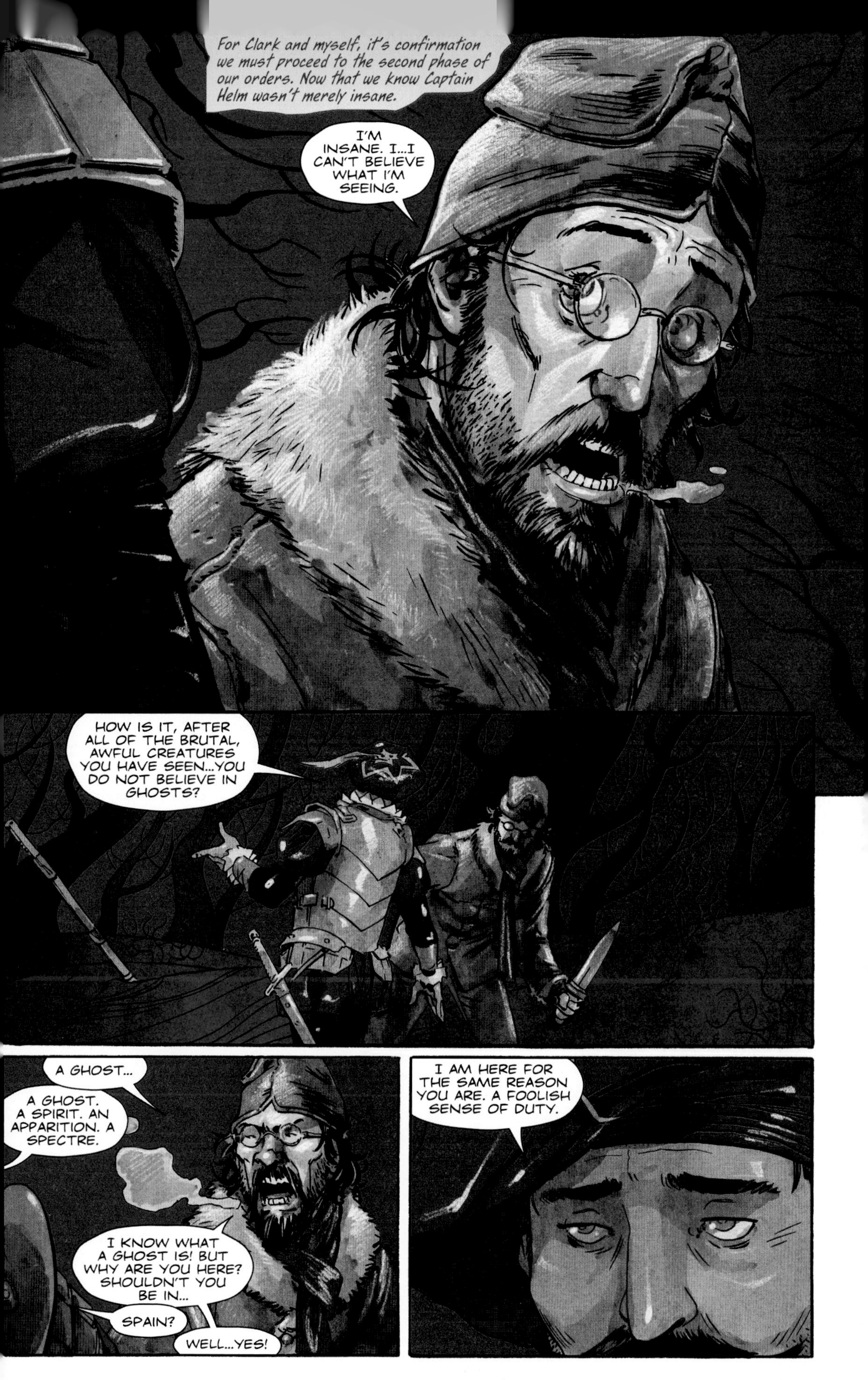
For Clark and myself, it's confirmation we must proceed to the second phase of our orders. Now that we know Captain Helm wasn't merely insane.
I'M INSANE. I...I CAN'T BELIEVE WHAT I'M SEEING.
HOW IS IT, AFTER ALL OF THE BRUTAL, AWFUL CREATURES YOU HAVE SEEN...YOU DO NOT BELIEVE IN GHOSTS?
A GHOST...
A GHOST. A SPIRIT. AN APPARITION. A SPECTRE.
I KNOW WHAT A GHOST IS! BUT WHY ARE YOU HERE? SHOULDN'T YOU BE IN...
SPAIN?
WELL...YES!
I AM HERE FOR THE SAME REASON YOU ARE. A FOOLISH SENSE OF DUTY.

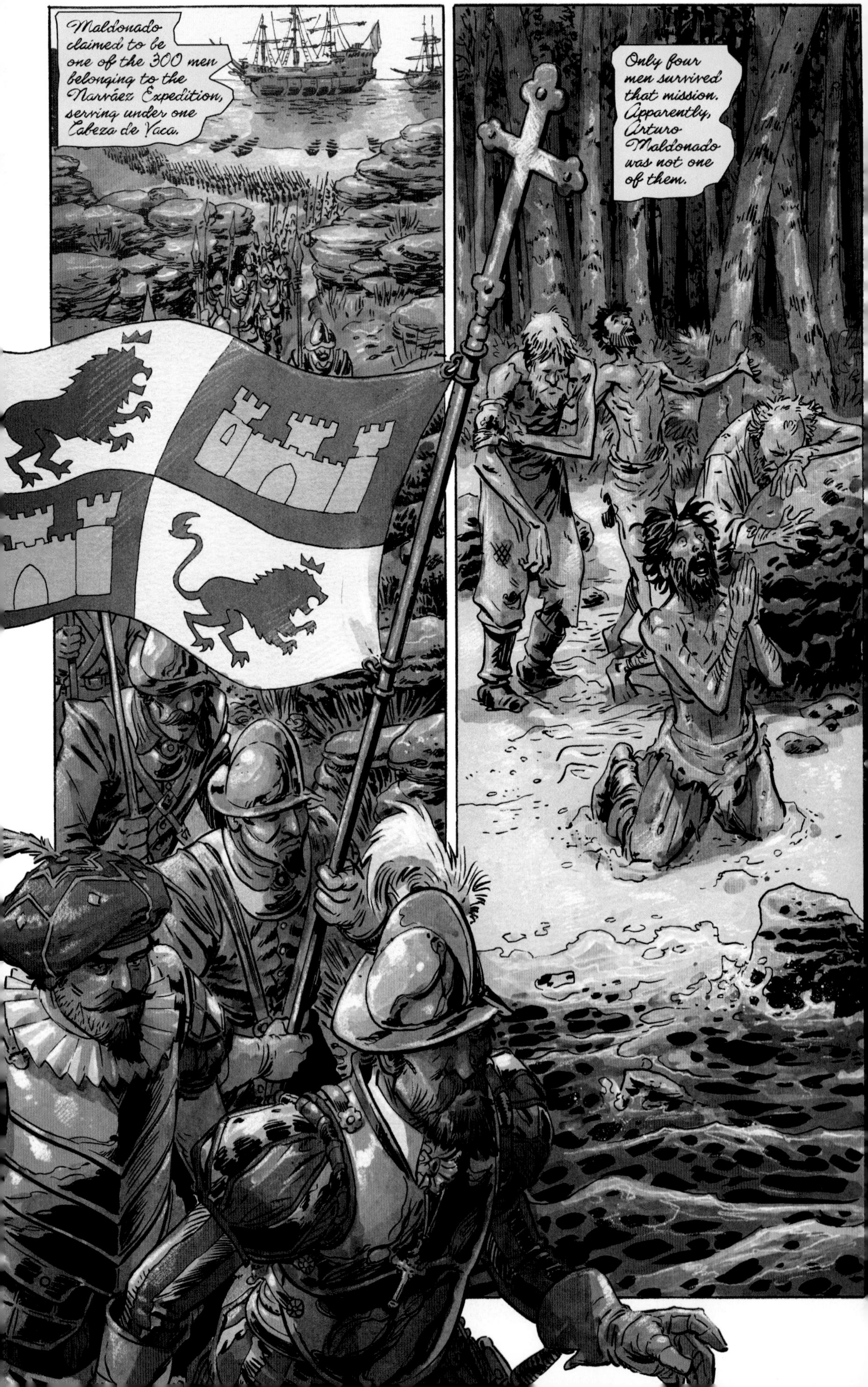
Maldonado claimed to be one of the 300 men belonging to the Narváez Expedition, serving under one Cabeza de Vaca.
Only four men survived that mission. Apparently, Arturo Maldonado was not one of them.

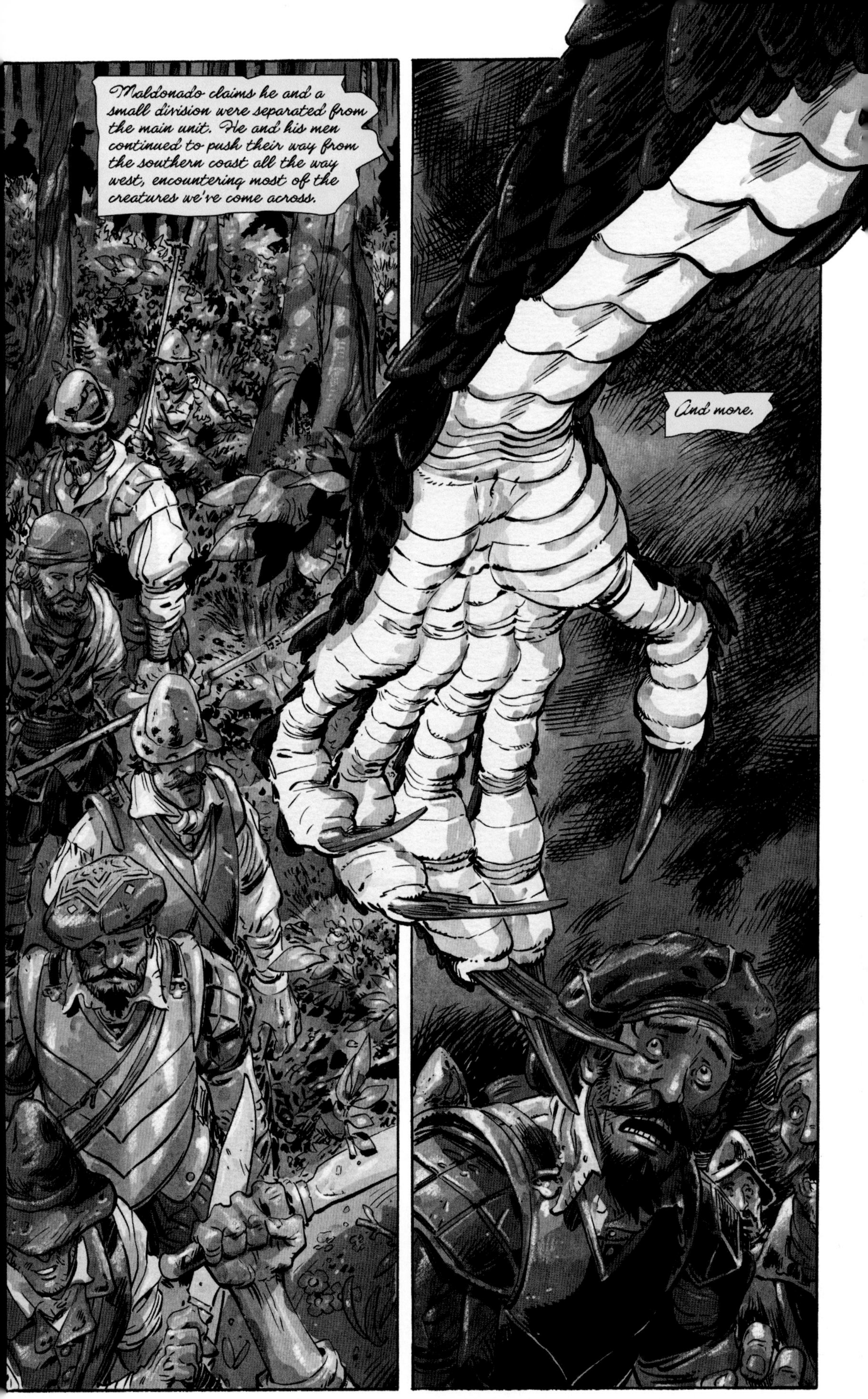
Maldonado claims he and a small division were separated from the main unit. He and his men continued to push their way from the southern coast all the way west, encountering most of the creatures we've come across.
And more.

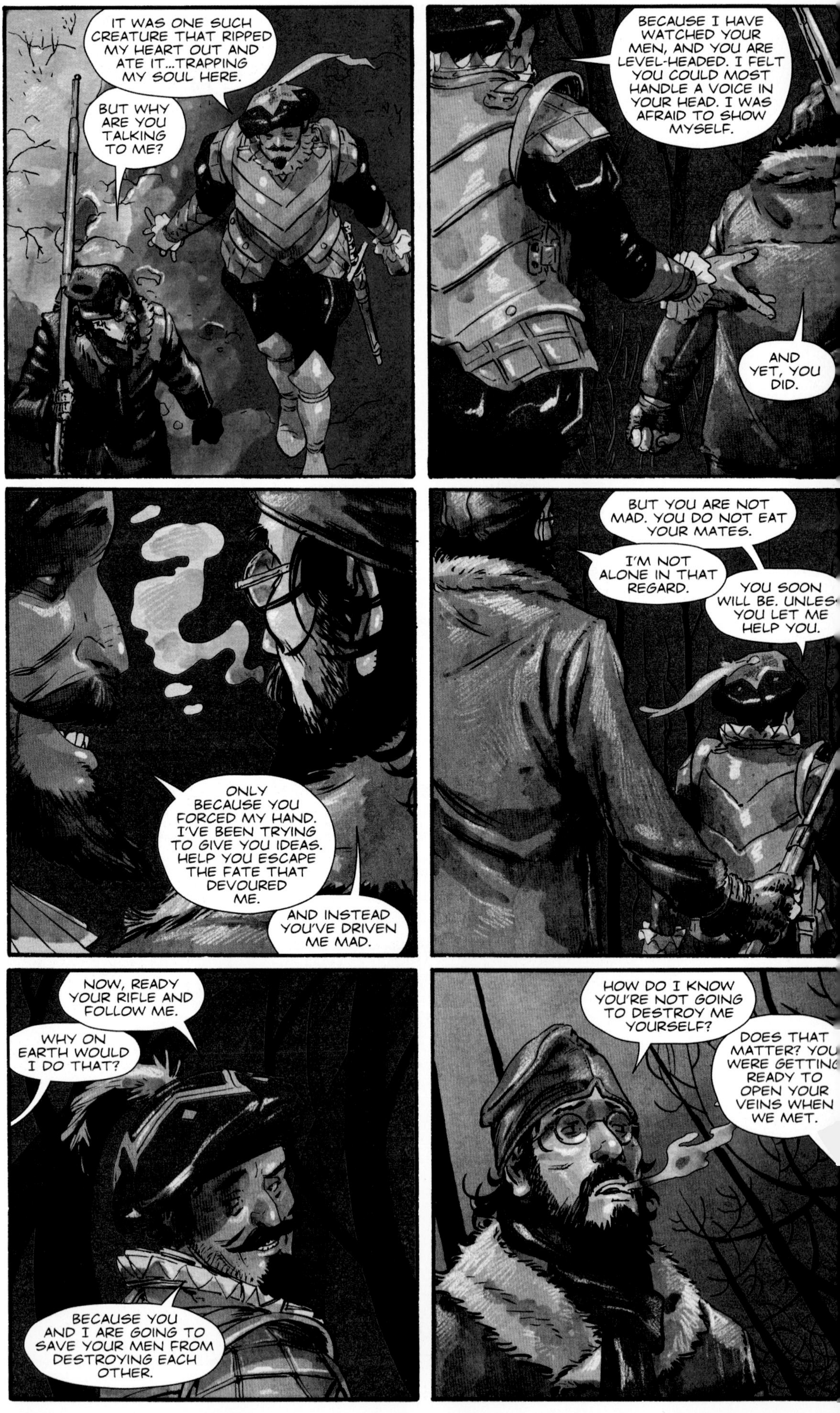
IT WAS ONE SUCH CREATURE THAT RIPPED MY HEART OUT AND ATE IT...TRAPPING MY SOUL HERE.
BUT WHY ARE YOU TALKING TO ME?
BECAUSE I HAVE WATCHED YOUR MEN, AND YOU ARE LEVEL-HEADED. I FELT YOU COULD MOST HANDLE A VOICE IN YOUR HEAD. I WAS AFRAID TO SHOW MYSELF.
AND YET, YOU DID.
ONLY BECAUSE YOU FORCED MY HAND. I'VE BEEN TRYING TO GIVE YOU IDEAS. HELP YOU ESCAPE THE FATE THAT DEVOURED ME.
AND INSTEAD YOU'VE DRIVEN ME MAD.
BUT YOU ARE NOT MAD. YOU DO NOT EAT YOUR MATES.
I'M NOT ALONE IN THAT REGARD.
YOU SOON WILL BE. UNLES YOU LET ME HELP YOU.
NOW, READY YOUR RIFLE AND FOLLOW ME.
WHY ON EARTH WOULD I DO THAT?
BECAUSE YOU AND I ARE GOING TO SAVE YOUR MEN FROM DESTROYING EACH OTHER.
HOW DO I KNOW YOU'RE NOT GOING TO DESTROY ME YOURSELF?
DOES THAT MATTER? YOU WERE GETTING READY TO OPEN YOUR VEINS WHEN WE MET.

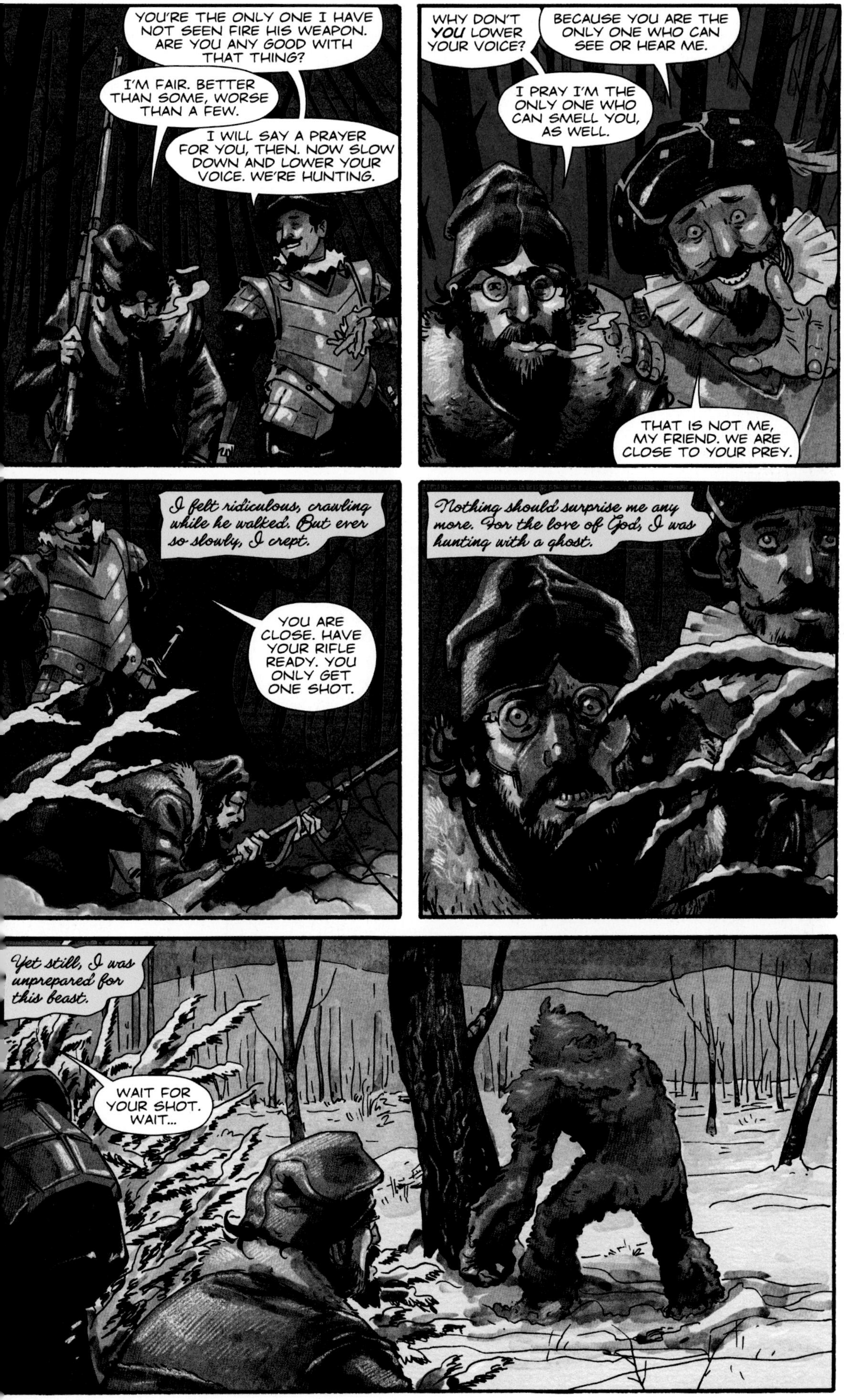

YOU'RE THE ONLY ONE I HAVE NOT SEEN FIRE HIS WEAPON. ARE YOU ANY GOOD WITH THAT THING?
I'M FAIR. BETTER THAN SOME, WORSE THAN A FEW.
I WILL SAY A PRAYER FOR YOU, THEN. NOW SLOW DOWN AND LOWER YOUR VOICE. WE'RE HUNTING.
WHY DON'T YOU LOWER YOUR VOICE?
BECAUSE YOU ARE THE ONLY ONE WHO CAN SEE OR HEAR ME.
I PRAY I'M THE ONLY ONE WHO CAN SMELL YOU, AS WELL.
THAT IS NOT ME, MY FRIEND. WE ARE CLOSE TO YOUR PREY.
I felt ridiculous, crawling while he walked. But ever so slowly, I crept.
YOU ARE CLOSE. HAVE YOUR RIFLE READY. YOU ONLY GET ONE SHOT.
Nothing should surprise me any more. For the love of God, I was hunting with a ghost.
Yet still, I was unprepared for this beast.
WAIT FOR YOUR SHOT. WAIT...

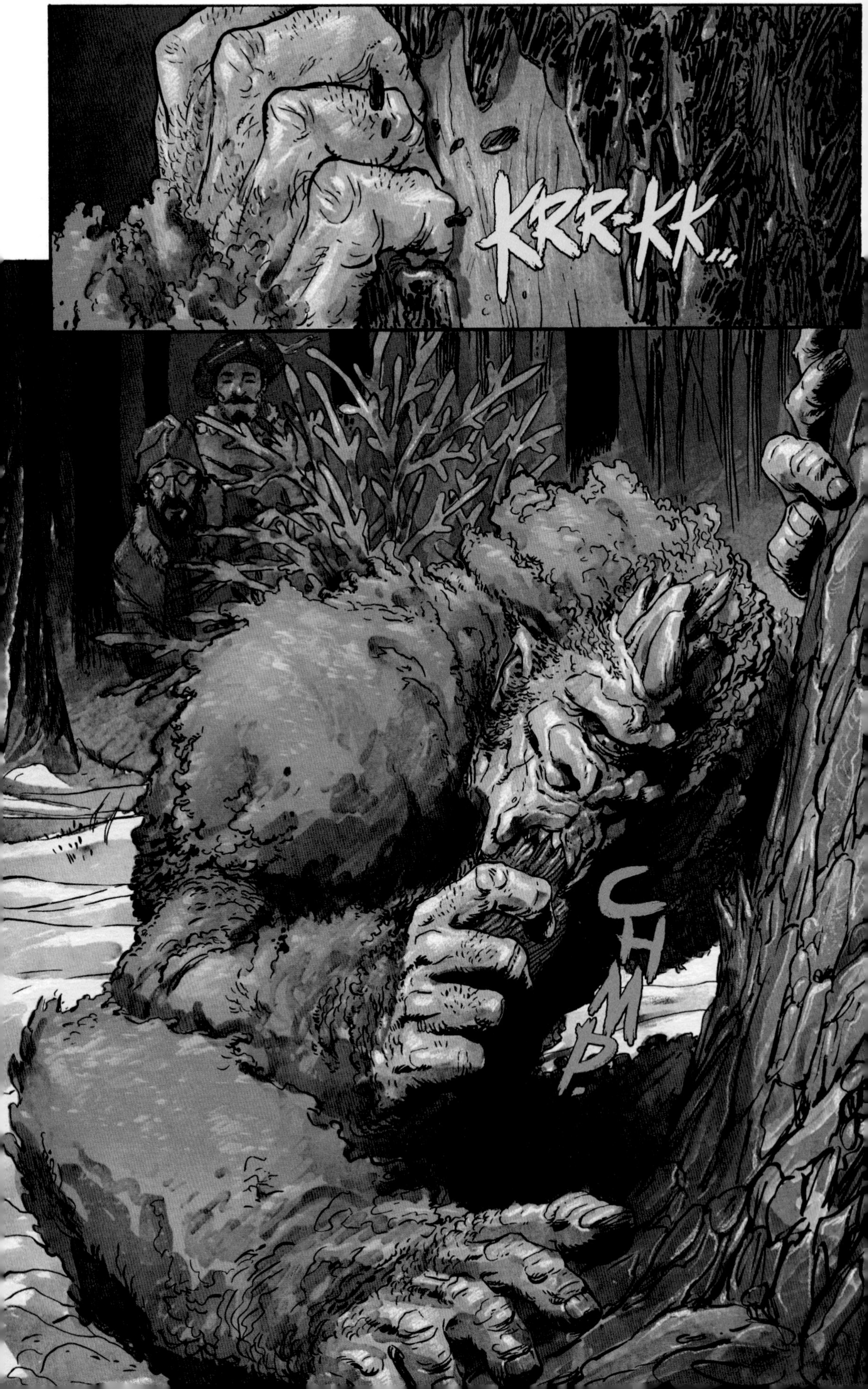
KRR-KK...
CHMB

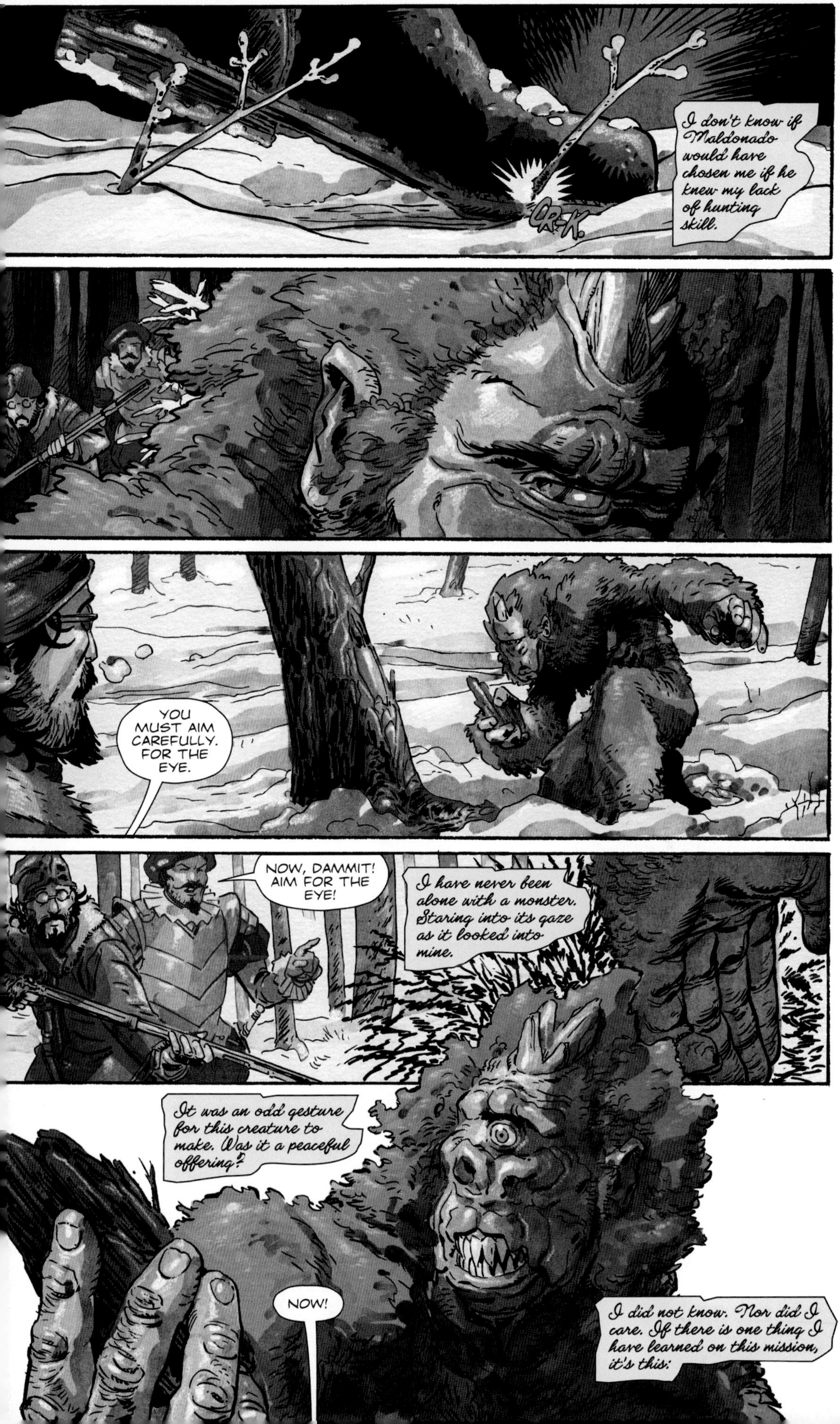

CR-K.
I don't know if Maldonado would have chosen me if he knew my lack of hunting skill.
YOU MUST AIM CAREFULLY. FOR THE EYE.
NOW, DAMMIT! AIM FOR THE EYE!
I have never been alone with a monster. Staring into its gaze as it looked into mine.
It was an odd gesture for this creature to make. Was it a peaceful offering?
NOW!
I did not know. Nor did I care. If there is one thing I have learned on this mission, it's this:

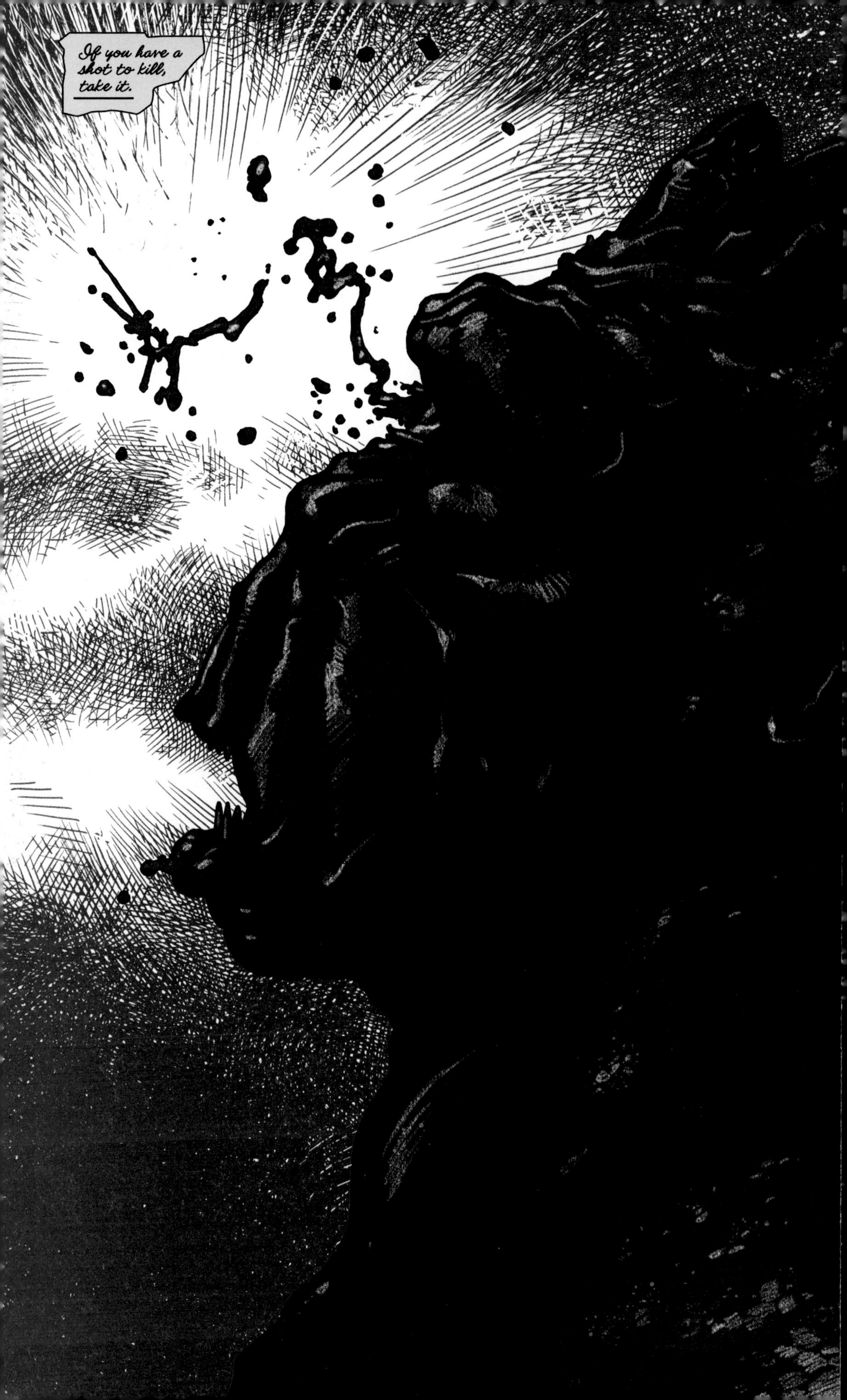
If you have a shot to kill, take it.

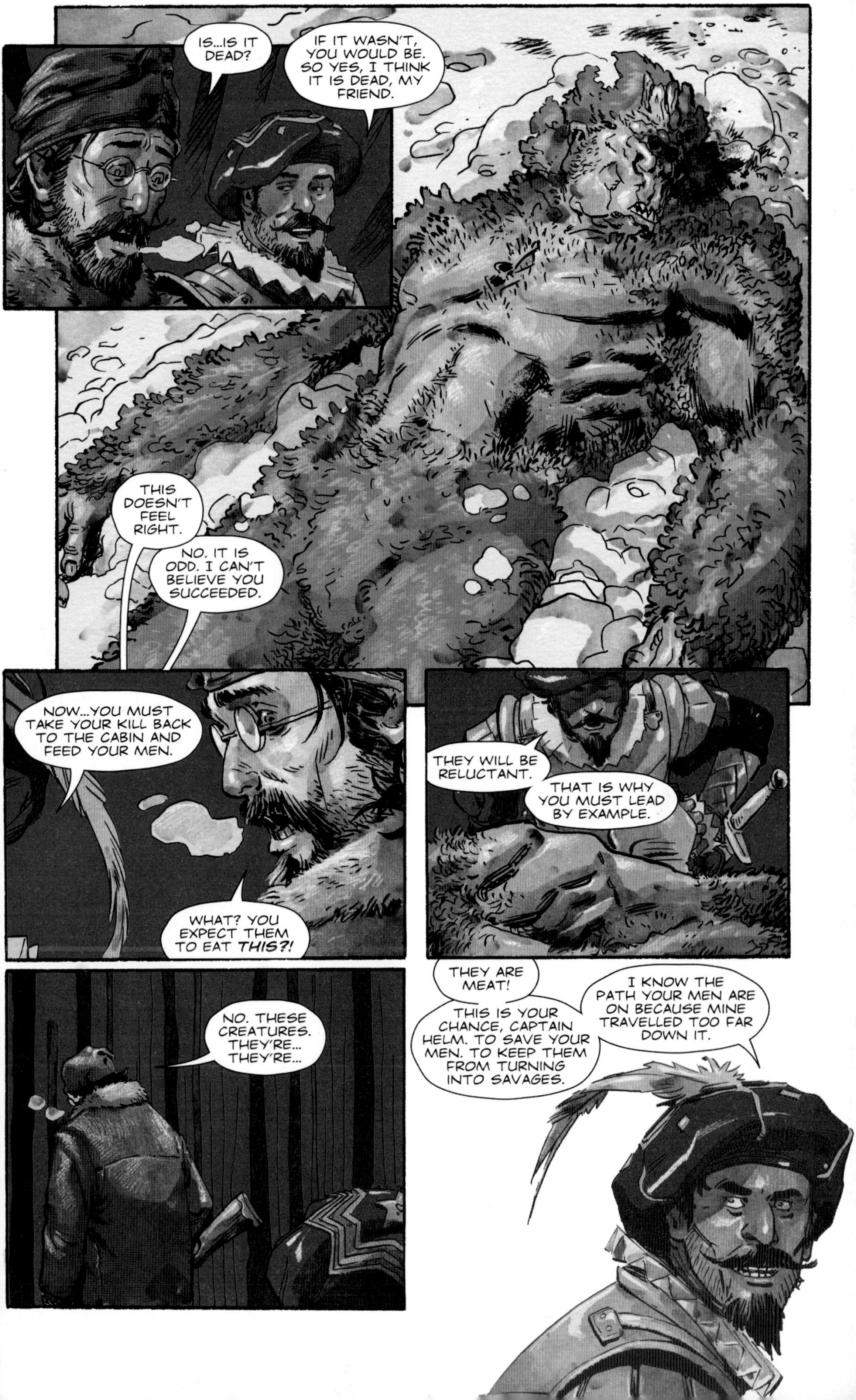
IS...IS IT DEAD?
IF IT WASN'T, YOU WOULD BE. SO YES, I THINK IT IS DEAD, MY FRIEND.
THIS DOESN'T FEEL RIGHT.
NO. IT IS ODD. I CAN'T BELIEVE YOU SUCCEEDED.
NOW...YOU MUST TAKE YOUR KILL BACK TO THE CABIN AND FEED YOUR MEN.
WHAT? YOU EXPECT THEM TO EAT ***THIS?!***
THEY WILL BE RELUCTANT.
THAT IS WHY YOU MUST LEAD BY EXAMPLE.
NO. THESE CREATURES. THEY'RE... THEY'RE...
THEY ARE MEAT!
THIS IS YOUR CHANCE, CAPTAIN HELM. TO SAVE YOUR MEN. TO KEEP THEM FROM TURNING INTO SAVAGES.
I KNOW THE PATH YOUR MEN ARE ON BECAUSE MINE TRAVELLED TOO FAR DOWN IT.

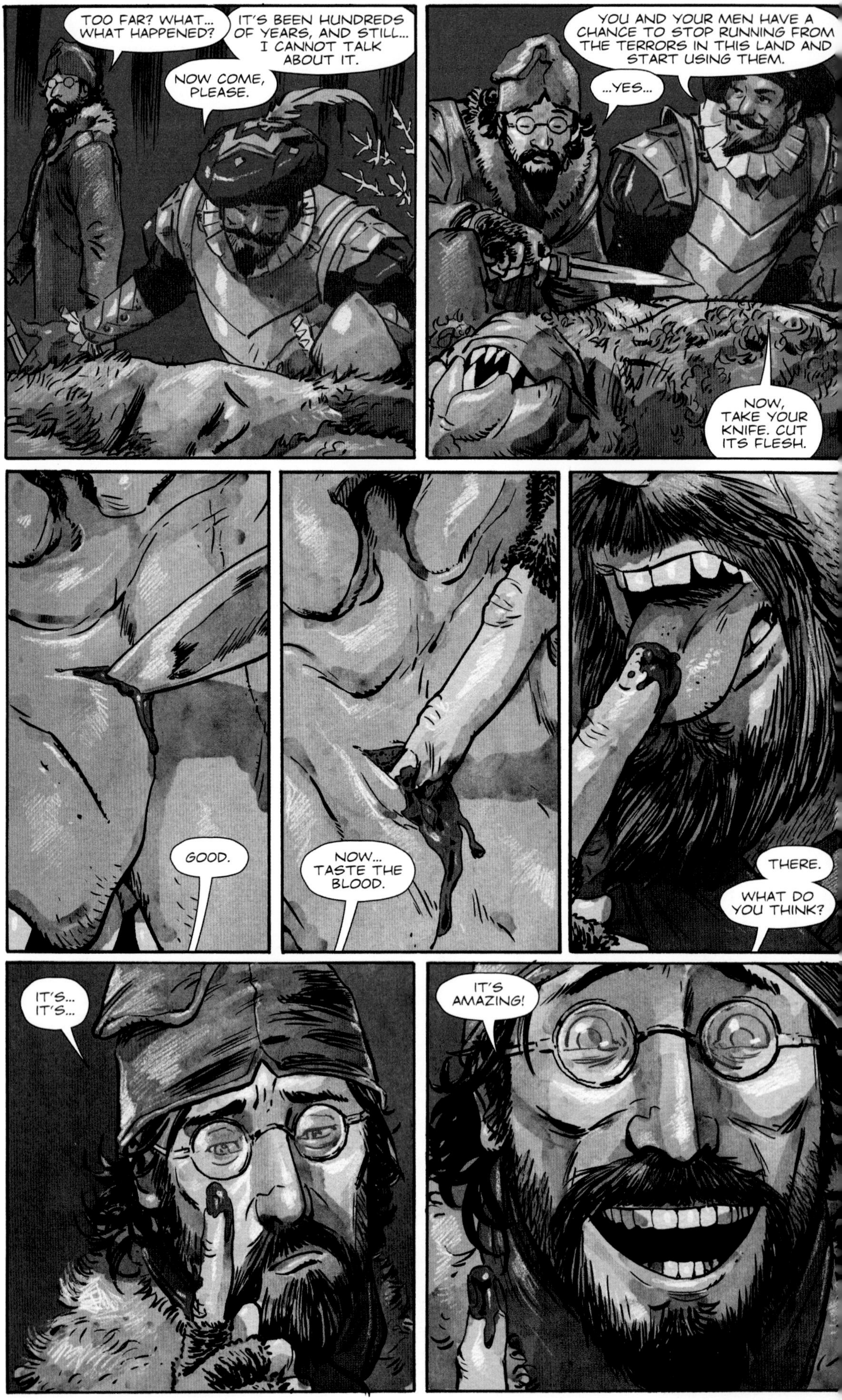
TOO FAR? WHAT... WHAT HAPPENED?
IT'S BEEN HUNDREDS OF YEARS, AND STILL... I CANNOT TALK ABOUT IT.
NOW COME, PLEASE.
YOU AND YOUR MEN HAVE A CHANCE TO STOP RUNNING FROM THE TERRORS IN THIS LAND AND START USING THEM.
...YES...
NOW, TAKE YOUR KNIFE. CUT ITS FLESH.
GOOD.
NOW... TASTE THE BLOOD.
THERE.
WHAT DO YOU THINK?
IT'S... IT'S...
IT'S AMAZING!

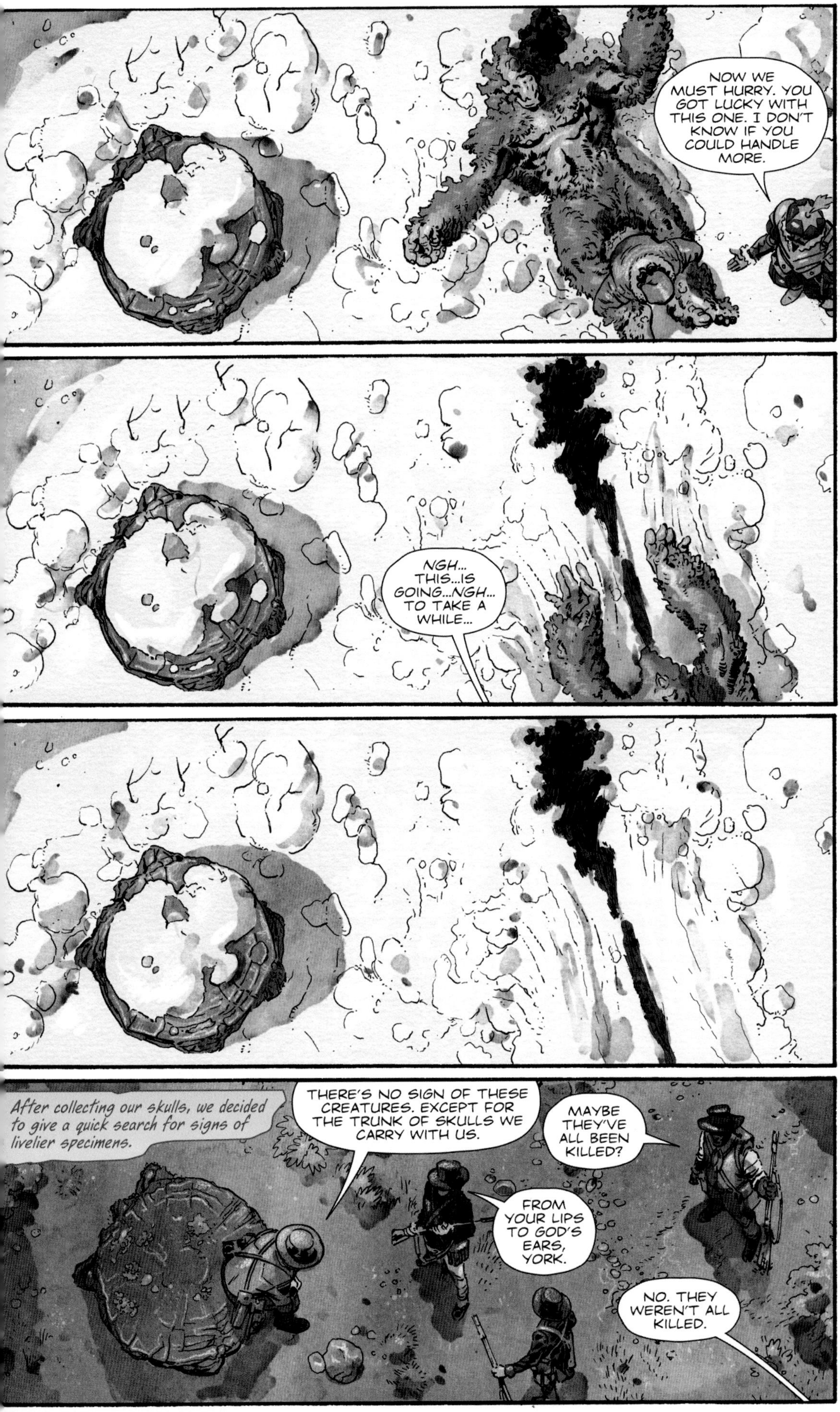
NOW WE MUST HURRY. YOU GOT LUCKY WITH THIS ONE. I DON'T KNOW IF YOU COULD HANDLE MORE.
NGH... THIS...IS GOING...NGH... TO TAKE A WHILE...
After collecting our skulls, we decided to give a quick search for signs of livelier specimens.
THERE'S NO SIGN OF THESE CREATURES. EXCEPT FOR THE TRUNK OF SKULLS WE CARRY WITH US.
MAYBE THEY'VE ALL BEEN KILLED?
FROM YOUR LIPS TO GOD'S EARS, YORK.
NO. THEY WEREN'T ALL KILLED.

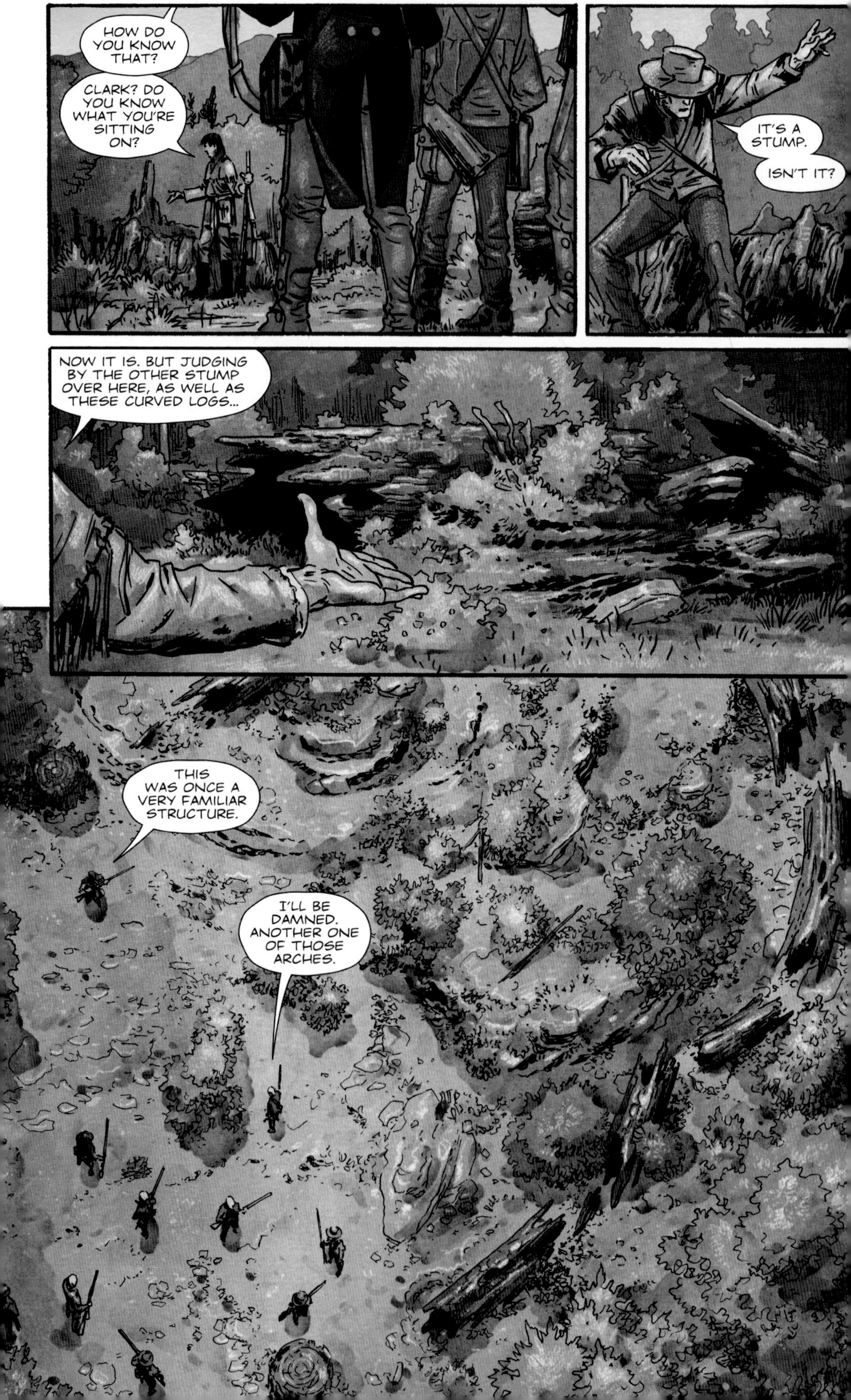
HOW DO YOU KNOW THAT?
CLARK? DO YOU KNOW WHAT YOU'RE SITTING ON?
IT'S A STUMP.
ISN'T IT?
NOW IT IS. BUT JUDGING BY THE OTHER STUMP OVER HERE, AS WELL AS THESE CURVED LOGS...
THIS WAS ONCE A VERY FAMILIAR STRUCTURE.
I'LL BE DAMNED. ANOTHER ONE OF THOSE ARCHES.

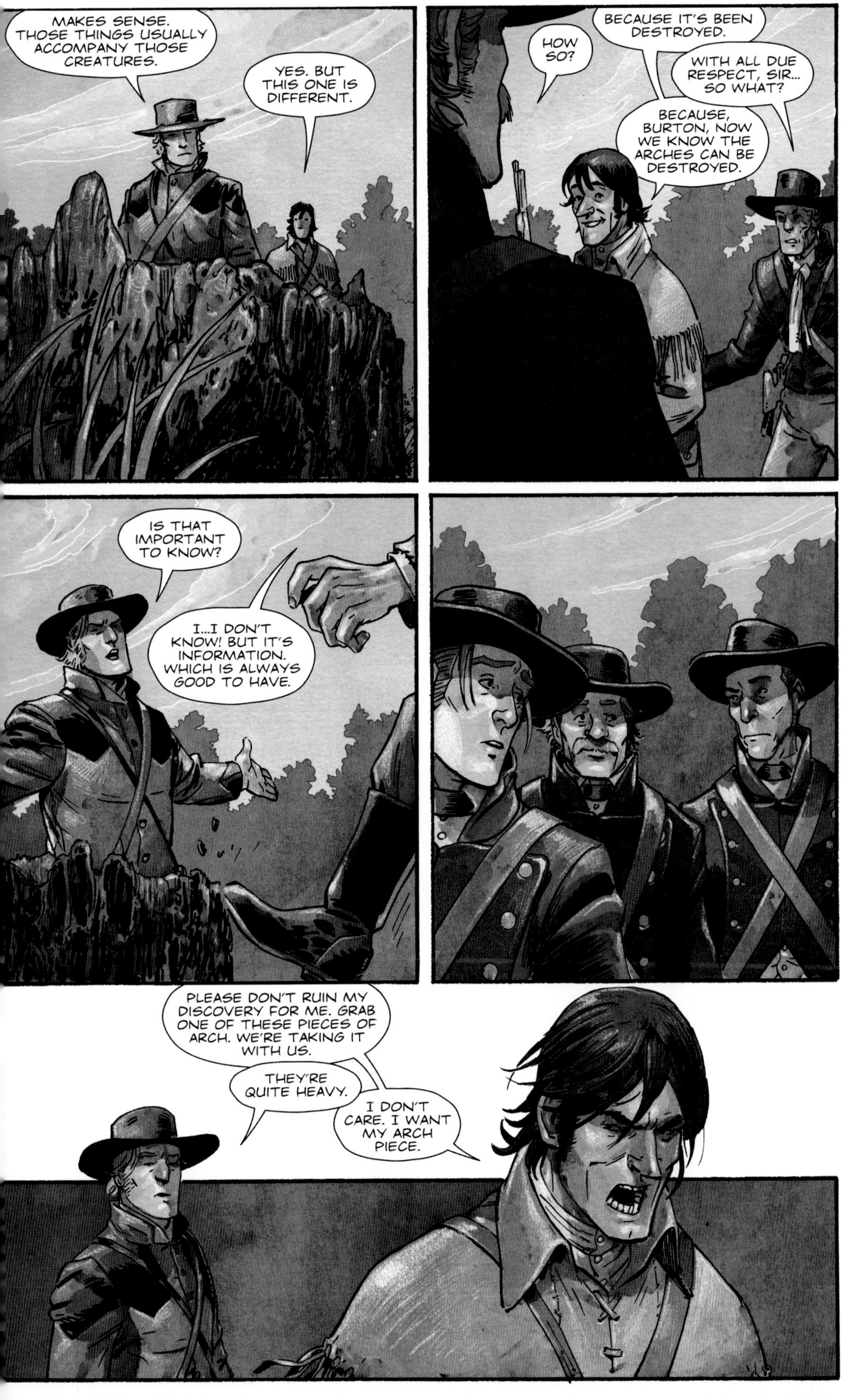

MAKES SENSE. THOSE THINGS USUALLY ACCOMPANY THOSE CREATURES.
YES. BUT THIS ONE IS DIFFERENT.
HOW SO?
BECAUSE IT'S BEEN DESTROYED.
WITH ALL DUE RESPECT, SIR... SO WHAT?
BECAUSE, BURTON, NOW WE KNOW THE ARCHES CAN BE DESTROYED.
IS THAT IMPORTANT TO KNOW?
I...I DON'T KNOW! BUT IT'S INFORMATION. WHICH IS ALWAYS GOOD TO HAVE.
PLEASE DON'T RUIN MY DISCOVERY FOR ME. GRAB ONE OF THESE PIECES OF ARCH. WE'RE TAKING IT WITH US.
THEY'RE QUITE HEAVY.
I DON'T CARE. I WANT MY ARCH PIECE.

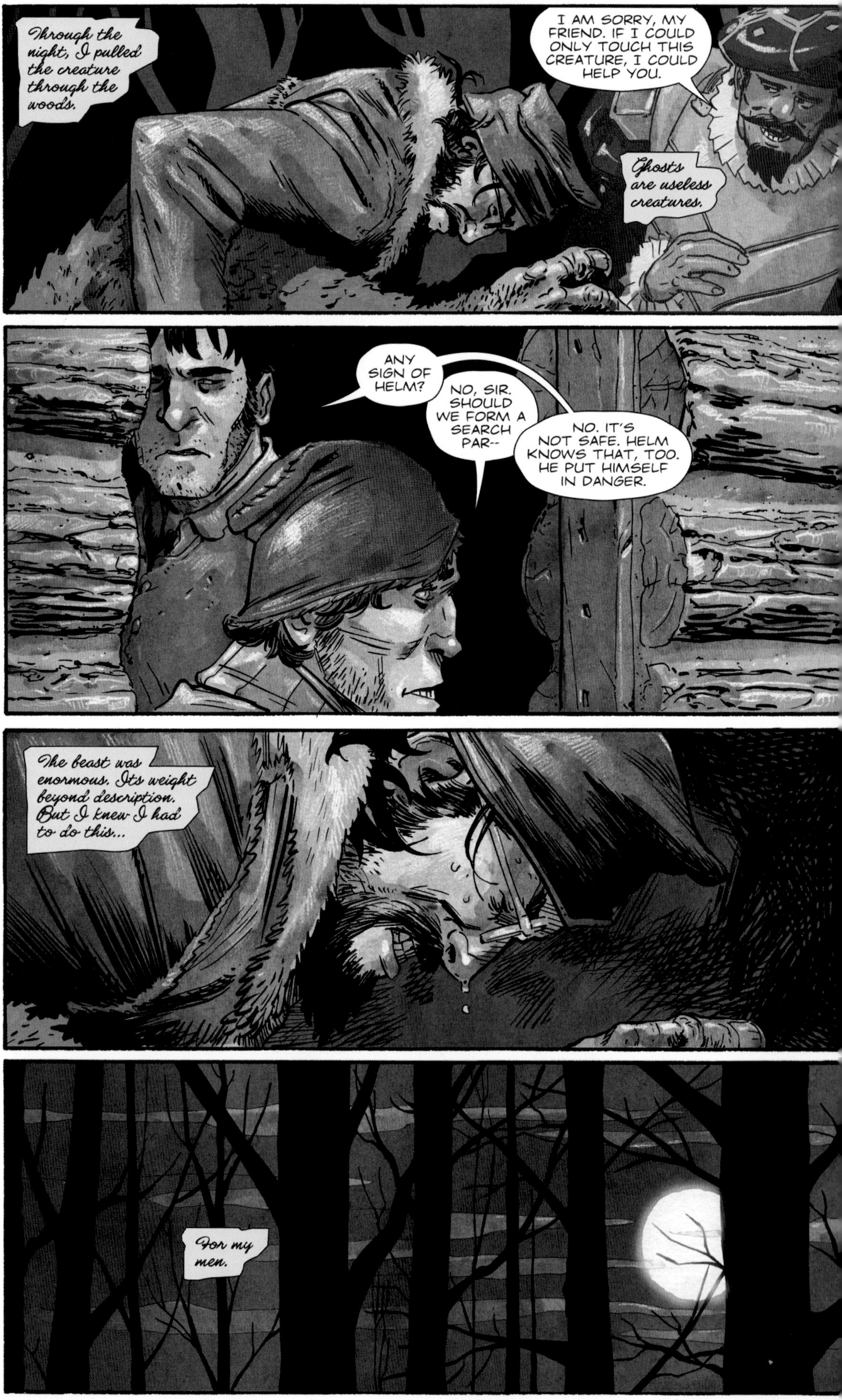

Through the night, I pulled the creature through the woods.
I AM SORRY, MY FRIEND. IF I COULD ONLY TOUCH THIS CREATURE, I COULD HELP YOU.
Ghosts are useless creatures.
ANY SIGN OF HELM?
NO, SIR. SHOULD WE FORM A SEARCH PAR--
NO. IT'S NOT SAFE. HELM KNOWS THAT, TOO. HE PUT HIMSELF IN DANGER.
The beast was enormous. Its weight beyond description. But I knew I had to do this...
For my men.

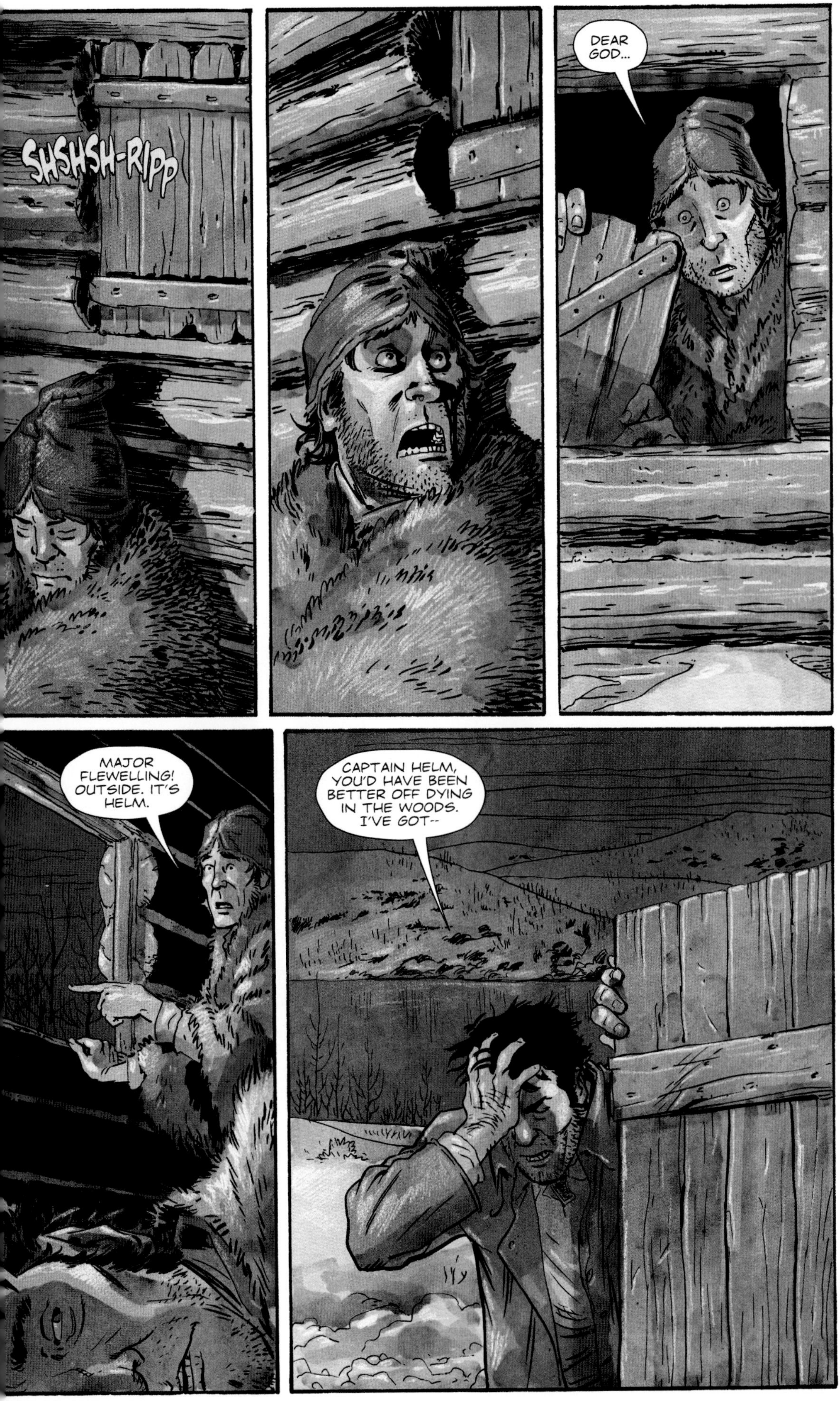
SHSHSH-RIPP
DEAR GOD...
MAJOR FLEWELLING! OUTSIDE. IT'S HELM.
CAPTAIN HELM, YOU'D HAVE BEEN BETTER OFF DYING IN THE WOODS. I'VE GOT--

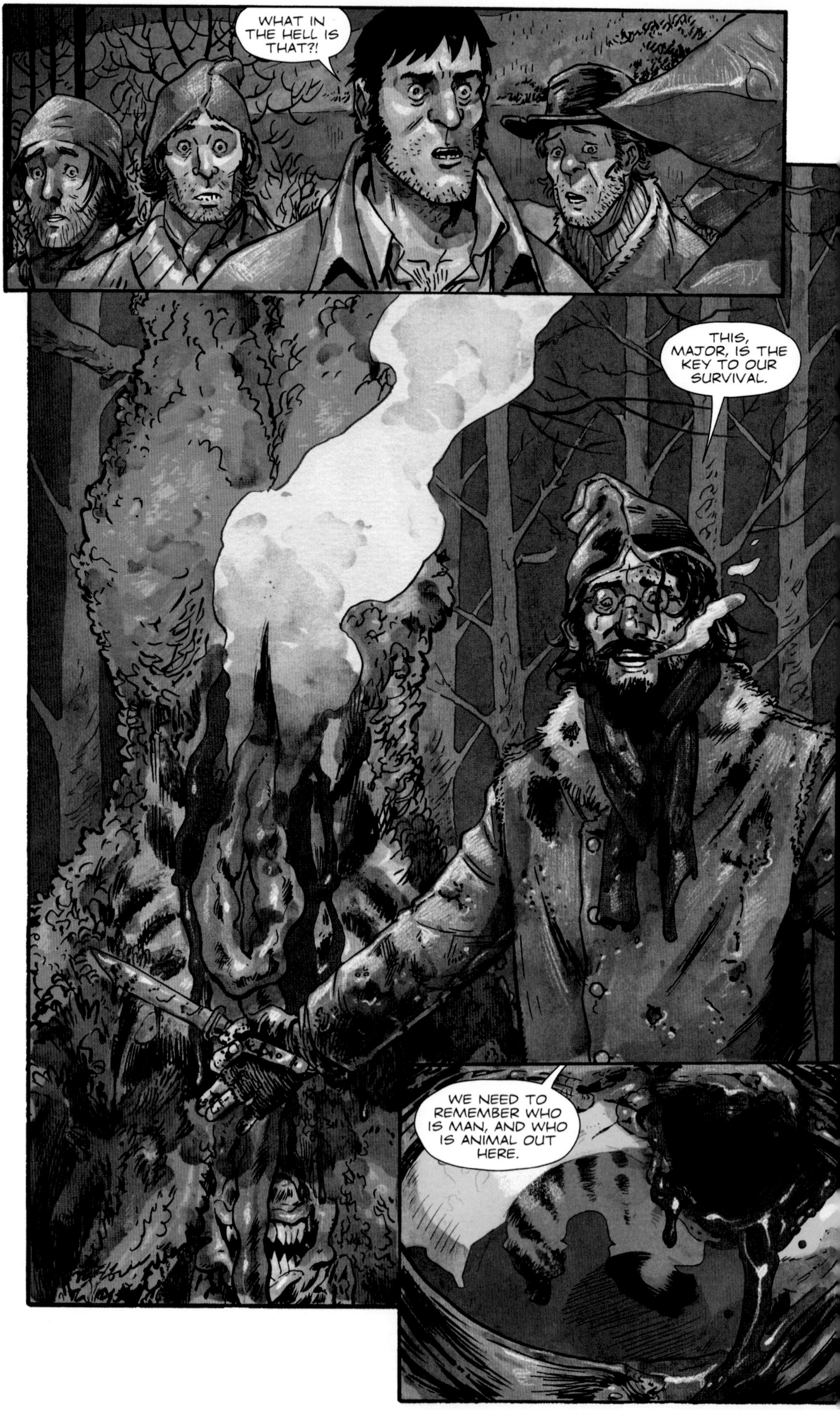
WHAT IN THE HELL IS THAT?!
THIS, MAJOR, IS THE KEY TO OUR SURVIVAL.
WE NEED TO REMEMBER WHO IS MAN, AND WHO IS ANIMAL OUT HERE.

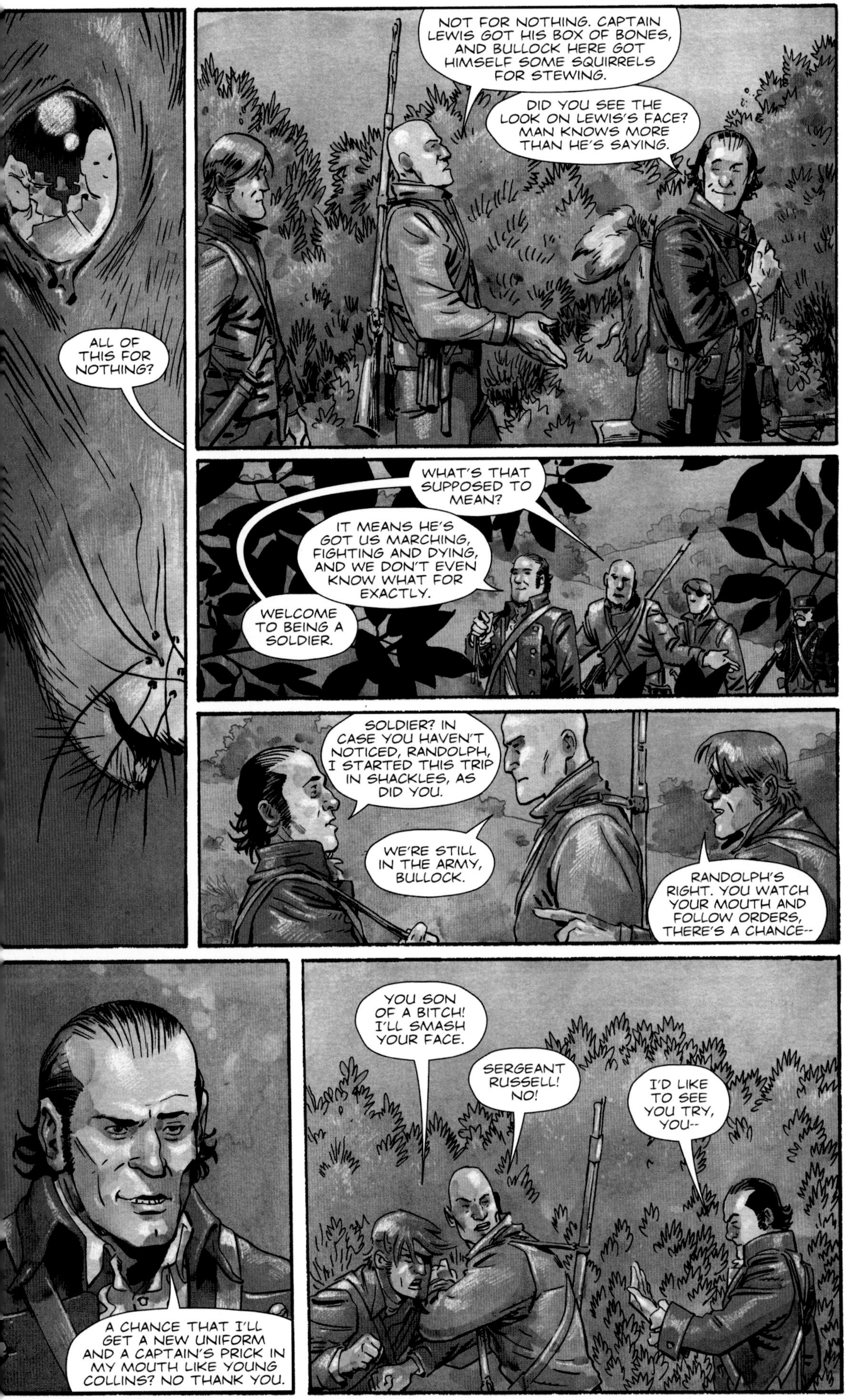
NOT FOR NOTHING. CAPTAIN LEWIS GOT HIS BOX OF BONES, AND BULLOCK HERE GOT HIMSELF SOME SQUIRRELS FOR STEWING.
DID YOU SEE THE LOOK ON LEWIS'S FACE? MAN KNOWS MORE THAN HE'S SAYING.
ALL OF THIS FOR NOTHING?
WHAT'S THAT SUPPOSED TO MEAN?
IT MEANS HE'S GOT US MARCHING, FIGHTING AND DYING, AND WE DON'T EVEN KNOW WHAT FOR EXACTLY.
WELCOME TO BEING A SOLDIER.
SOLDIER? IN CASE YOU HAVEN'T NOTICED, RANDOLPH, I STARTED THIS TRIP IN SHACKLES, AS DID YOU.
WE'RE STILL IN THE ARMY, BULLOCK.
RANDOLPH'S RIGHT. YOU WATCH YOUR MOUTH AND FOLLOW ORDERS, THERE'S A CHANCE--
A CHANCE THAT I'LL GET A NEW UNIFORM AND A CAPTAIN'S PRICK IN MY MOUTH LIKE YOUNG COLLINS? NO THANK YOU.
YOU SON OF A BITCH! I'LL SMASH YOUR FACE.
SERGEANT RUSSELL! NO!
I'D LIKE TO SEE YOU TRY, YOU--

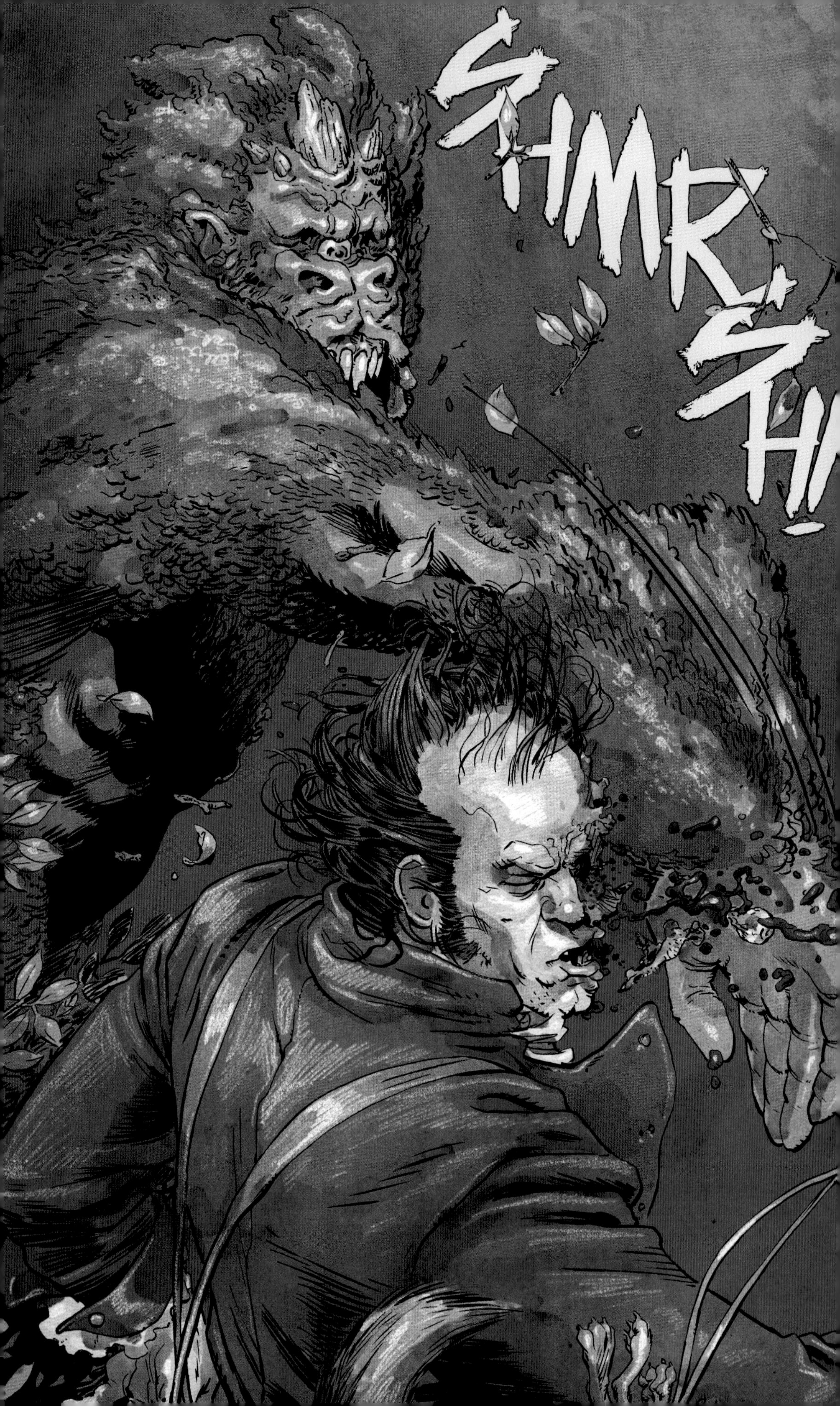
SHMRSH!!

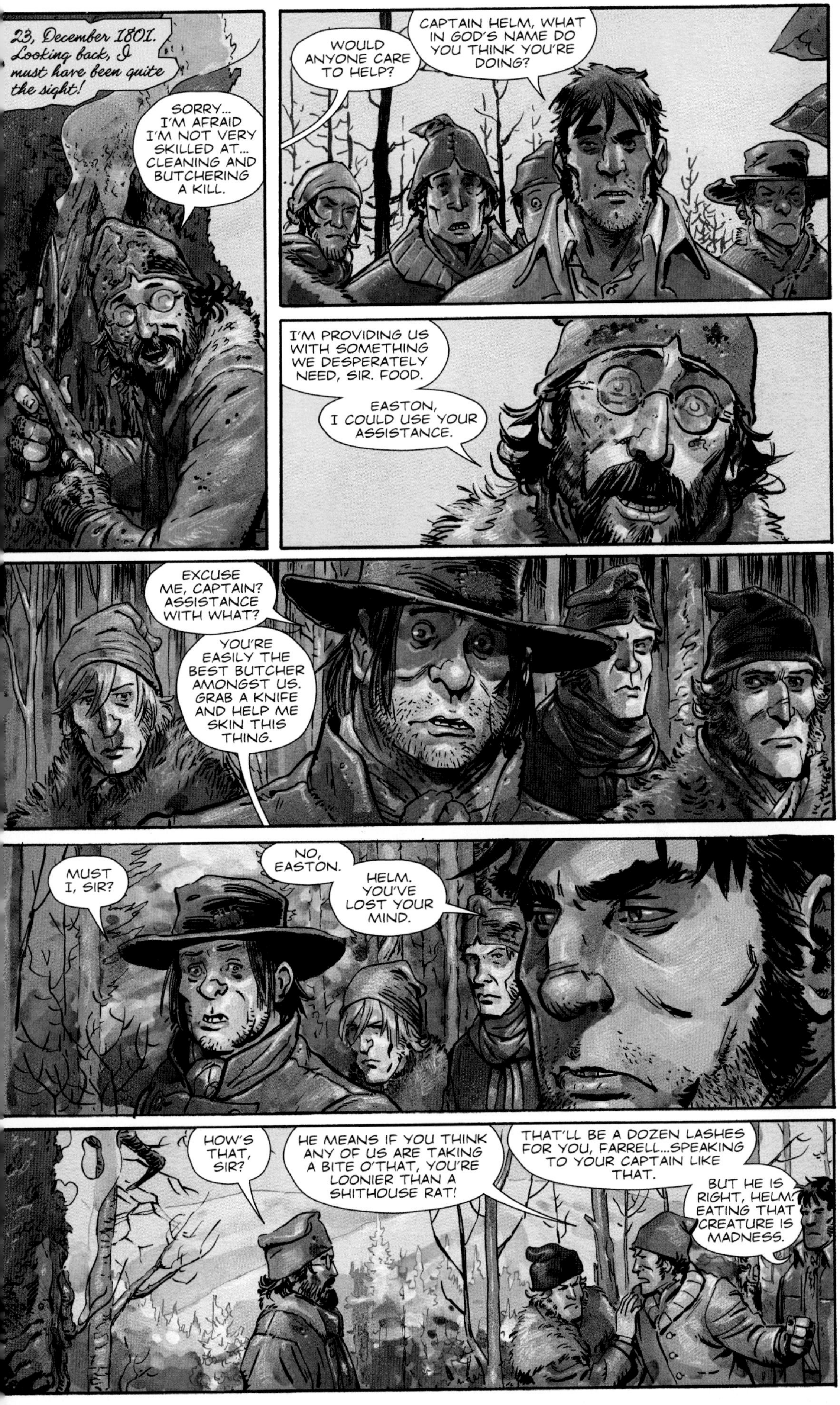

23, December 1801. Looking back, I must have been quite the sight!
SORRY... I'M AFRAID I'M NOT VERY SKILLED AT... CLEANING AND BUTCHERING A KILL.
WOULD ANYONE CARE TO HELP?
CAPTAIN HELM, WHAT IN GOD'S NAME DO YOU THINK YOU'RE DOING?
I'M PROVIDING US WITH SOMETHING WE DESPERATELY NEED, SIR. FOOD.
EASTON, I COULD USE YOUR ASSISTANCE.
EXCUSE ME, CAPTAIN? ASSISTANCE WITH WHAT?
YOU'RE EASILY THE BEST BUTCHER AMONGST US. GRAB A KNIFE AND HELP ME SKIN THIS THING.
MUST I, SIR?
NO, EASTON.
HELM. YOU'VE LOST YOUR MIND.
HOW'S THAT, SIR?
HE MEANS IF YOU THINK ANY OF US ARE TAKING A BITE O'THAT, YOU'RE LOONIER THAN A SHITHOUSE RAT!
THAT'LL BE A DOZEN LASHES FOR YOU, FARRELL...SPEAKING TO YOUR CAPTAIN LIKE THAT.
BUT HE IS RIGHT, HELM. EATING THAT CREATURE IS MADNESS.

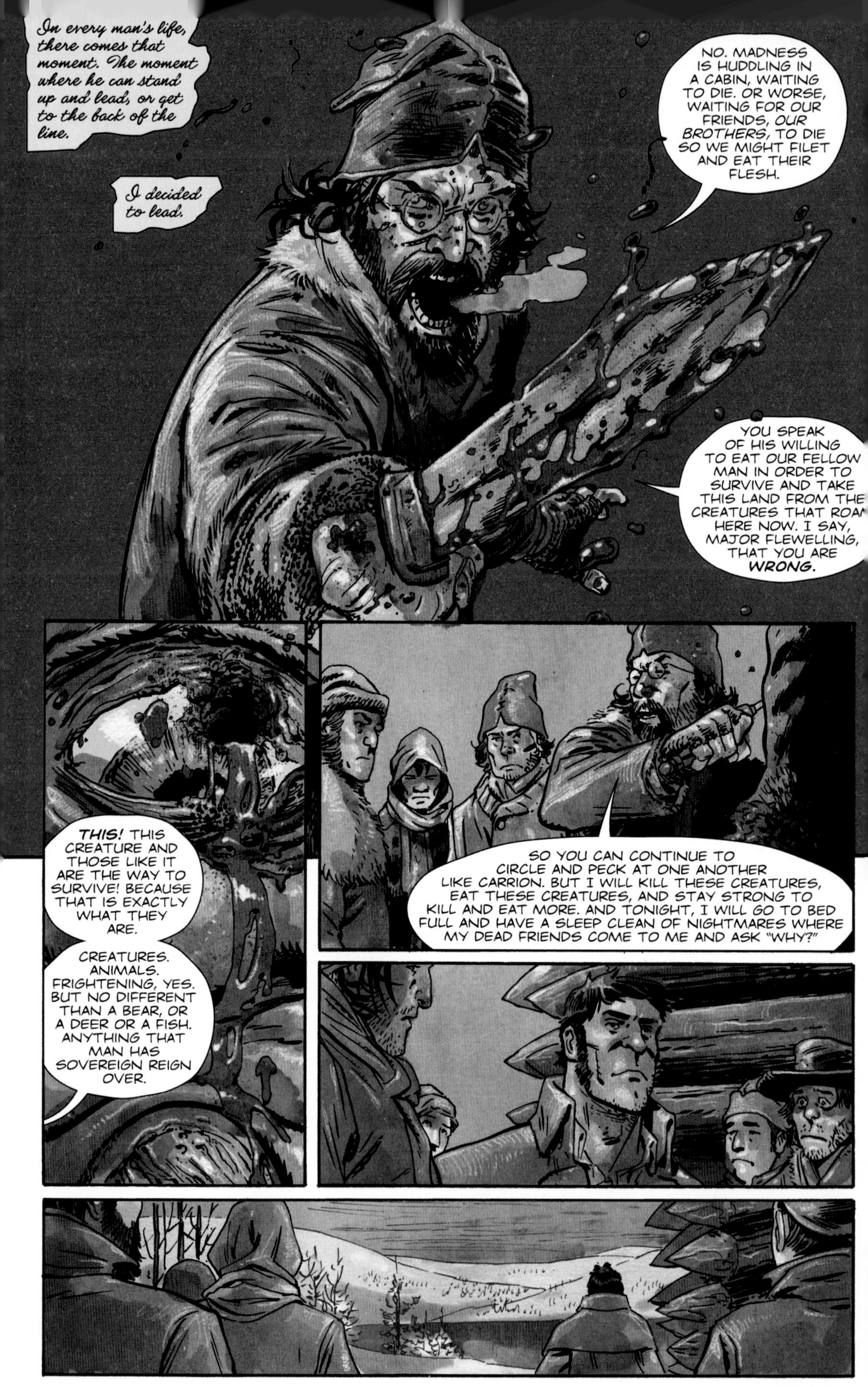

In every man's life, there comes that moment. The moment where he can stand up and lead, or get to the back of the line.
I decided to lead.
NO. MADNESS IS HUDDLING IN A CABIN, WAITING TO DIE. OR WORSE, WAITING FOR OUR FRIENDS, OUR BROTHERS, TO DIE SO WE MIGHT FILET AND EAT THEIR FLESH.
YOU SPEAK OF HIS WILLING TO EAT OUR FELLOW MAN IN ORDER TO SURVIVE AND TAKE THIS LAND FROM THE CREATURES THAT ROAM HERE NOW. I SAY, MAJOR FLEWELLING, THAT YOU ARE **WRONG.**
THIS! THIS CREATURE AND THOSE LIKE IT ARE THE WAY TO SURVIVE! BECAUSE THAT IS EXACTLY WHAT THEY ARE.
CREATURES. ANIMALS. FRIGHTENING, YES. BUT NO DIFFERENT THAN A BEAR, OR A DEER OR A FISH. ANYTHING THAT MAN HAS SOVEREIGN REIGN OVER.
SO YOU CAN CONTINUE TO CIRCLE AND PECK AT ONE ANOTHER LIKE CARRION. BUT I WILL KILL THESE CREATURES, EAT THESE CREATURES, AND STAY STRONG TO KILL AND EAT MORE. AND TONIGHT, I WILL GO TO BED FULL AND HAVE A SLEEP CLEAN OF NIGHTMARES WHERE MY DEAD FRIENDS COME TO ME AND ASK "WHY?"

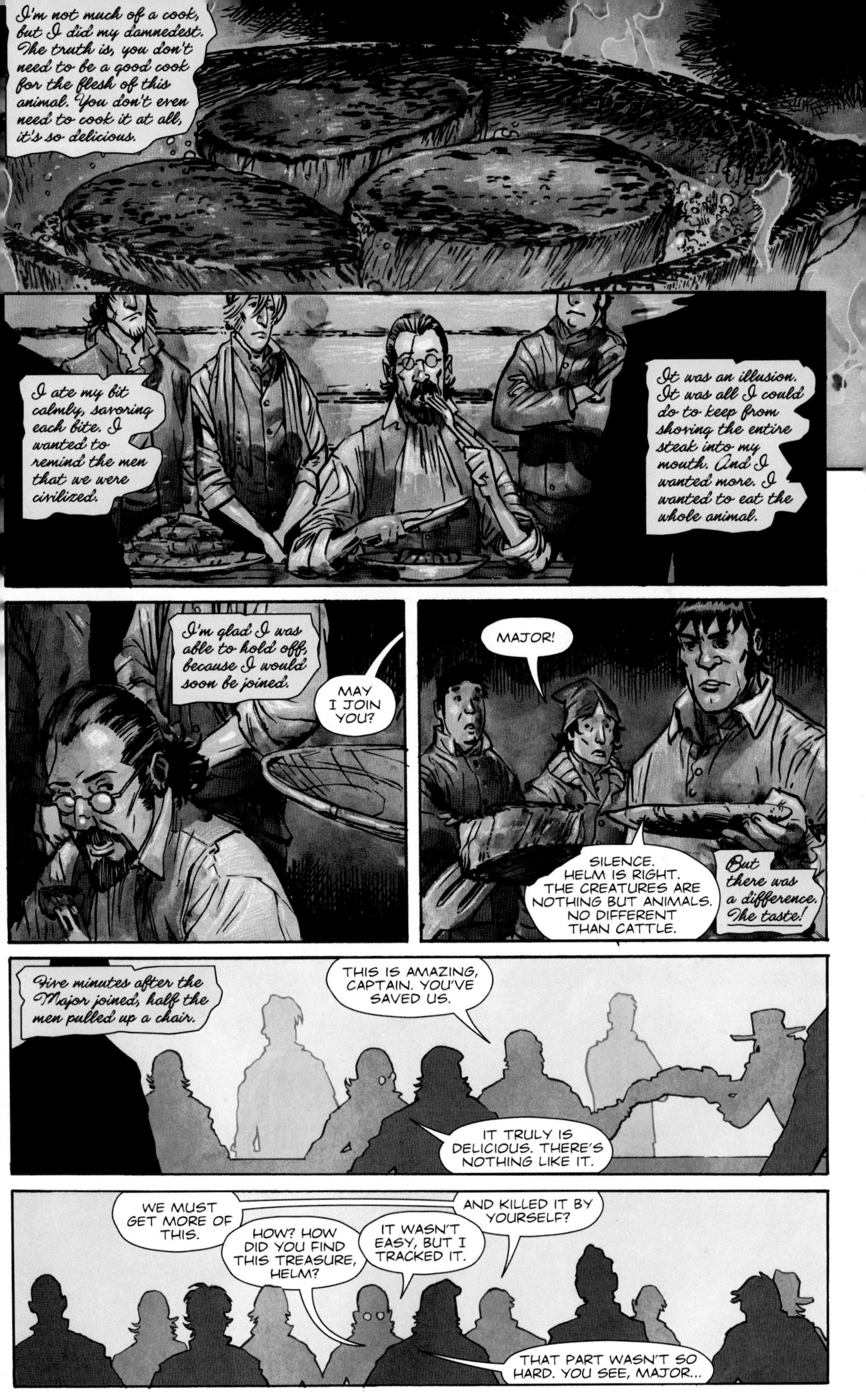
I'm not much of a cook, but I did my damnedest. The truth is, you don't need to be a good cook for the flesh of this animal. You don't even need to cook it at all, it's so delicious.
I ate my bit calmly, savoring each bite. I wanted to remind the men that we were civilized.
It was an illusion. It was all I could do to keep from shoving the entire steak into my mouth. And I wanted more. I wanted to eat the whole animal.
I'm glad I was able to hold off, because I would soon be joined.
MAY I JOIN YOU?
MAJOR!
SILENCE. HELM IS RIGHT. THE CREATURES ARE NOTHING BUT ANIMALS. NO DIFFERENT THAN CATTLE.
But there was a difference. The taste!
Five minutes after the Major joined, half the men pulled up a chair.
THIS IS AMAZING, CAPTAIN. YOU'VE SAVED US.
IT TRULY IS DELICIOUS. THERE'S NOTHING LIKE IT.
WE MUST GET MORE OF THIS.
HOW? HOW DID YOU FIND THIS TREASURE, HELM?
IT WASN'T EASY, BUT I TRACKED IT.
AND KILLED IT BY YOURSELF?
THAT PART WASN'T SO HARD. YOU SEE, MAJOR...

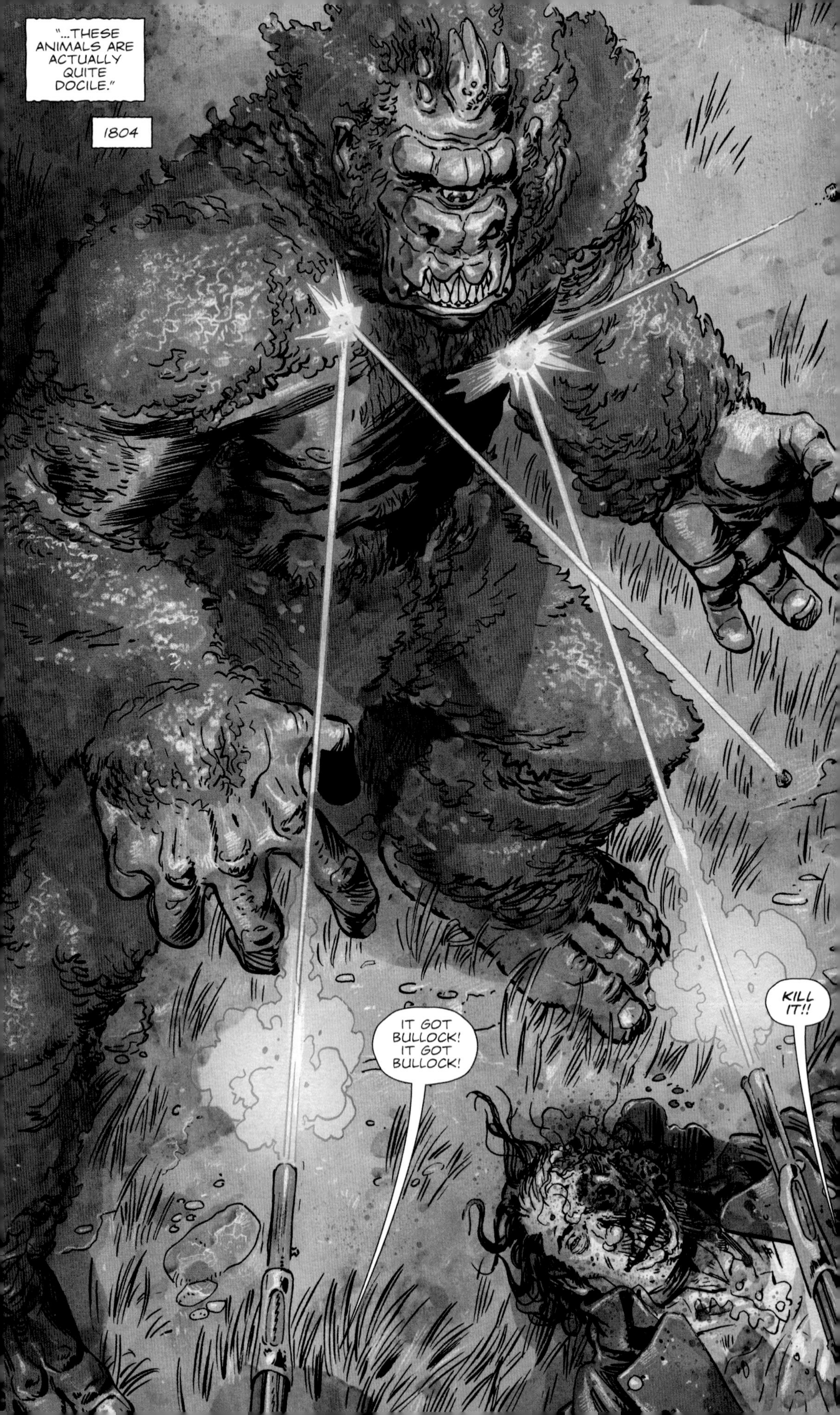
"...THESE ANIMALS ARE ACTUALLY QUITE DOCILE."
1804
IT GOT BULLOCK! IT GOT BULLOCK!
KILL IT!!

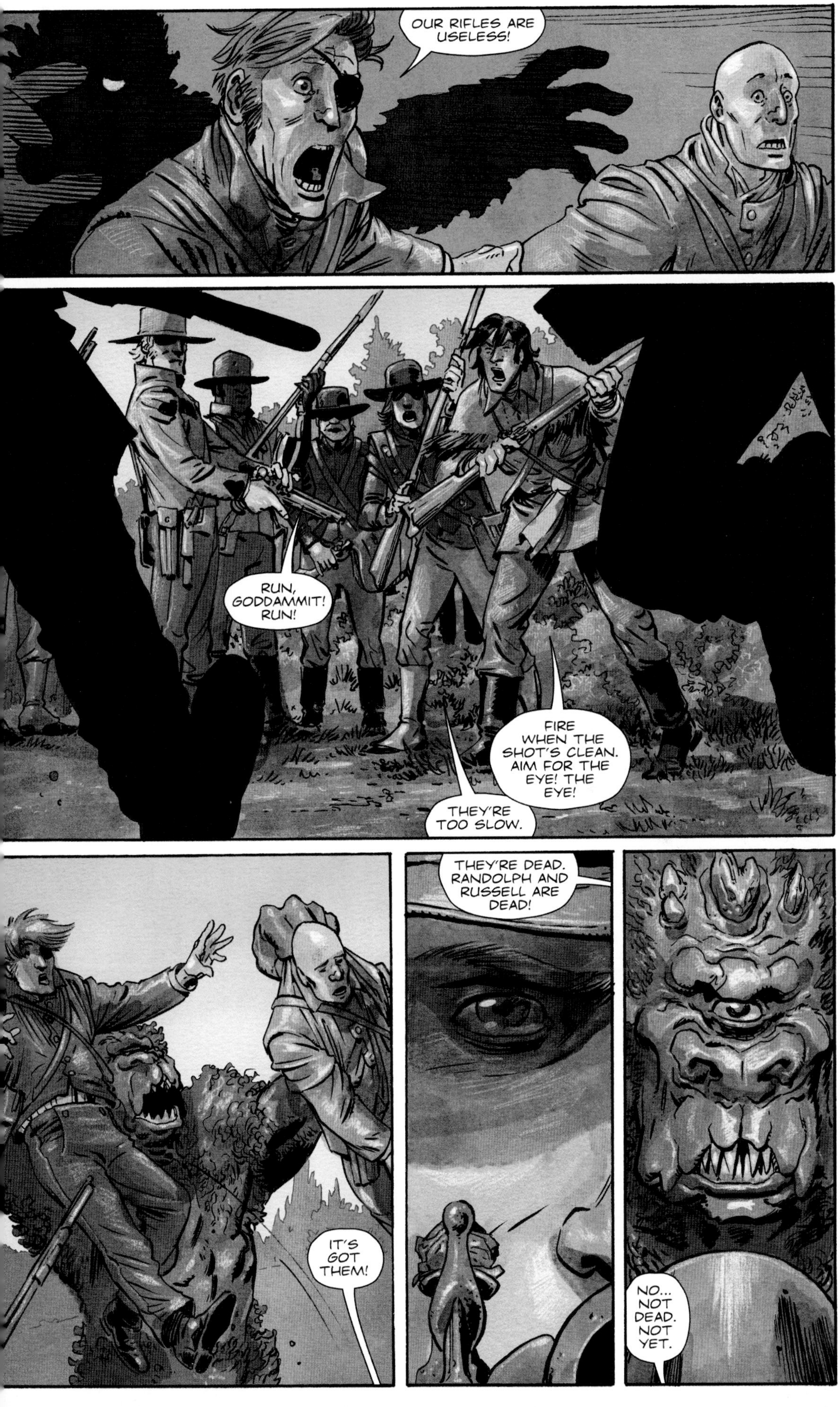
OUR RIFLES ARE USELESS!
RUN, GODDAMMIT! RUN!
FIRE WHEN THE SHOT'S CLEAN. AIM FOR THE EYE! THE EYE!
THEY'RE TOO SLOW.
IT'S GOT THEM!
THEY'RE DEAD. RANDOLPH AND RUSSELL ARE DEAD!
NO... NOT DEAD. NOT YET.

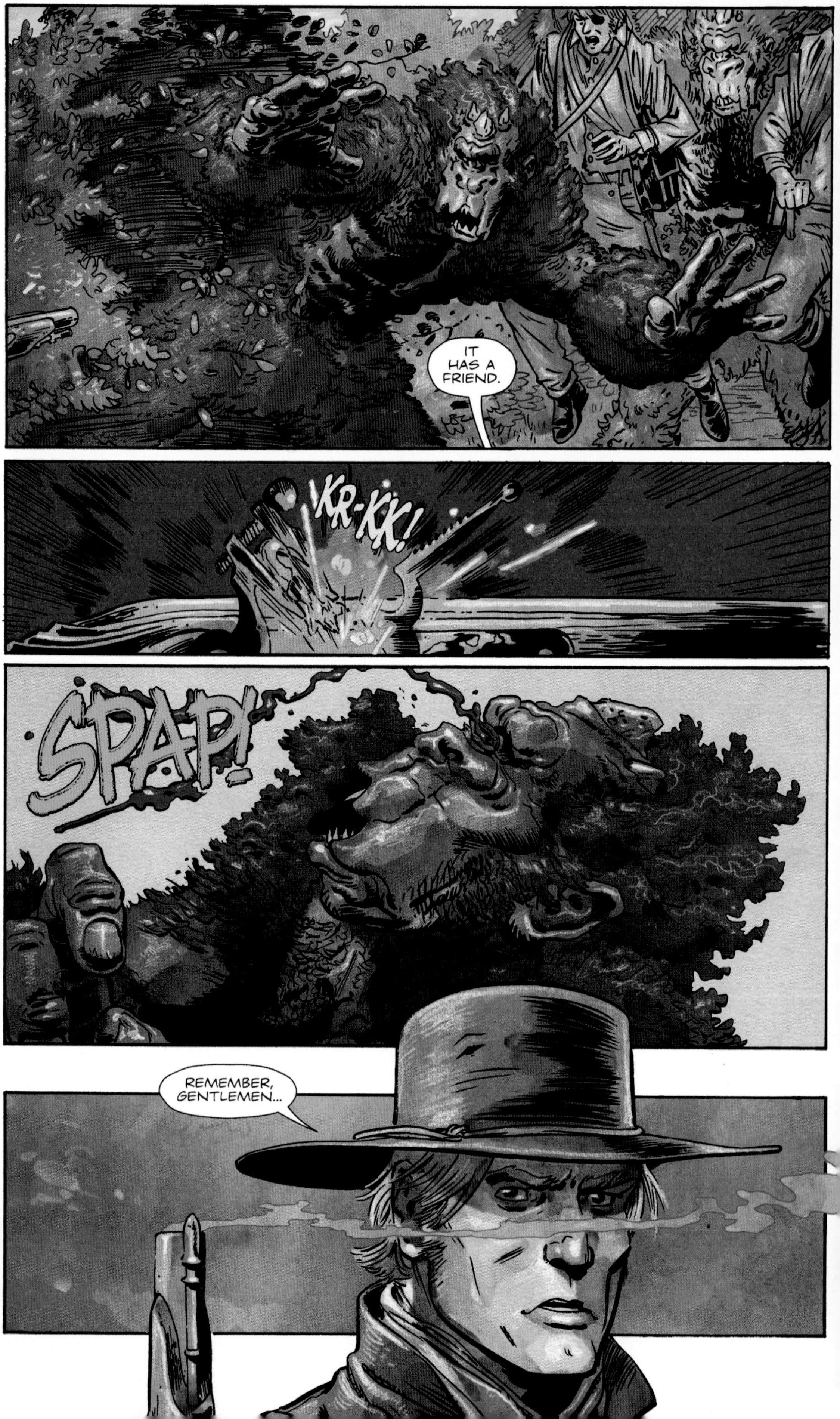
IT HAS A FRIEND.
KR-KK!
SPAP!
REMEMBER, GENTLEMEN...

THE EYE.

AAAAOOOOGH!!!

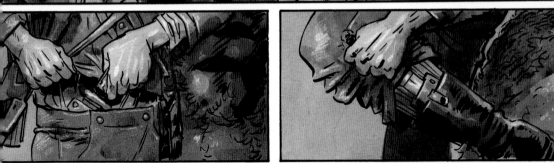

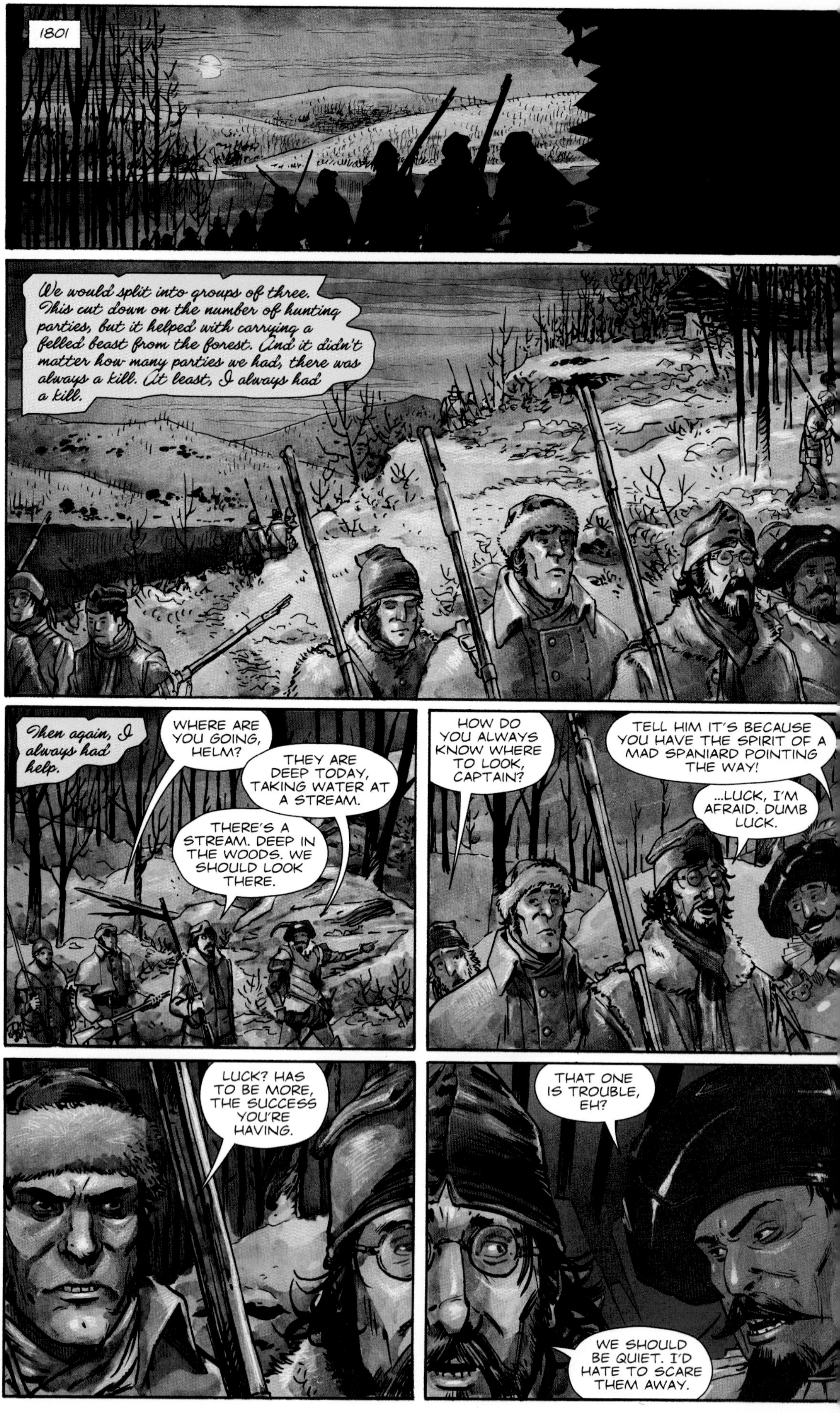
1801
We would split into groups of three. This cut down on the number of hunting parties, but it helped with carrying a felled beast from the forest. And it didn't matter how many parties we had, there was always a kill. At least, I always had a kill.
Then again, I always had help.
WHERE ARE YOU GOING, HELM?
THEY ARE DEEP TODAY, TAKING WATER AT A STREAM.
THERE'S A STREAM. DEEP IN THE WOODS. WE SHOULD LOOK THERE.
HOW DO YOU ALWAYS KNOW WHERE TO LOOK, CAPTAIN?
TELL HIM IT'S BECAUSE YOU HAVE THE SPIRIT OF A MAD SPANIARD POINTING THE WAY!
...LUCK, I'M AFRAID. DUMB LUCK.
LUCK? HAS TO BE MORE, THE SUCCESS YOU'RE HAVING.
THAT ONE IS TROUBLE, EH?
WE SHOULD BE QUIET. I'D HATE TO SCARE THEM AWAY.

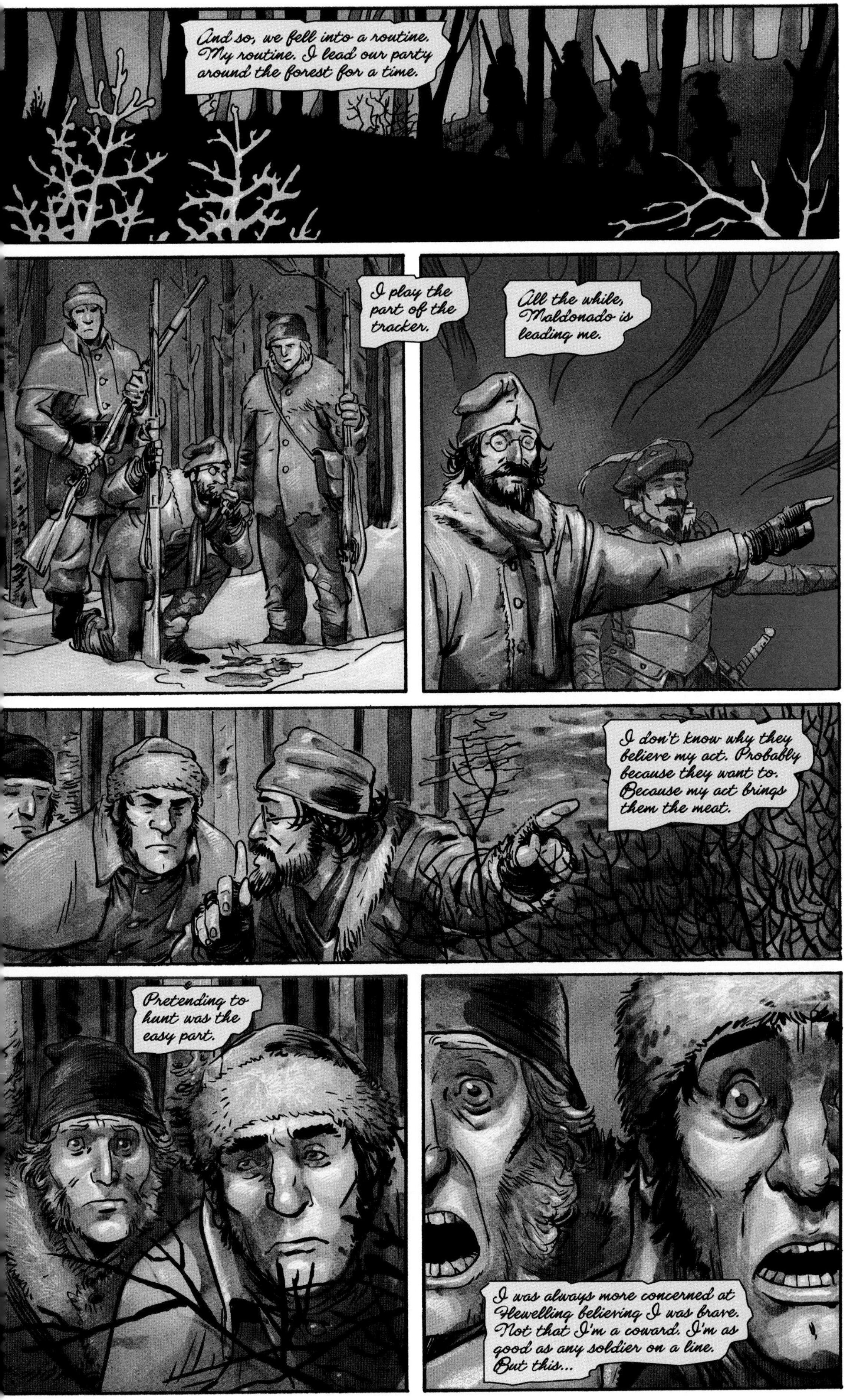
And so, we fell into a routine. My routine. I lead our party around the forest for a time.
I play the part of the tracker.
All the while, Maldonado is leading me.
I don't know why they believe my act. Probably because they want to. Because my act brings them the meat.
Pretending to hunt was the easy part.
I was always more concerned at Hewelling believing I was brave. Not that I'm a coward. I'm as good as any soldier on a line. But this...

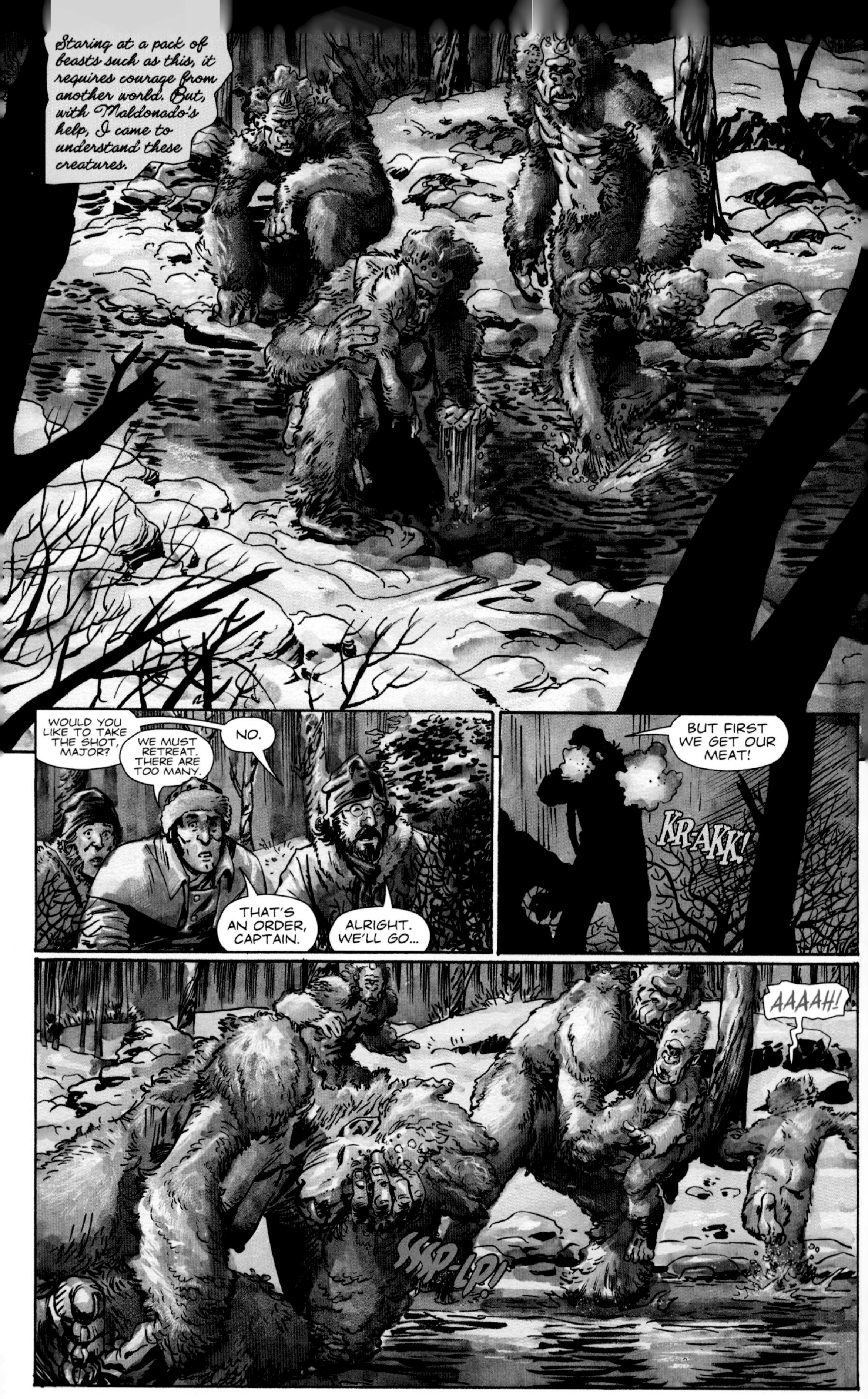
Staring at a pack of beasts such as this, it requires courage from another world. But, with Maldonado's help, I came to understand these creatures.
WOULD YOU LIKE TO TAKE THE SHOT, MAJOR?
WE MUST RETREAT. THERE ARE TOO MANY.
NO.
THAT'S AN ORDER, CAPTAIN.
ALRIGHT. WE'LL GO...
BUT FIRST WE GET OUR MEAT!
KR-AKK!
AAAAH!
SSSP-LP!

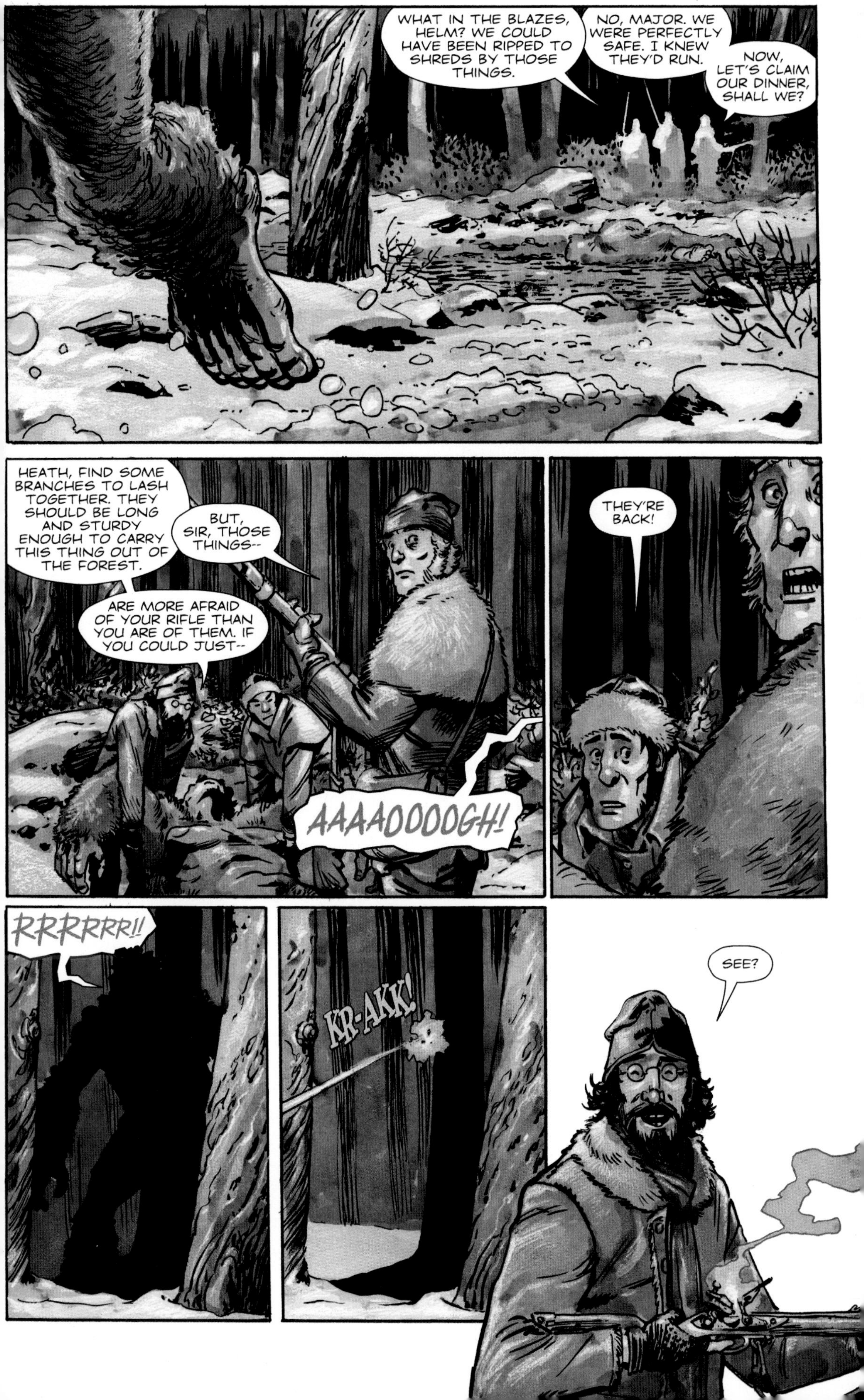
WHAT IN THE BLAZES, HELM? WE COULD HAVE BEEN RIPPED TO SHREDS BY THOSE THINGS.
NO, MAJOR. WE WERE PERFECTLY SAFE. I KNEW THEY'D RUN.
NOW, LET'S CLAIM OUR DINNER, SHALL WE?
HEATH, FIND SOME BRANCHES TO LASH TOGETHER. THEY SHOULD BE LONG AND STURDY ENOUGH TO CARRY THIS THING OUT OF THE FOREST.
BUT, SIR, THOSE THINGS--
ARE MORE AFRAID OF YOUR RIFLE THAN YOU ARE OF THEM. IF YOU COULD JUST--
AAAAOOOOGH!
THEY'RE BACK!
RRRRRR!!
KR-AKK!
SEE?

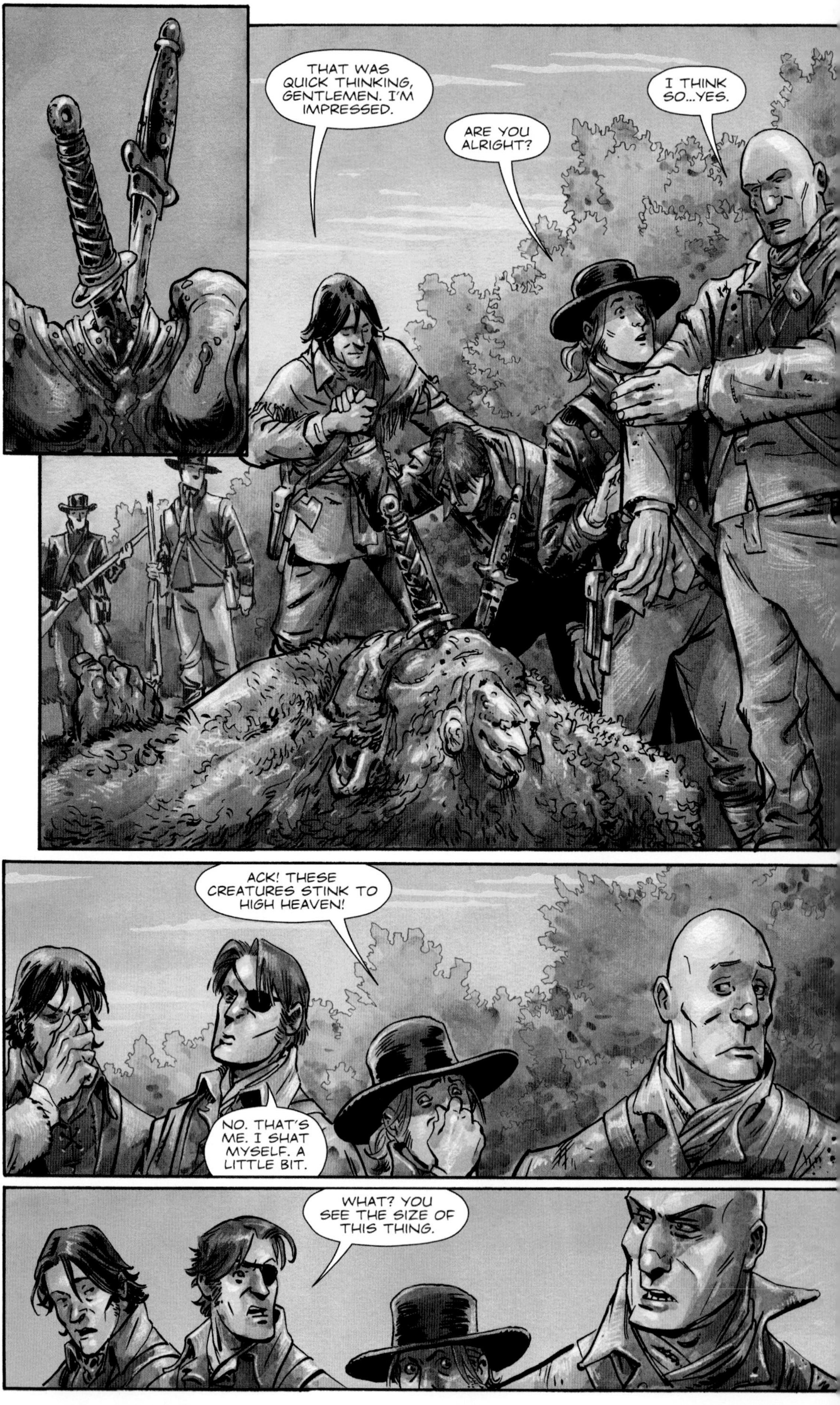
THAT WAS QUICK THINKING, GENTLEMEN. I'M IMPRESSED.
ARE YOU ALRIGHT?
I THINK SO...YES.
ACK! THESE CREATURES STINK TO HIGH HEAVEN!
NO. THAT'S ME. I SHAT MYSELF. A LITTLE BIT.
WHAT? YOU SEE THE SIZE OF THIS THING.

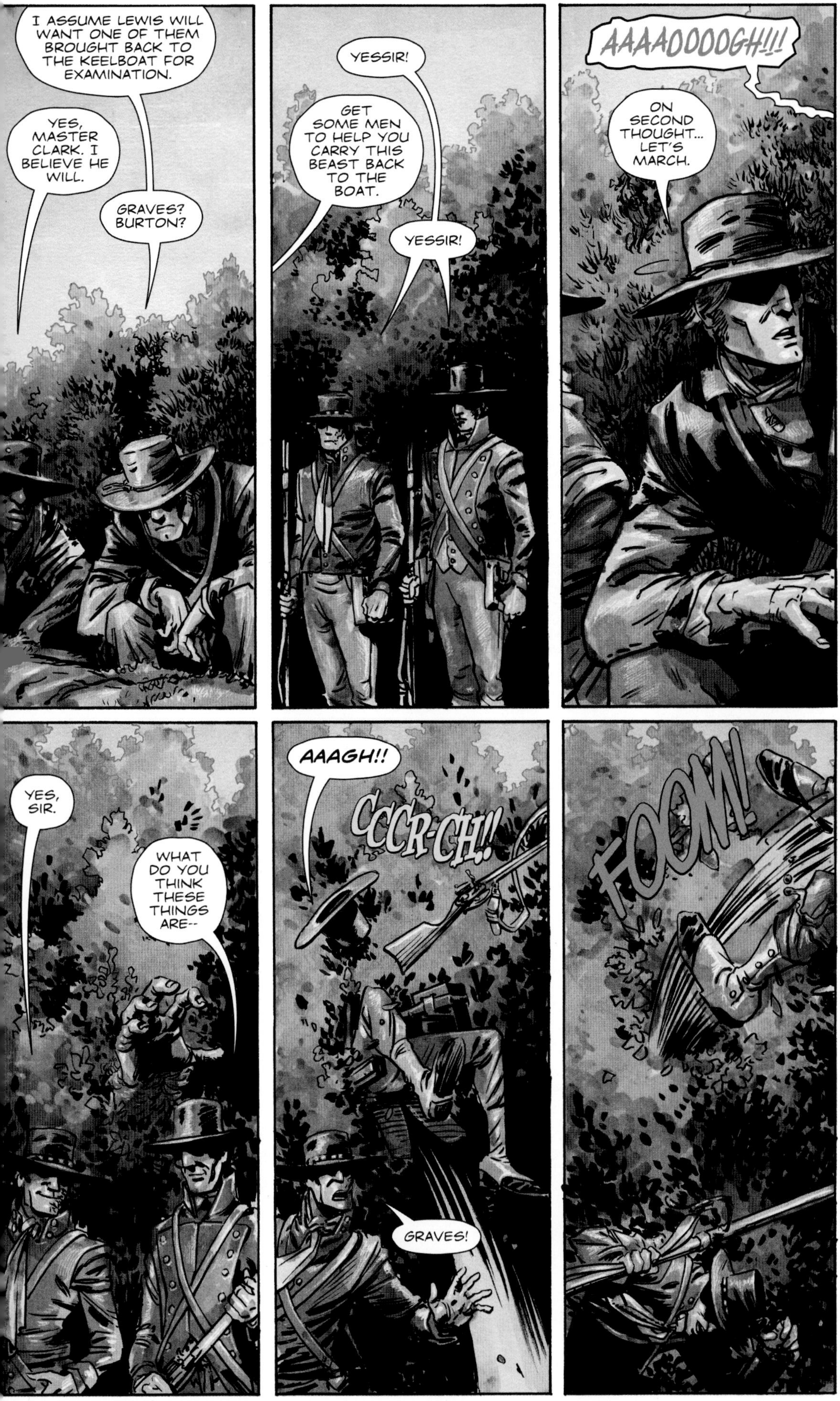
I ASSUME LEWIS WILL WANT ONE OF THEM BROUGHT BACK TO THE KEELBOAT FOR EXAMINATION.
YES, MASTER CLARK. I BELIEVE HE WILL.
GRAVES? BURTON?
YESSIR!
GET SOME MEN TO HELP YOU CARRY THIS BEAST BACK TO THE BOAT.
YESSIR!
AAAAOOOOGH!!!
ON SECOND THOUGHT... LET'S MARCH.
YES, SIR.
WHAT DO YOU THINK THESE THINGS ARE--
AAAGH!!
CCCR-CH!!
GRAVES!
FOOM!

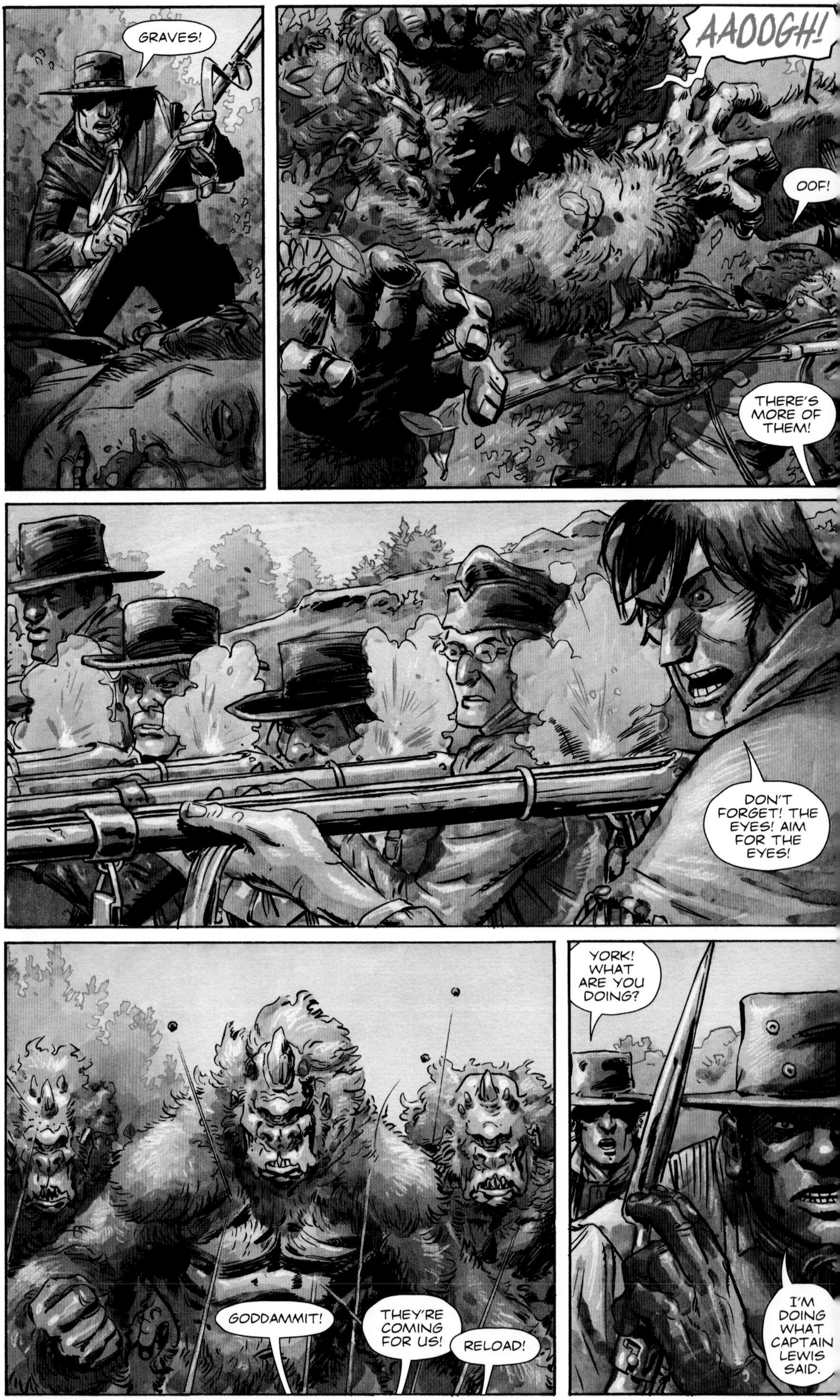
GRAVES!
AAOOGH!
OOF!
THERE'S MORE OF THEM!
DON'T FORGET! THE EYES! AIM FOR THE EYES!
GODDAMMIT!
THEY'RE COMING FOR US!
RELOAD!
YORK! WHAT ARE YOU DOING?
I'M DOING WHAT CAPTAIN LEWIS SAID.

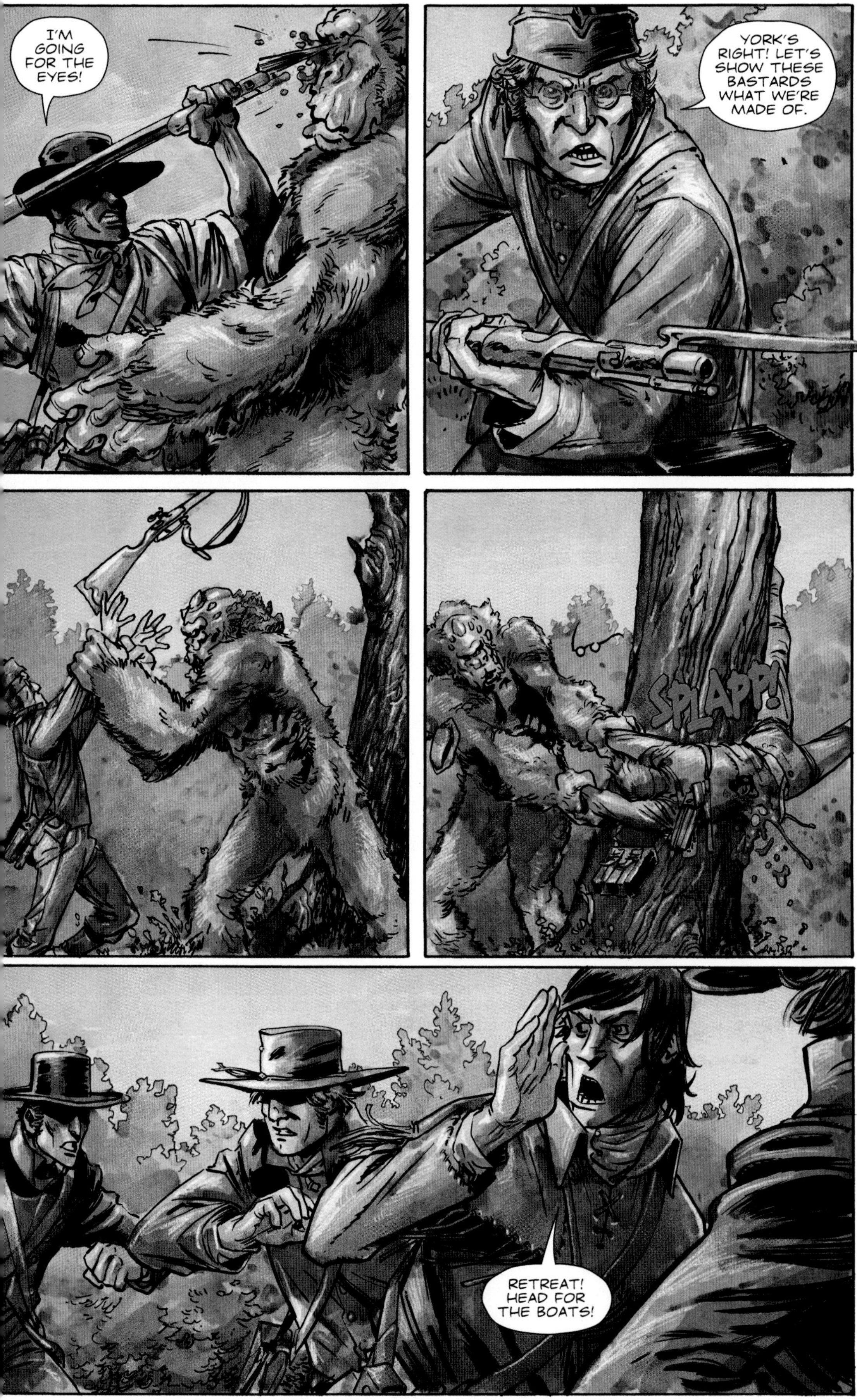
I'M GOING FOR THE EYES!
YORK'S RIGHT! LET'S SHOW THESE BASTARDS WHAT WE'RE MADE OF.
SPLAPP!
RETREAT! HEAD FOR THE BOATS!

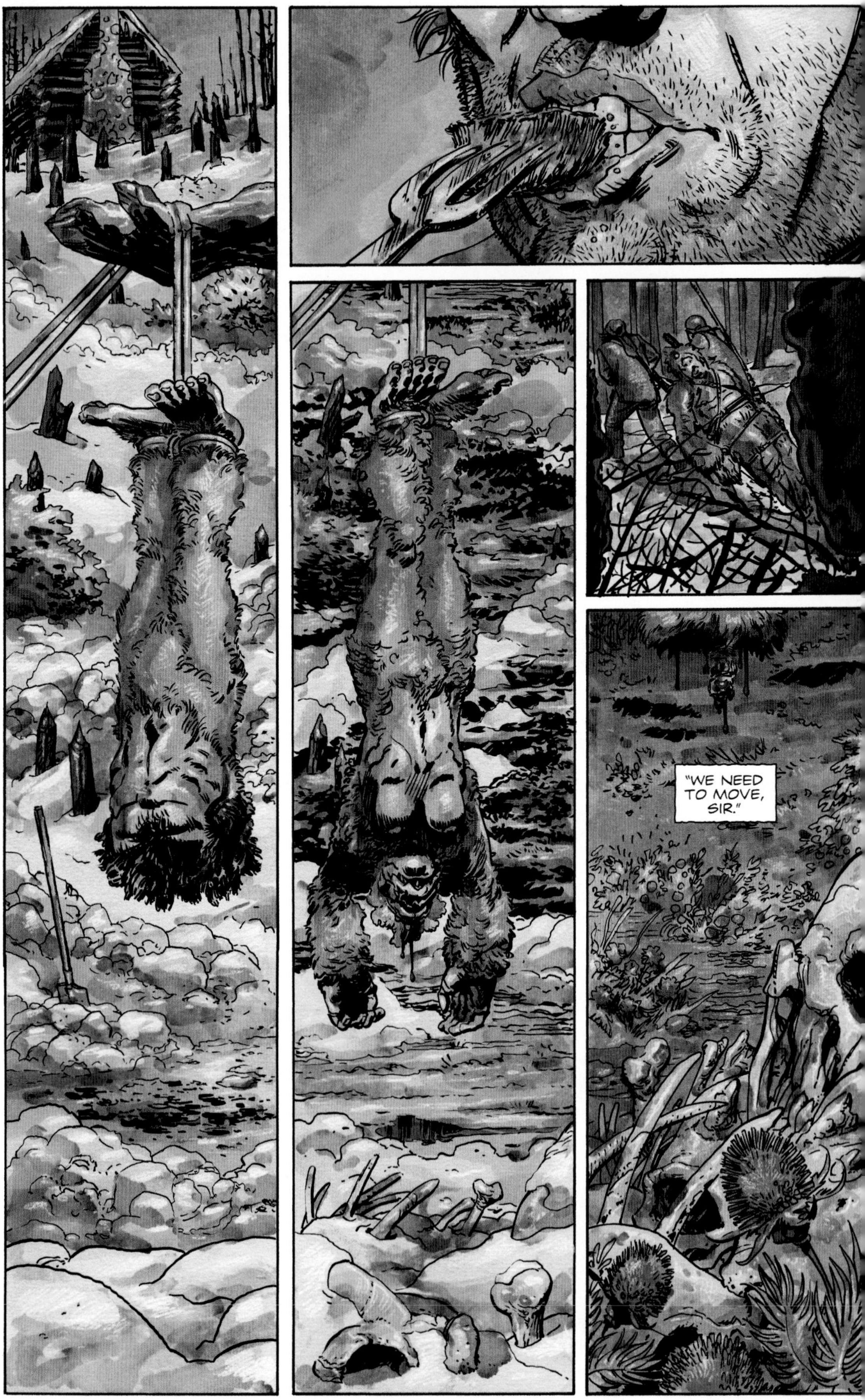
"WE NEED
TO MOVE,
SIR."

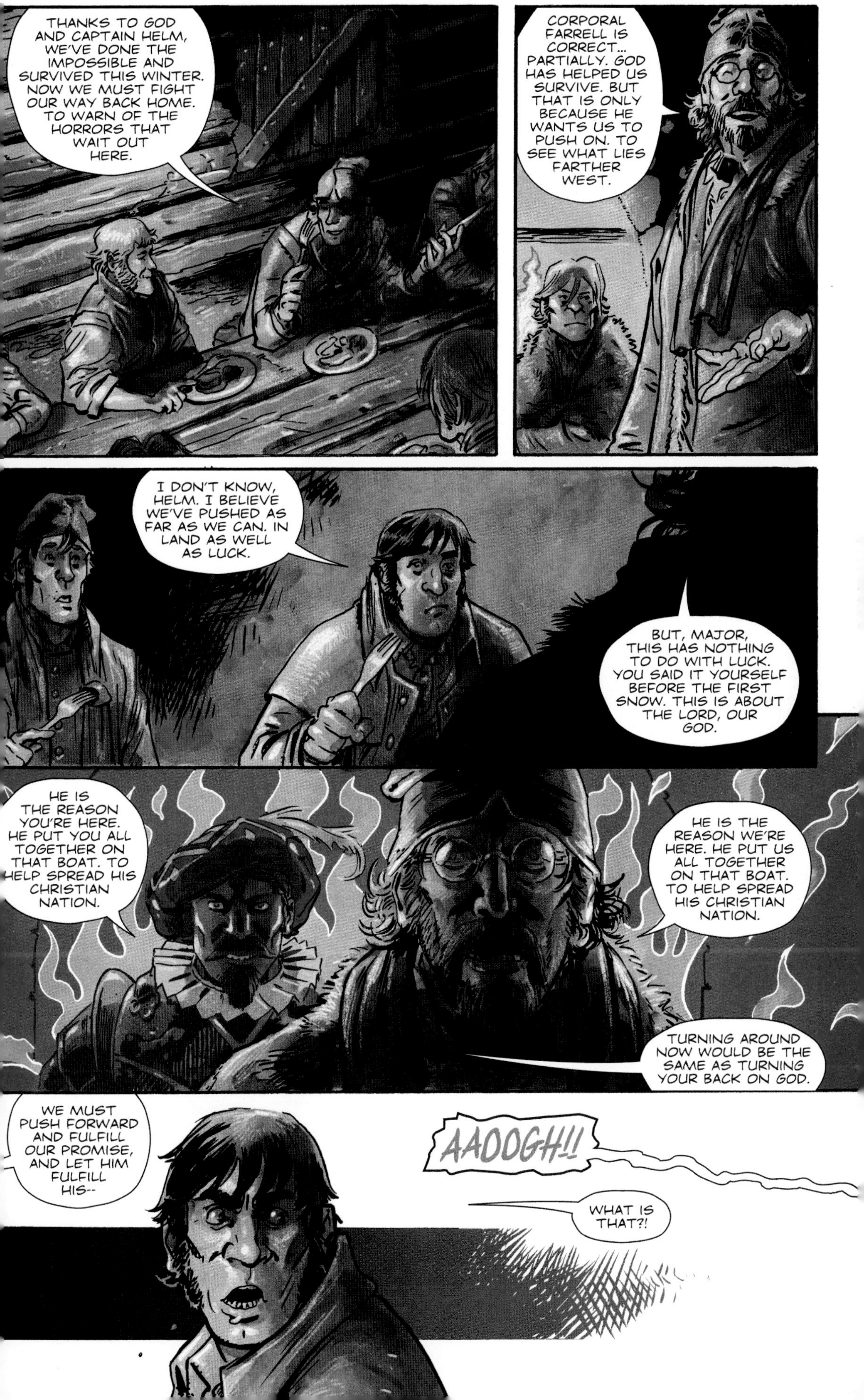

THANKS TO GOD AND CAPTAIN HELM, WE'VE DONE THE IMPOSSIBLE AND SURVIVED THIS WINTER. NOW WE MUST FIGHT OUR WAY BACK HOME. TO WARN OF THE HORRORS THAT WAIT OUT HERE.
CORPORAL FARRELL IS CORRECT... PARTIALLY. GOD HAS HELPED US SURVIVE. BUT THAT IS ONLY BECAUSE HE WANTS US TO PUSH ON. TO SEE WHAT LIES FARTHER WEST.
I DON'T KNOW, HELM. I BELIEVE WE'VE PUSHED AS FAR AS WE CAN. IN LAND AS WELL AS LUCK.
BUT, MAJOR, THIS HAS NOTHING TO DO WITH LUCK. YOU SAID IT YOURSELF BEFORE THE FIRST SNOW. THIS IS ABOUT THE LORD, OUR GOD.
HE IS THE REASON YOU'RE HERE. HE PUT YOU ALL TOGETHER ON THAT BOAT. TO HELP SPREAD HIS CHRISTIAN NATION.
HE IS THE REASON WE'RE HERE. HE PUT US ALL TOGETHER ON THAT BOAT. TO HELP SPREAD HIS CHRISTIAN NATION.
TURNING AROUND NOW WOULD BE THE SAME AS TURNING YOUR BACK ON GOD.
WE MUST PUSH FORWARD AND FULFILL OUR PROMISE, AND LET HIM FULFILL HIS--
AAOOGH!!
WHAT IS THAT?!

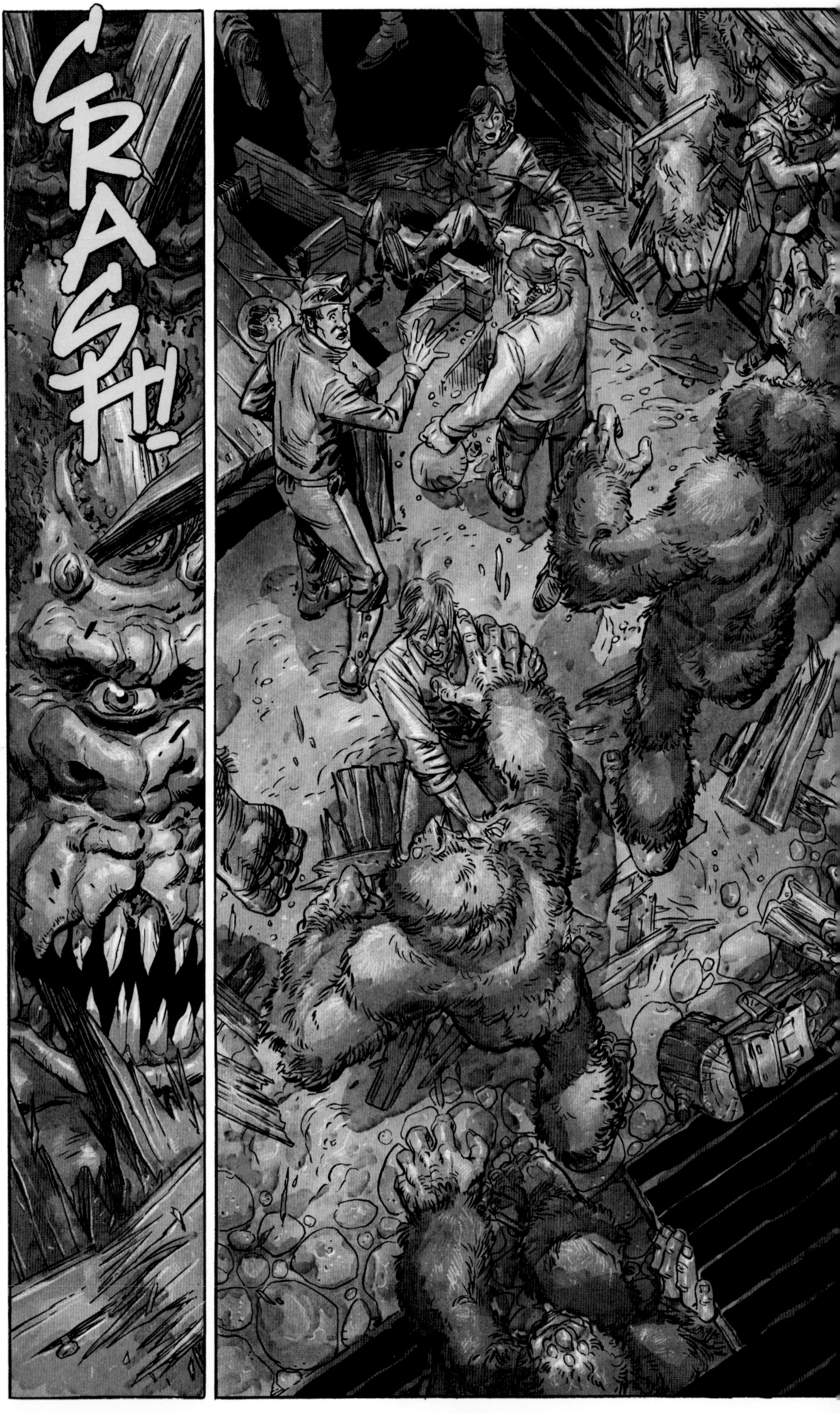
CRASH!

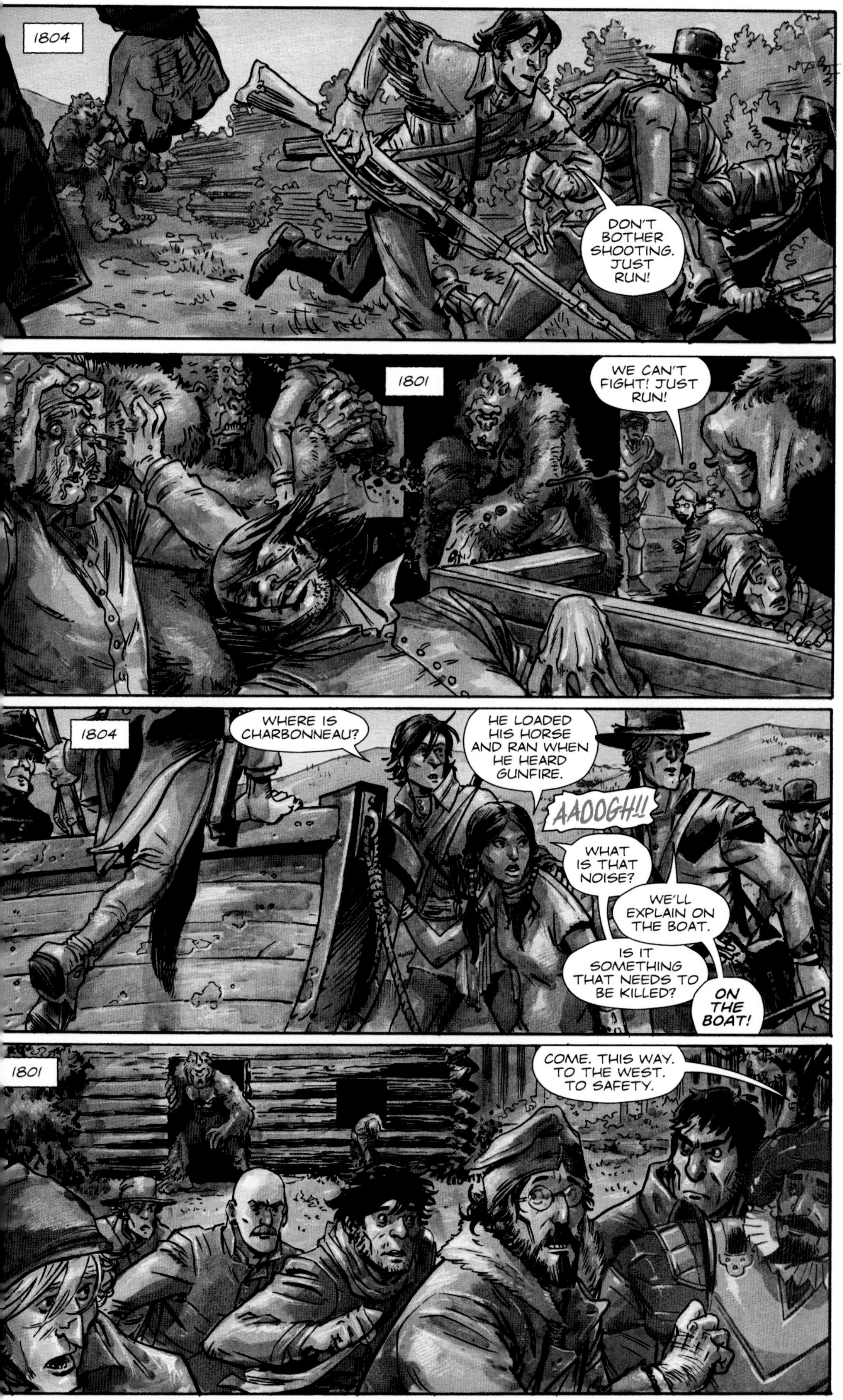
1804
DON'T BOTHER SHOOTING. JUST RUN!
1801
WE CAN'T FIGHT! JUST RUN!
1804
WHERE IS CHARBONNEAU?
HE LOADED HIS HORSE AND RAN WHEN HE HEARD GUNFIRE.
AAOOGH!!
WHAT IS THAT NOISE?
WE'LL EXPLAIN ON THE BOAT.
IS IT SOMETHING THAT NEEDS TO BE KILLED?
ON THE BOAT!
1801
COME. THIS WAY. TO THE WEST. TO SAFETY.

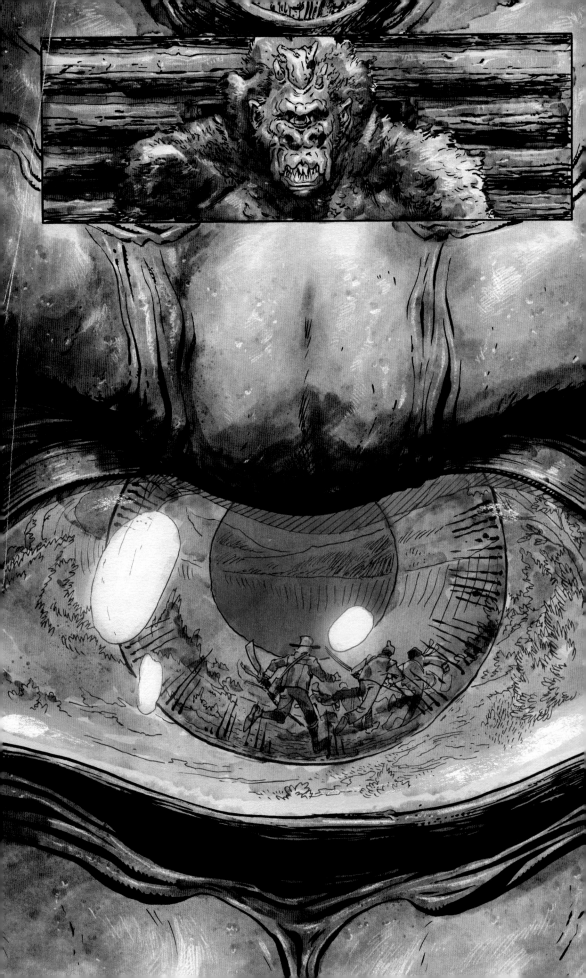

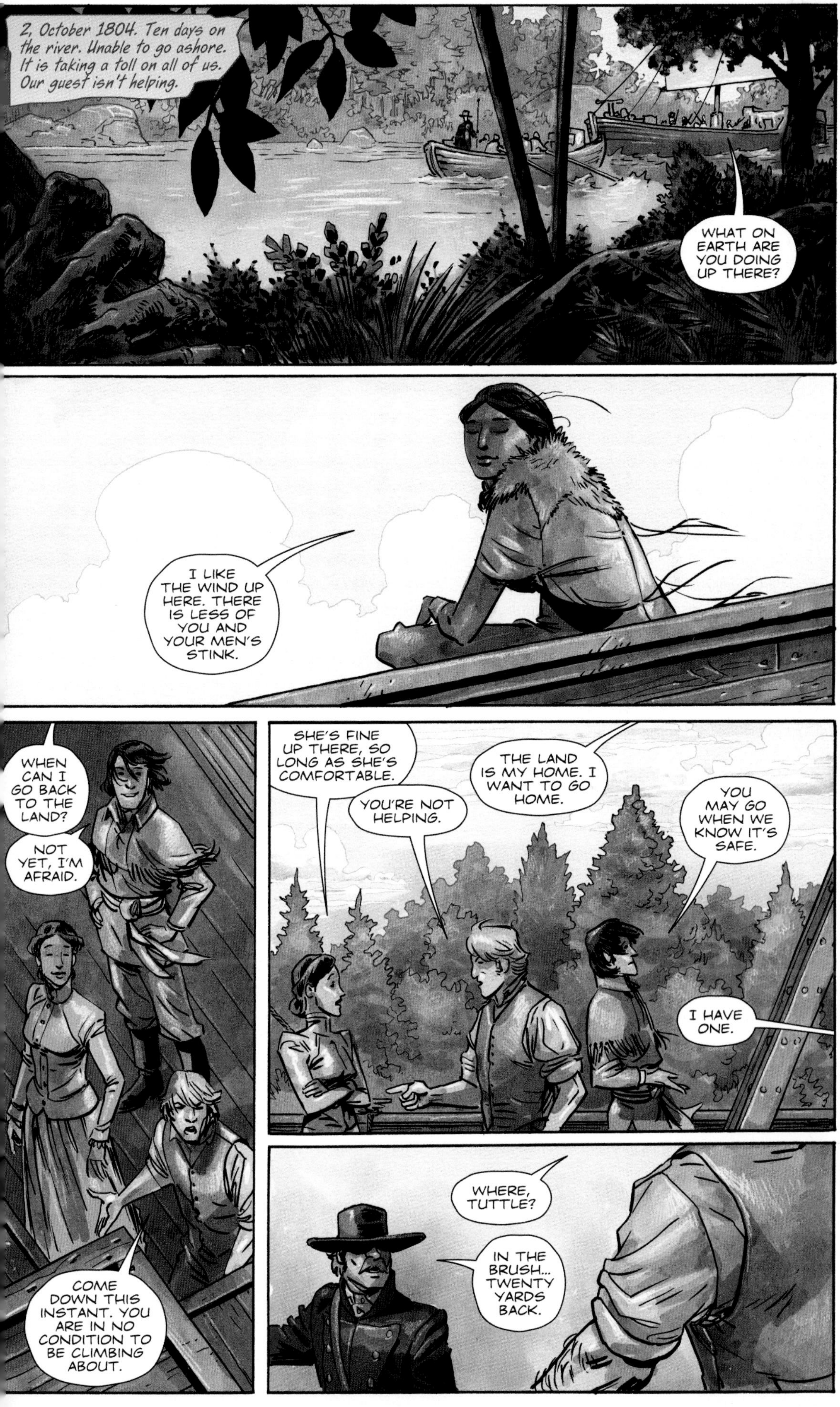
2, October 1804. Ten days on the river. Unable to go ashore. It is taking a toll on all of us. Our guest isn't helping.
WHAT ON EARTH ARE YOU DOING UP THERE?
I LIKE THE WIND UP HERE. THERE IS LESS OF YOU AND YOUR MEN'S STINK.
WHEN CAN I GO BACK TO THE LAND?
NOT YET, I'M AFRAID.
COME DOWN THIS INSTANT. YOU ARE IN NO CONDITION TO BE CLIMBING ABOUT.
SHE'S FINE UP THERE, SO LONG AS SHE'S COMFORTABLE.
YOU'RE NOT HELPING.
THE LAND IS MY HOME. I WANT TO GO HOME.
YOU MAY GO WHEN WE KNOW IT'S SAFE.
I HAVE ONE.
WHERE, TUTTLE?
IN THE BRUSH... TWENTY YARDS BACK.

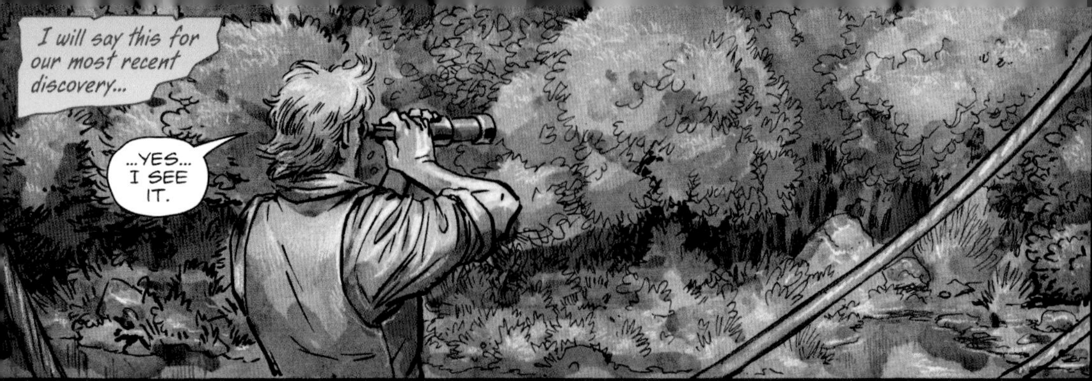
I will say this for our most recent discovery...
...YES... I SEE IT.

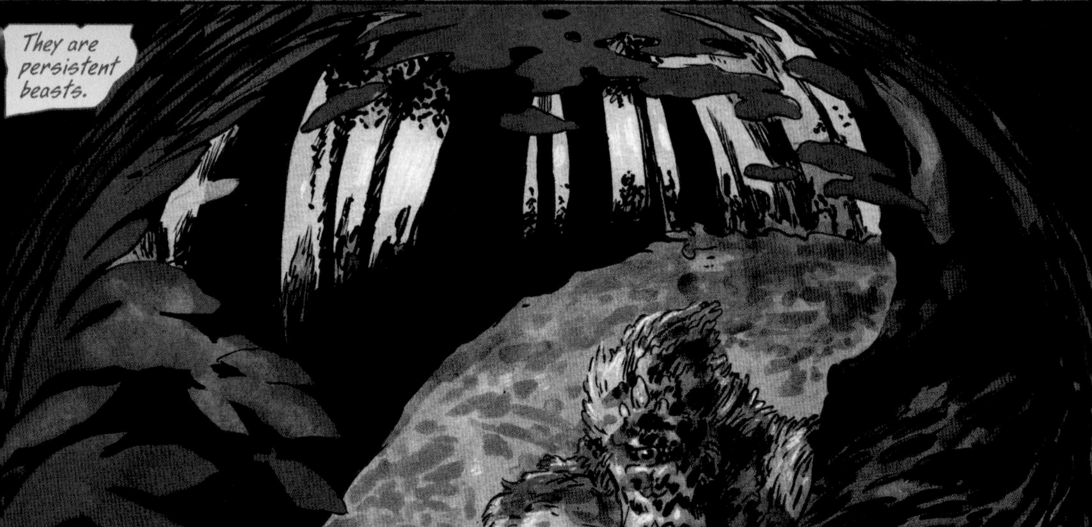
They are persistent beasts.
HE'S WELL HIDDEN. GOOD EYE, TUTTLE.

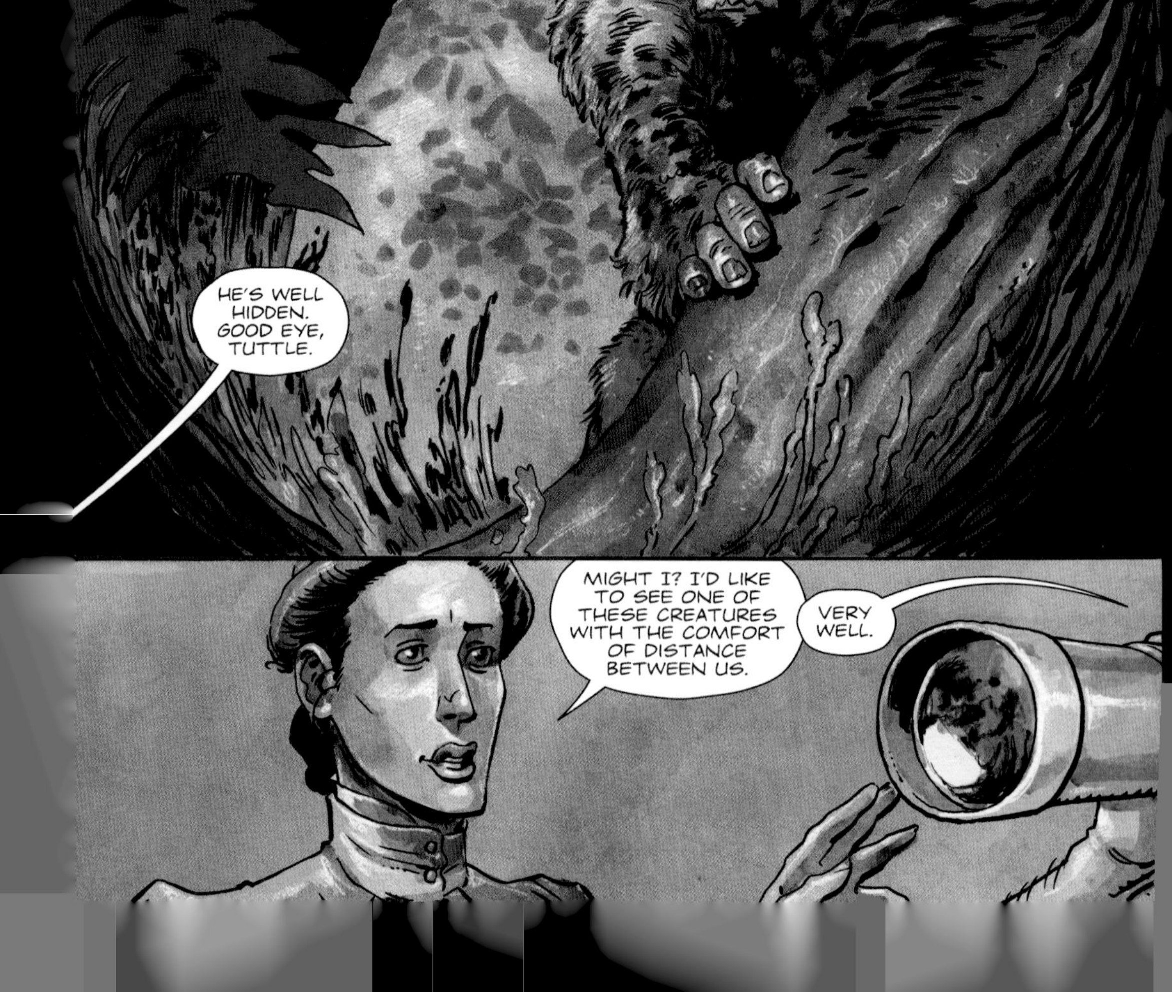
MIGHT I? I'D LIKE TO SEE ONE OF THESE CREATURES WITH THE COMFORT OF DISTANCE BETWEEN US.
VERY WELL.

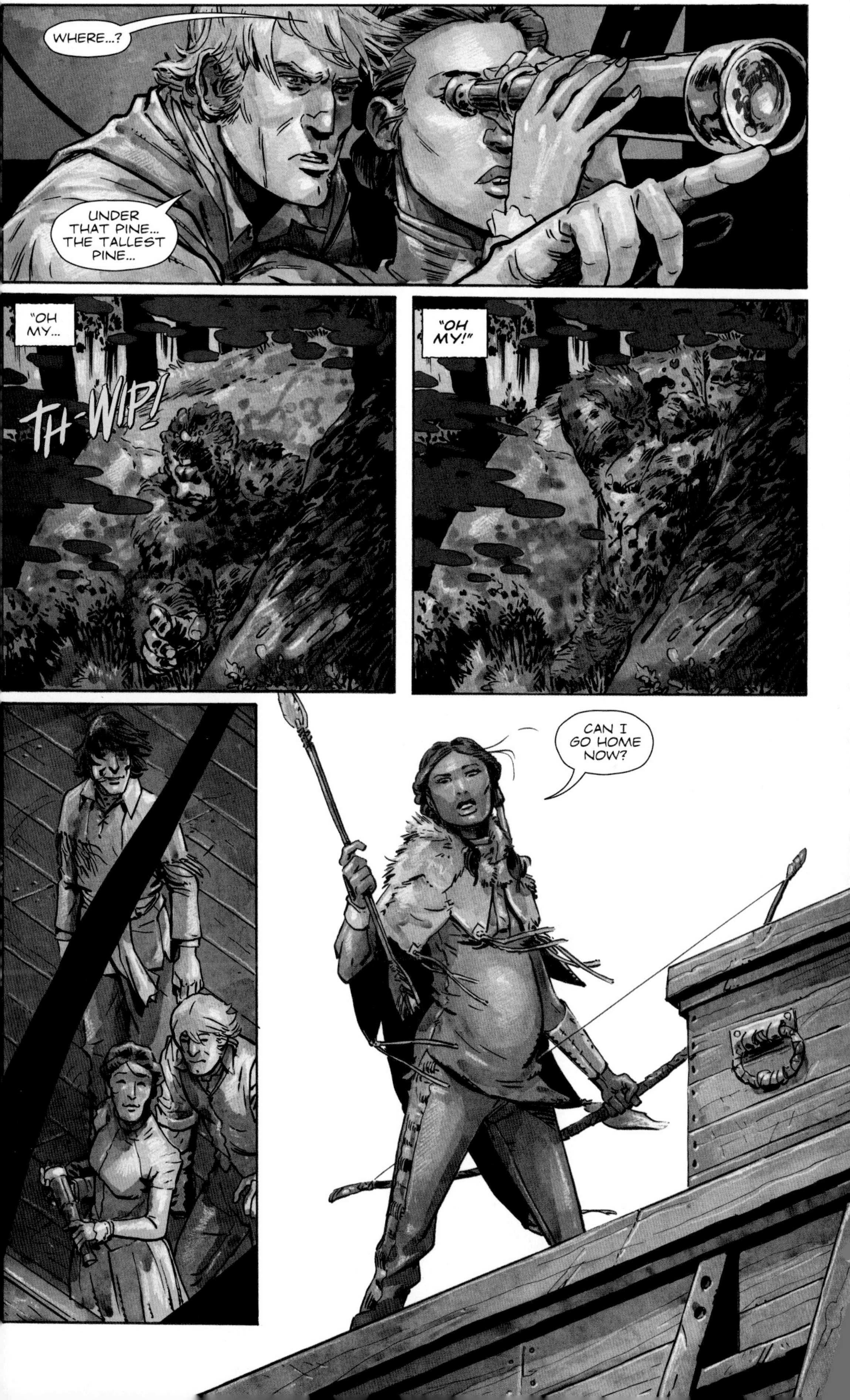
WHERE...?
UNDER THAT PINE... THE TALLEST PINE...
"OH MY...
TH-WIP!
"OH MY!"
CAN I GO HOME NOW?

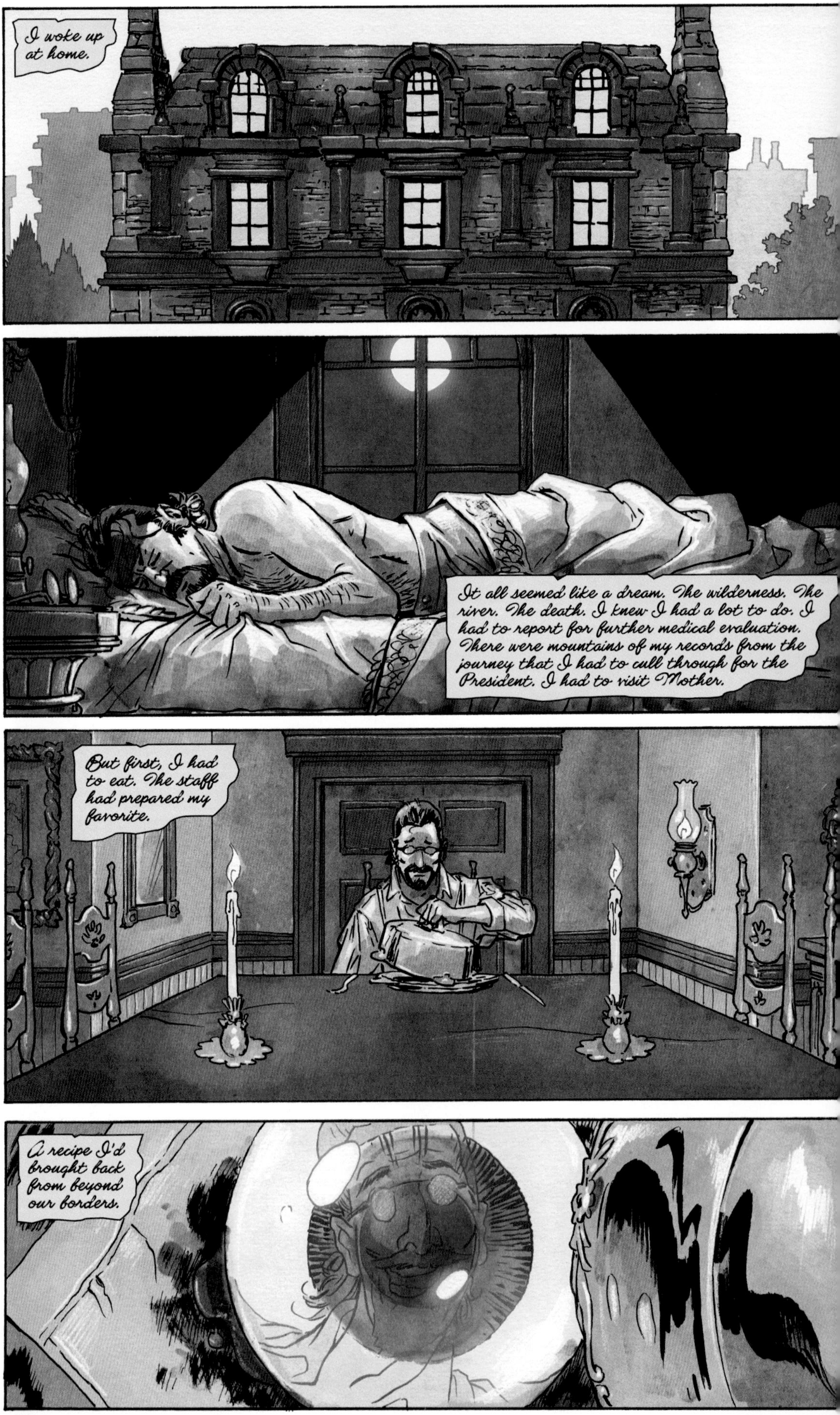
I woke up at home.
It all seemed like a dream. The wilderness. The river. The death. I knew I had a lot to do. I had to report for further medical evaluation. There were mountains of my records from the journey that I had to cull through for the President. I had to visit Mother.
But first, I had to eat. The staff had prepared my favorite.
A recipe I'd brought back from beyond our borders.

It was a feast fit for a king. As soon as I would devour one morsel...

More would appear!

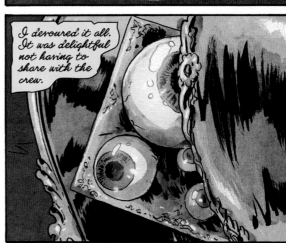

I devoured it all. It was delightful not having to share with the crew.

My gluttony knew no bounds. I could not get full.

Until I found myself too full.

KNOCK-KNOCK-KNOCK...

CAPTAIN HELM?

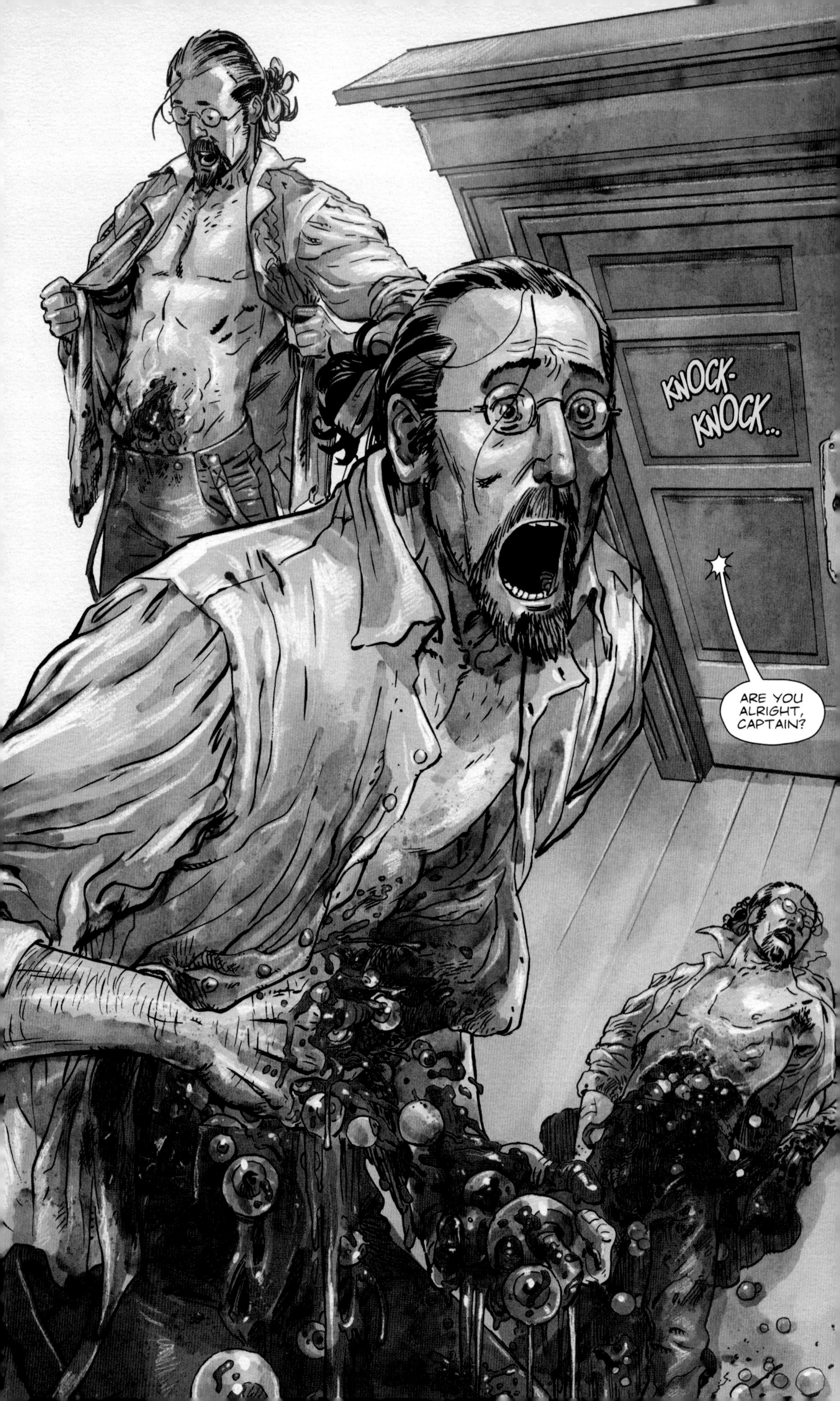
KNOCK-
KNOCK...
ARE YOU
ALRIGHT,
CAPTAIN?

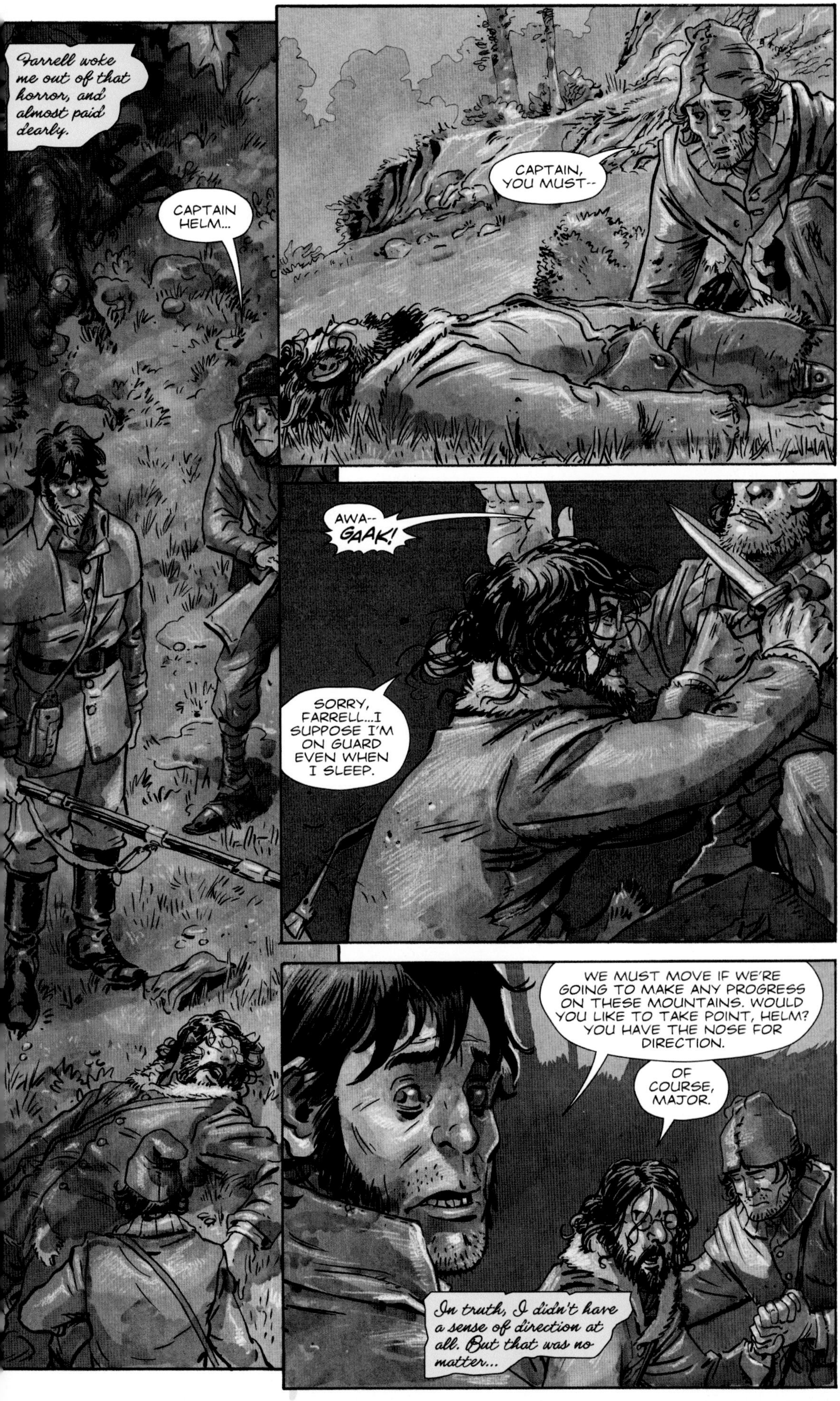
Farrell woke me out of that horror, and almost paid dearly.
CAPTAIN HELM...
CAPTAIN, YOU MUST--
AWA-- GAAK!
SORRY, FARRELL...I SUPPOSE I'M ON GUARD EVEN WHEN I SLEEP.
WE MUST MOVE IF WE'RE GOING TO MAKE ANY PROGRESS ON THESE MOUNTAINS. WOULD YOU LIKE TO TAKE POINT, HELM? YOU HAVE THE NOSE FOR DIRECTION.
OF COURSE, MAJOR.
In truth, I didn't have a sense of direction at all. But that was no matter...

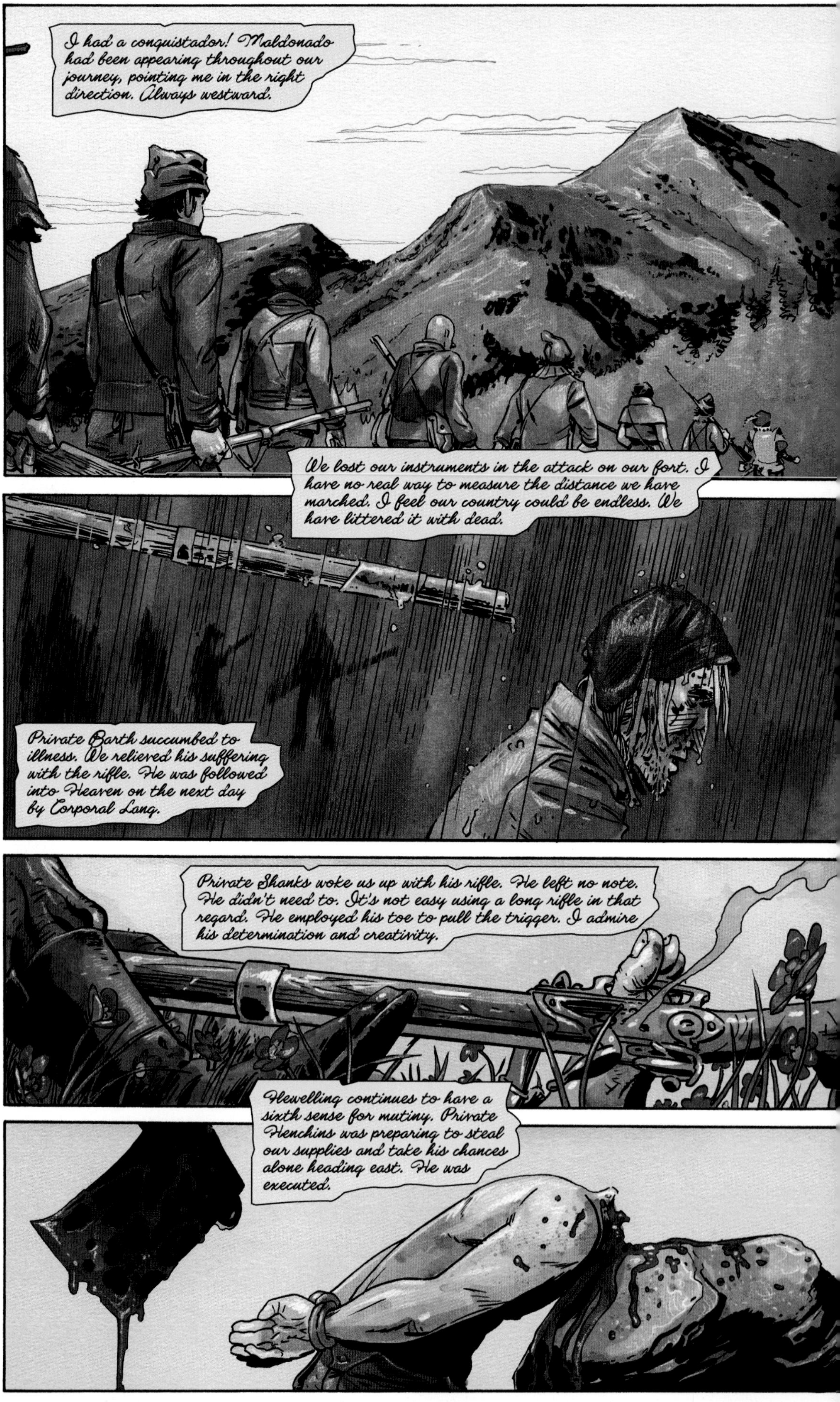
I had a conquistador! Maldonado had been appearing throughout our journey, pointing me in the right direction. Always westward.
We lost our instruments in the attack on our fort. I have no real way to measure the distance we have marched. I feel our country could be endless. We have littered it with dead.
Private Barth succumbed to illness. We relieved his suffering with the rifle. He was followed into Heaven on the next day by Corporal Lang.
Private Shanks woke us up with his rifle. He left no note. He didn't need to. It's not easy using a long rifle in that regard. He employed his toe to pull the trigger. I admire his determination and creativity.
Hewelling continues to have a sixth sense for mutiny. Private Henchins was preparing to steal our supplies and take his chances alone heading east. He was executed.

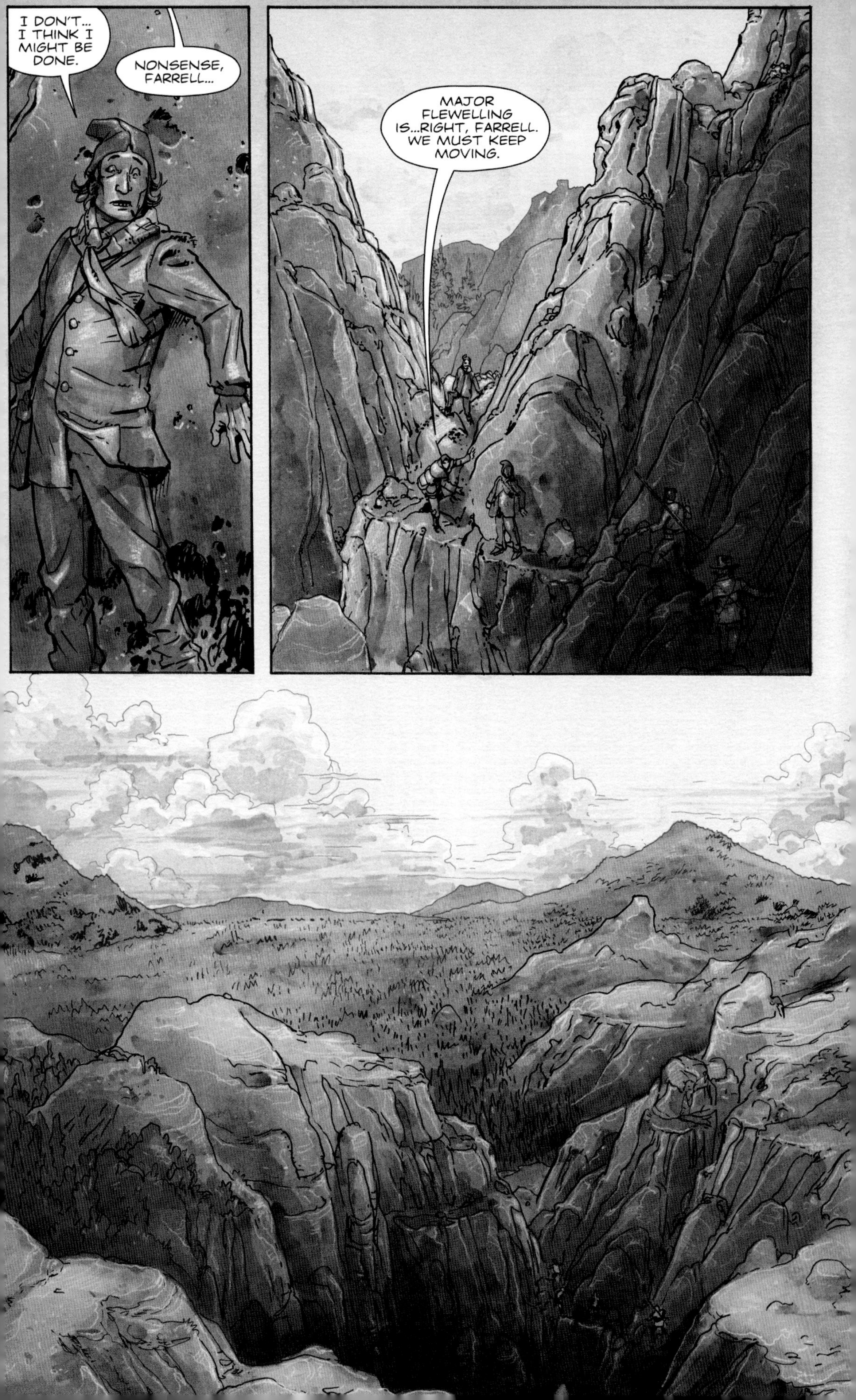
I DON'T...
I THINK I
MIGHT BE
DONE.
NONSENSE,
FARRELL...
MAJOR
FLEWELLING
IS...RIGHT, FARRELL.
WE MUST KEEP
MOVING.

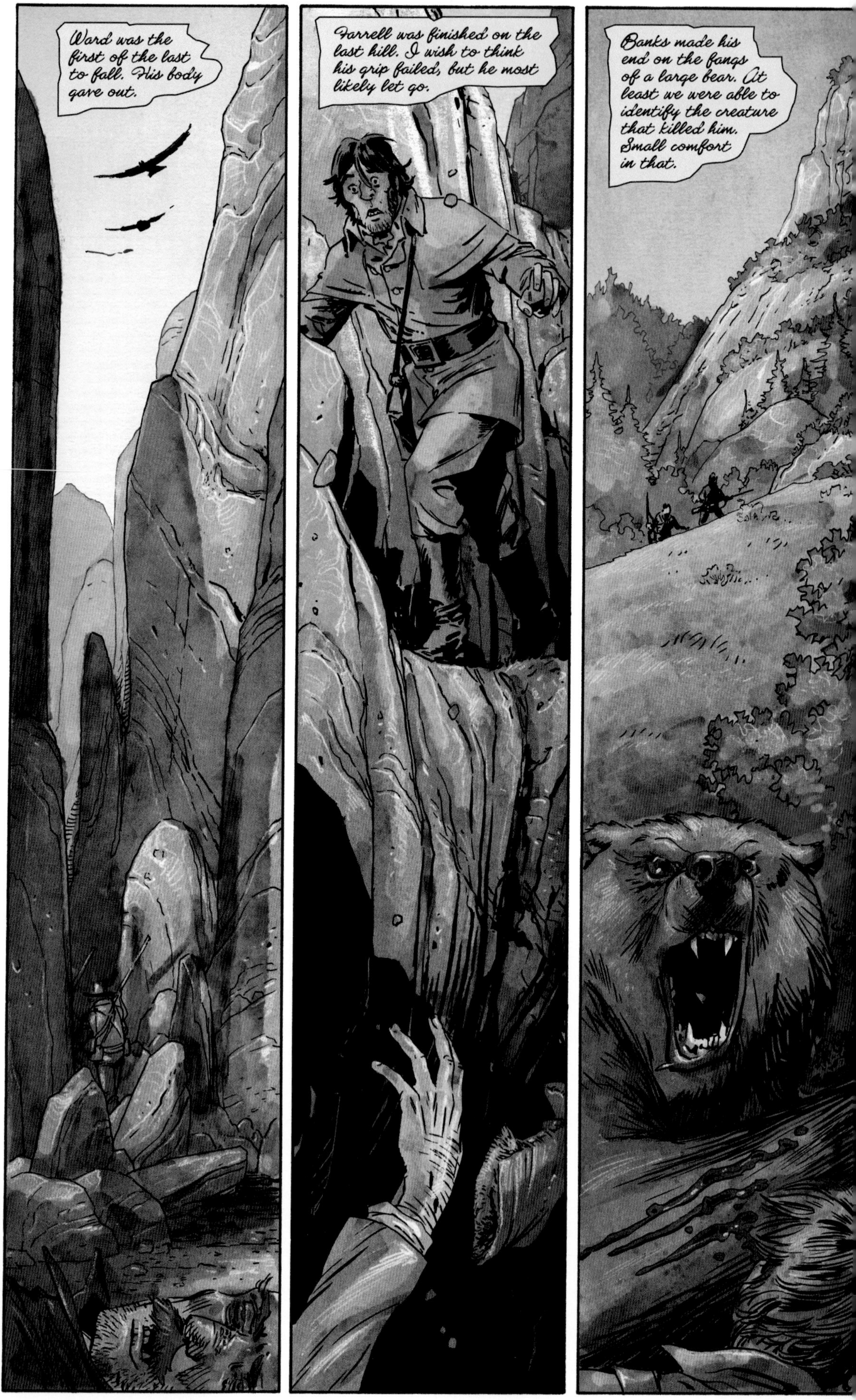
Ward was the first of the last to fall. His body gave out.
Farrell was finished on the last hill. I wish to think his grip failed, but he most likely let go.
Banks made his end on the fangs of a large bear. At least we were able to identify the creature that killed him. Small comfort in that.

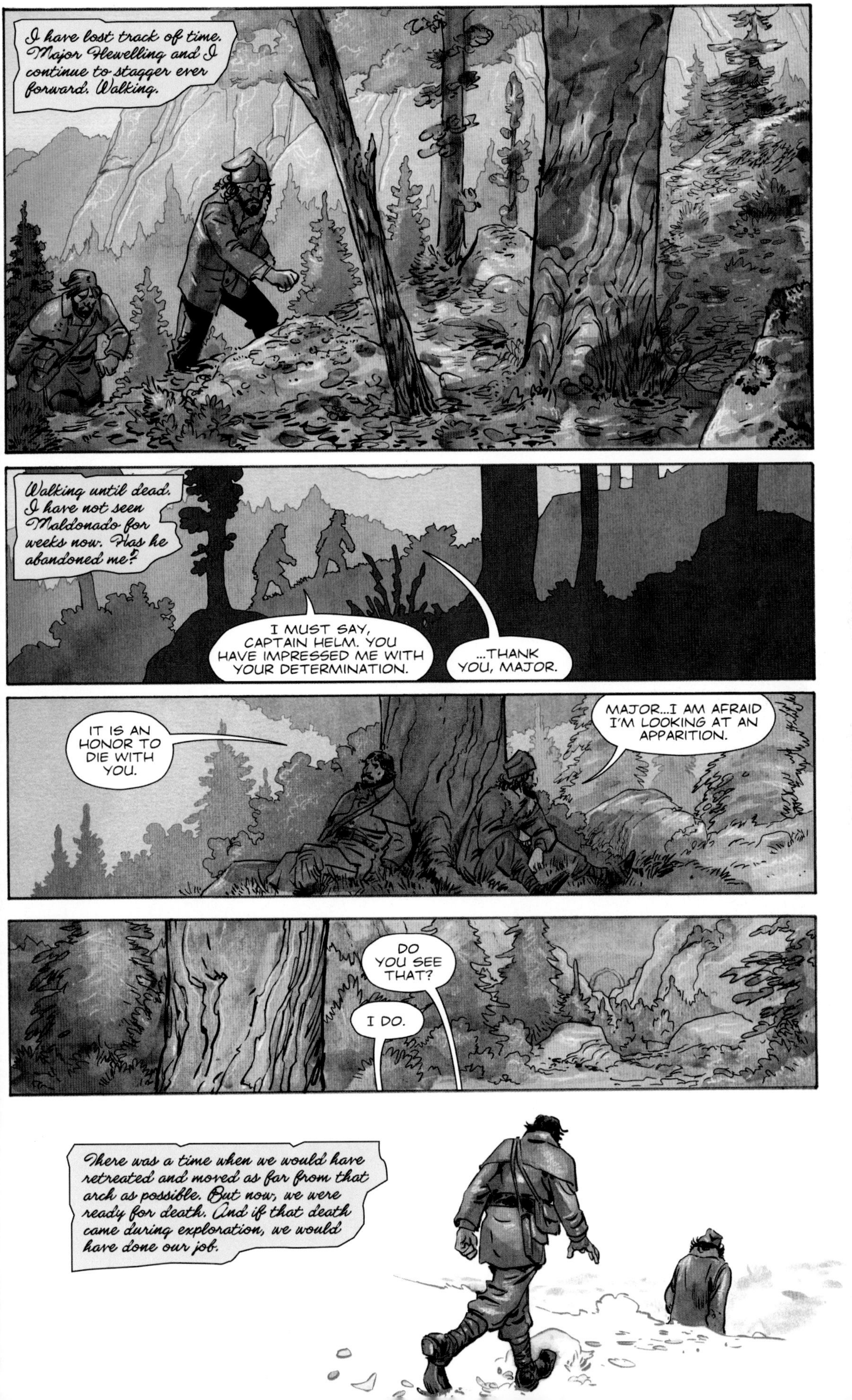
I have lost track of time. Major Flewelling and I continue to stagger ever forward. Walking.
Walking until dead. I have not seen Maldonado for weeks now. Has he abandoned me?
I MUST SAY, CAPTAIN HELM. YOU HAVE IMPRESSED ME WITH YOUR DETERMINATION.
...THANK YOU, MAJOR.
IT IS AN HONOR TO DIE WITH YOU.
MAJOR...I AM AFRAID I'M LOOKING AT AN APPARITION.
DO YOU SEE THAT?
I DO.
There was a time when we would have retreated and moved as far from that arch as possible. But now, we were ready for death. And if that death came during exploration, we would have done our job.

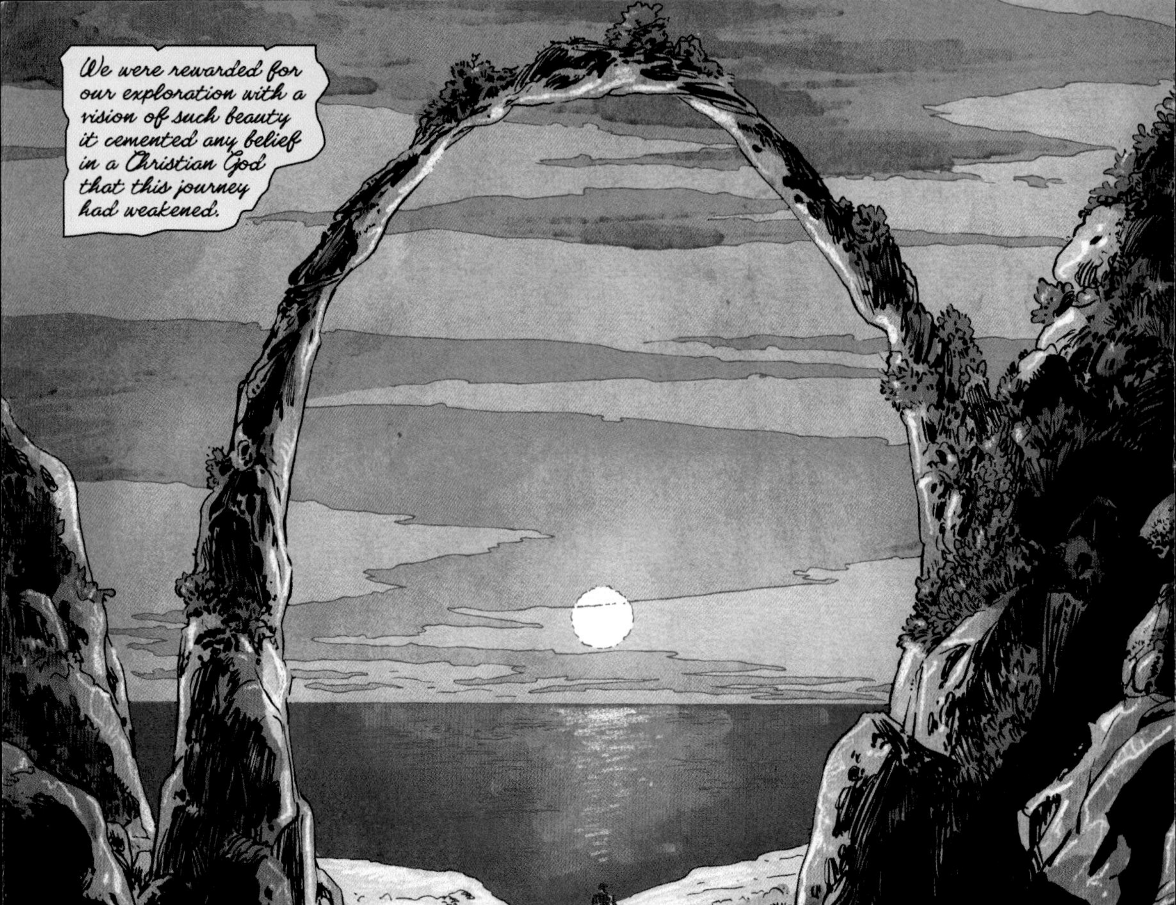
We were rewarded for our exploration with a vision of such beauty it cemented any belief in a Christian God that this journey had weakened.
IS THIS... HEAVEN?
NO, SIR... IT'S THE OCEAN.
WHO IS THAT?

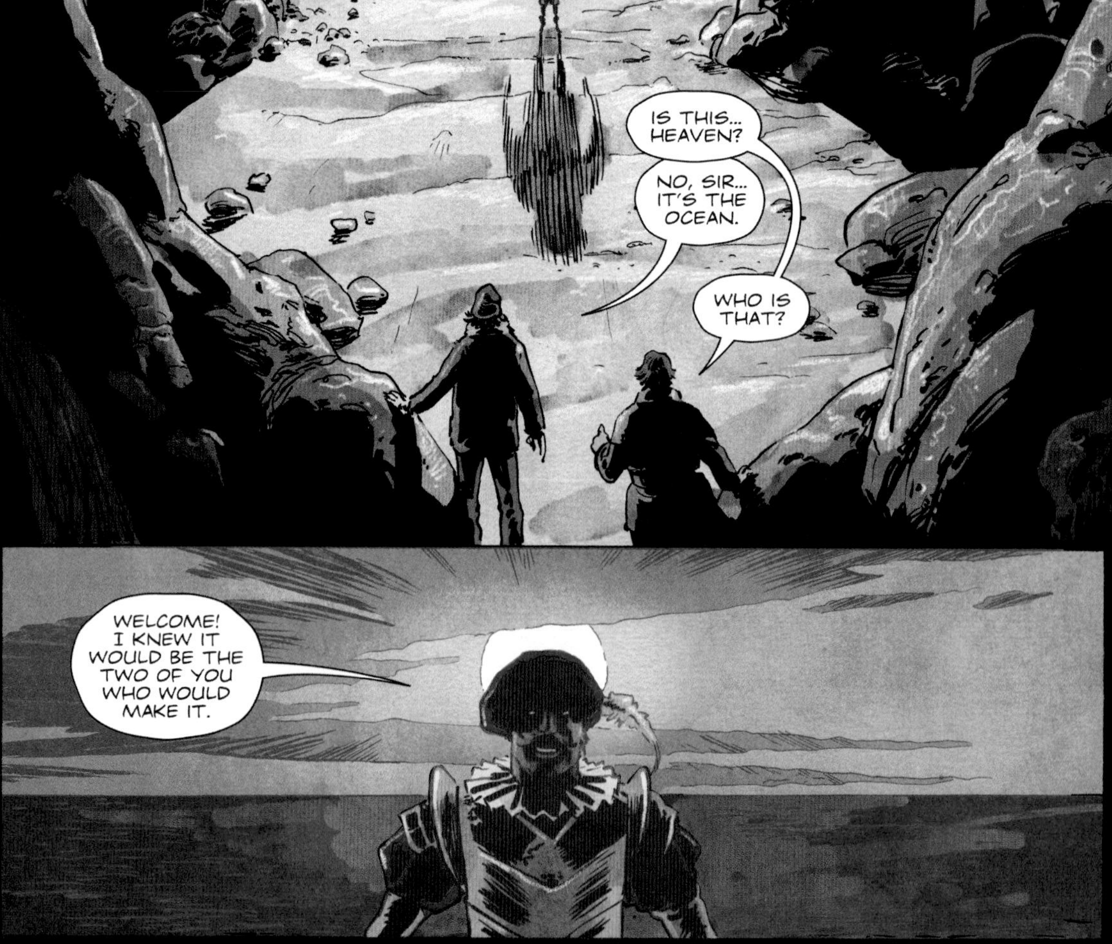
WELCOME! I KNEW IT WOULD BE THE TWO OF YOU WHO WOULD MAKE IT.

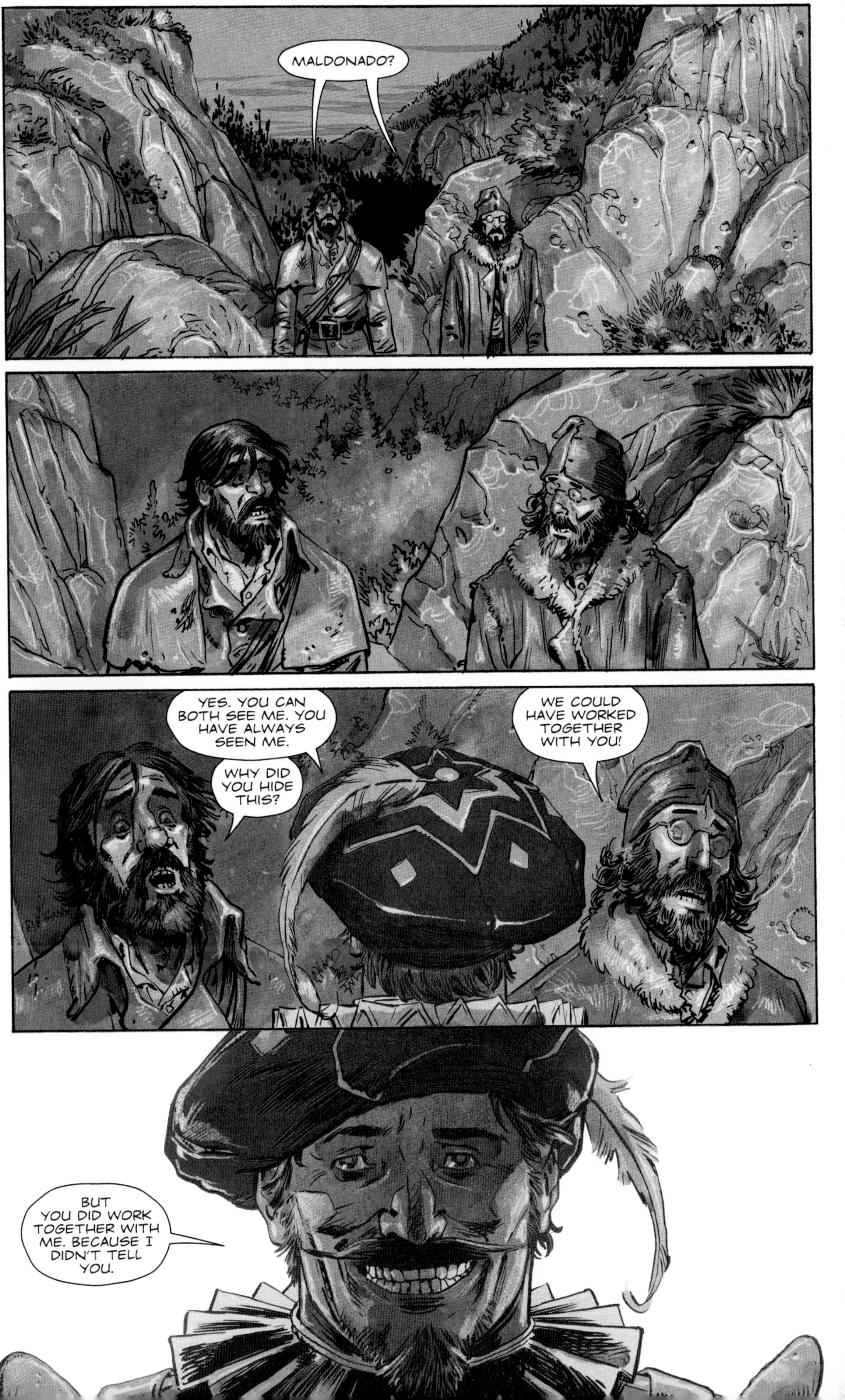
MALDONADO?
YES. YOU CAN BOTH SEE ME. YOU HAVE ALWAYS SEEN ME.
WHY DID YOU HIDE THIS?
WE COULD HAVE WORKED TOGETHER WITH YOU!
BUT YOU DID WORK TOGETHER WITH ME. BECAUSE I DIDN'T TELL YOU.

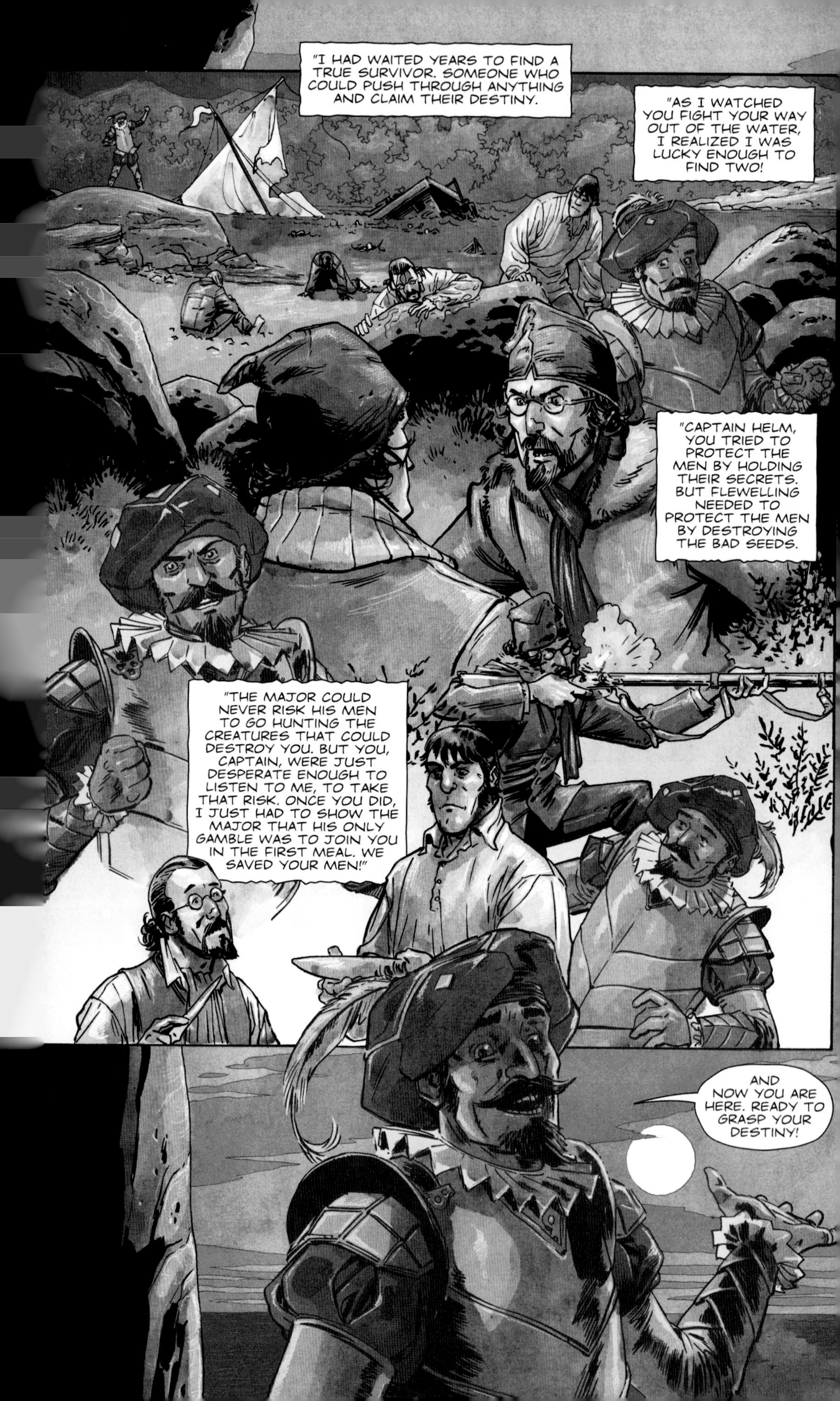
"I HAD WAITED YEARS TO FIND A TRUE SURVIVOR. SOMEONE WHO COULD PUSH THROUGH ANYTHING AND CLAIM THEIR DESTINY.
"AS I WATCHED YOU FIGHT YOUR WAY OUT OF THE WATER, I REALIZED I WAS LUCKY ENOUGH TO FIND TWO!
"CAPTAIN HELM, YOU TRIED TO PROTECT THE MEN BY HOLDING THEIR SECRETS. BUT FLEWELLING NEEDED TO PROTECT THE MEN BY DESTROYING THE BAD SEEDS.
"THE MAJOR COULD NEVER RISK HIS MEN TO GO HUNTING THE CREATURES THAT COULD DESTROY YOU. BUT YOU, CAPTAIN, WERE JUST DESPERATE ENOUGH TO LISTEN TO ME, TO TAKE THAT RISK. ONCE YOU DID, I JUST HAD TO SHOW THE MAJOR THAT HIS ONLY GAMBLE WAS TO JOIN YOU IN THE FIRST MEAL. WE SAVED YOUR MEN!"
AND NOW YOU ARE HERE. READY TO GRASP YOUR DESTINY!

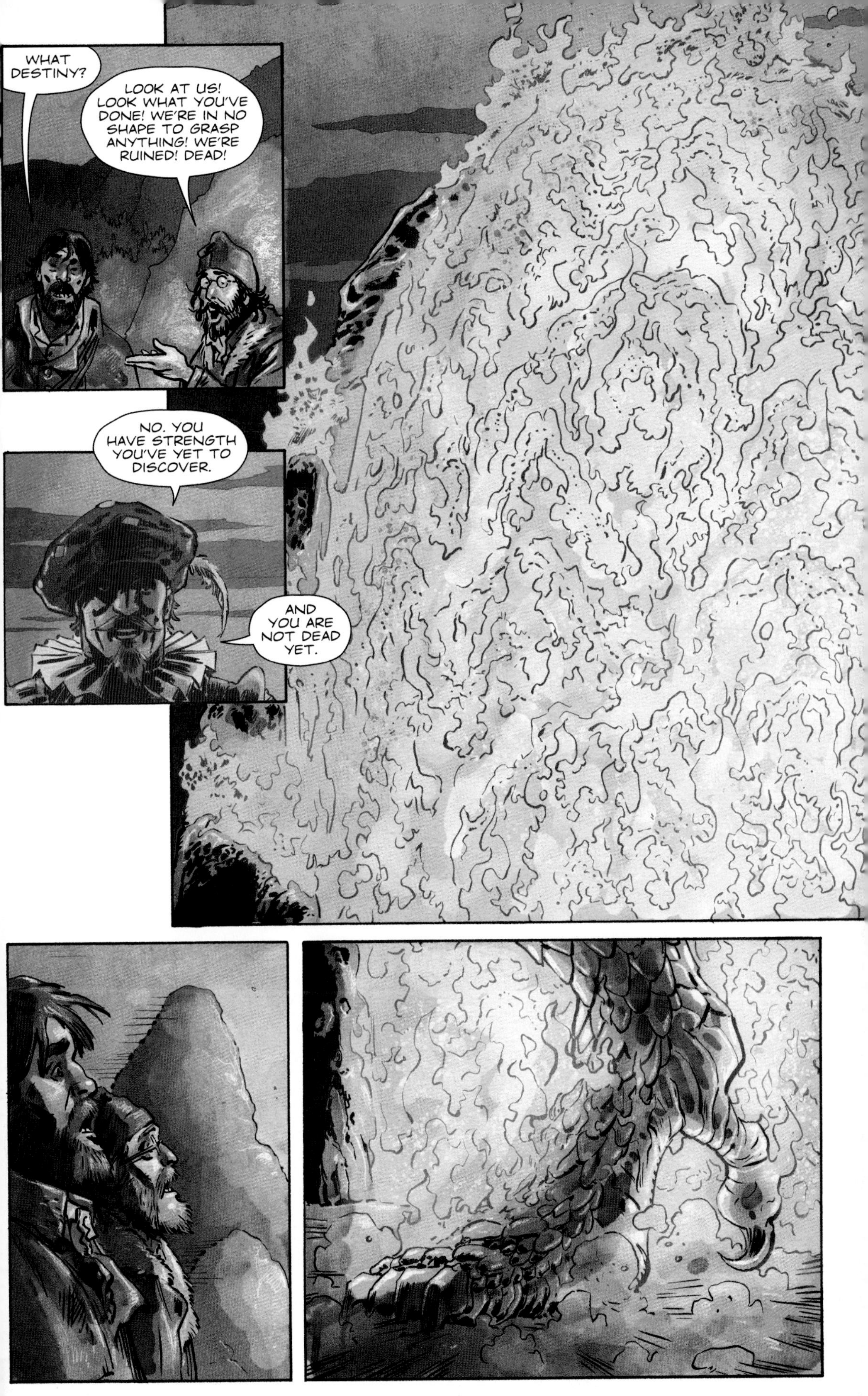
WHAT DESTINY?
LOOK AT US! LOOK WHAT YOU'VE DONE! WE'RE IN NO SHAPE TO GRASP ANYTHING! WE'RE RUINED! DEAD!
NO. YOU HAVE STRENGTH YOU'VE YET TO DISCOVER.
AND YOU ARE NOT DEAD YET.

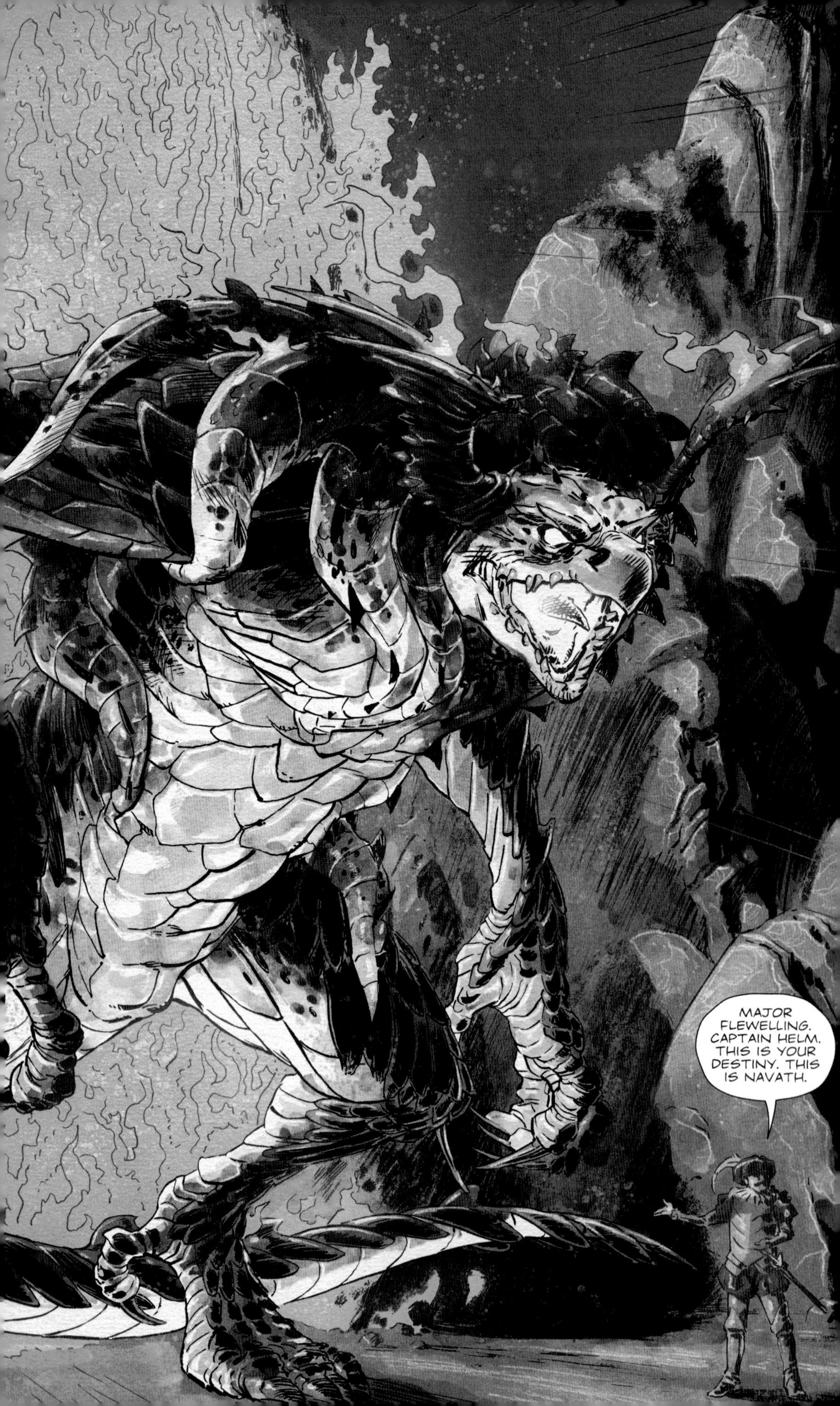
MAJOR FLEWELLING. CAPTAIN HELM. THIS IS YOUR DESTINY. THIS IS NAVATH.

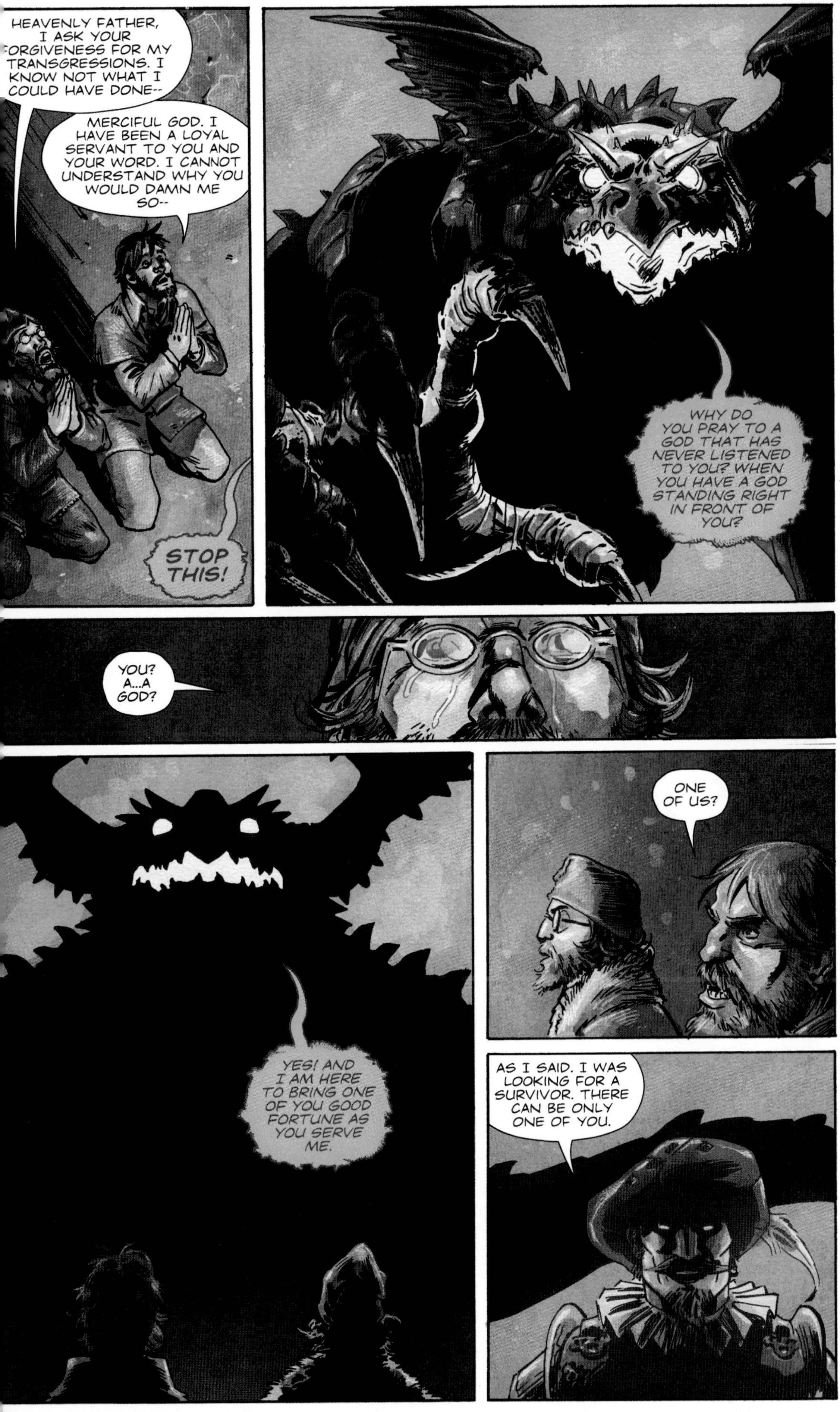
HEAVENLY FATHER, I ASK YOUR FORGIVENESS FOR MY TRANSGRESSIONS. I KNOW NOT WHAT I COULD HAVE DONE--
MERCIFUL GOD. I HAVE BEEN A LOYAL SERVANT TO YOU AND YOUR WORD. I CANNOT UNDERSTAND WHY YOU WOULD DAMN ME SO--
STOP THIS!
WHY DO YOU PRAY TO A GOD THAT HAS NEVER LISTENED TO YOU? WHEN YOU HAVE A GOD STANDING RIGHT IN FRONT OF YOU?
YOU? A...A GOD?
YES! AND I AM HERE TO BRING ONE OF YOU GOOD FORTUNE AS YOU SERVE ME.
ONE OF US?
AS I SAID. I WAS LOOKING FOR A SURVIVOR. THERE CAN BE ONLY ONE OF YOU.

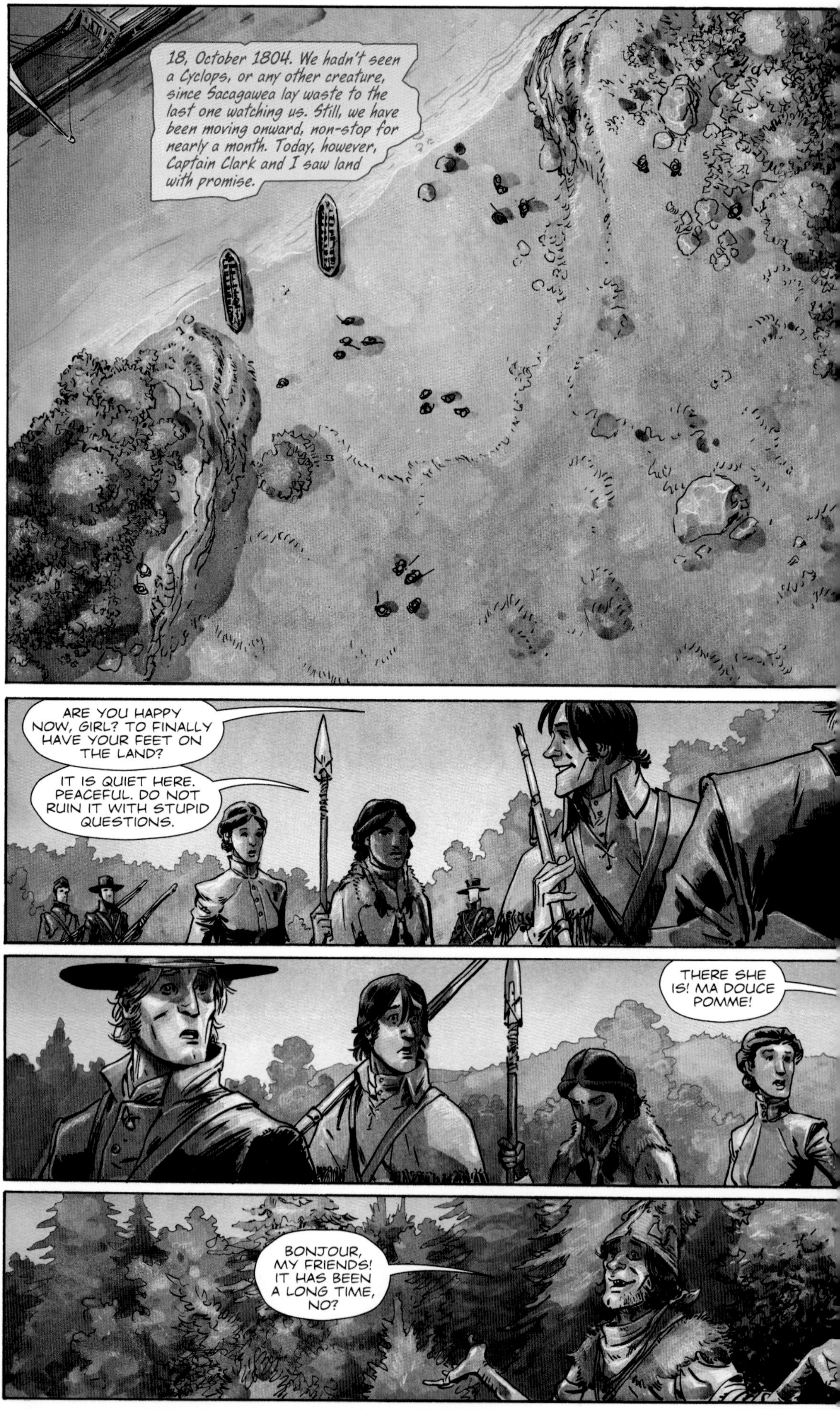
18, October 1804. We hadn't seen a Cyclops, or any other creature, since Sacagawea lay waste to the last one watching us. Still, we have been moving onward, non-stop for nearly a month. Today, however, Captain Clark and I saw land with promise.
ARE YOU HAPPY NOW, GIRL? TO FINALLY HAVE YOUR FEET ON THE LAND?
IT IS QUIET HERE. PEACEFUL. DO NOT RUIN IT WITH STUPID QUESTIONS.
THERE SHE IS! MA DOUCE POMME!
BONJOUR, MY FRIENDS! IT HAS BEEN A LONG TIME, NO?

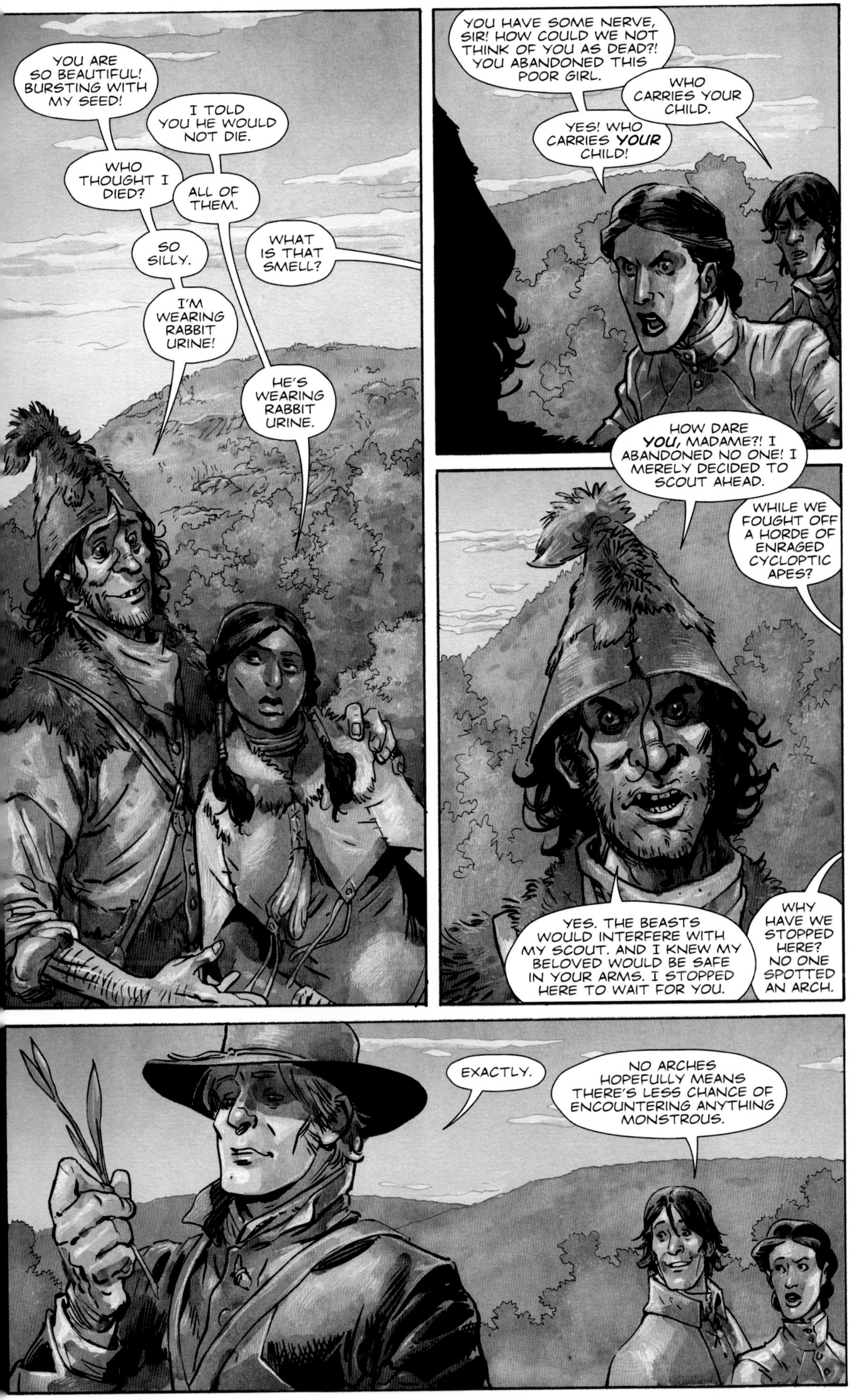

YOU ARE SO BEAUTIFUL! BURSTING WITH MY SEED!
I TOLD YOU HE WOULD NOT DIE.
WHO THOUGHT I DIED?
ALL OF THEM.
SO SILLY.
WHAT IS THAT SMELL?
I'M WEARING RABBIT URINE!
HE'S WEARING RABBIT URINE.
YOU HAVE SOME NERVE, SIR! HOW COULD WE NOT THINK OF YOU AS DEAD?! YOU ABANDONED THIS POOR GIRL.
WHO CARRIES YOUR CHILD.
YES! WHO CARRIES **YOUR** CHILD!
HOW DARE **YOU,** MADAME?! I ABANDONED NO ONE! I MERELY DECIDED TO SCOUT AHEAD.
WHILE WE FOUGHT OFF A HORDE OF ENRAGED CYCLOPTIC APES?
YES. THE BEASTS WOULD INTERFERE WITH MY SCOUT. AND I KNEW MY BELOVED WOULD BE SAFE IN YOUR ARMS. I STOPPED HERE TO WAIT FOR YOU.
WHY HAVE WE STOPPED HERE? NO ONE SPOTTED AN ARCH.
EXACTLY.
NO ARCHES HOPEFULLY MEANS THERE'S LESS CHANCE OF ENCOUNTERING ANYTHING MONSTROUS.

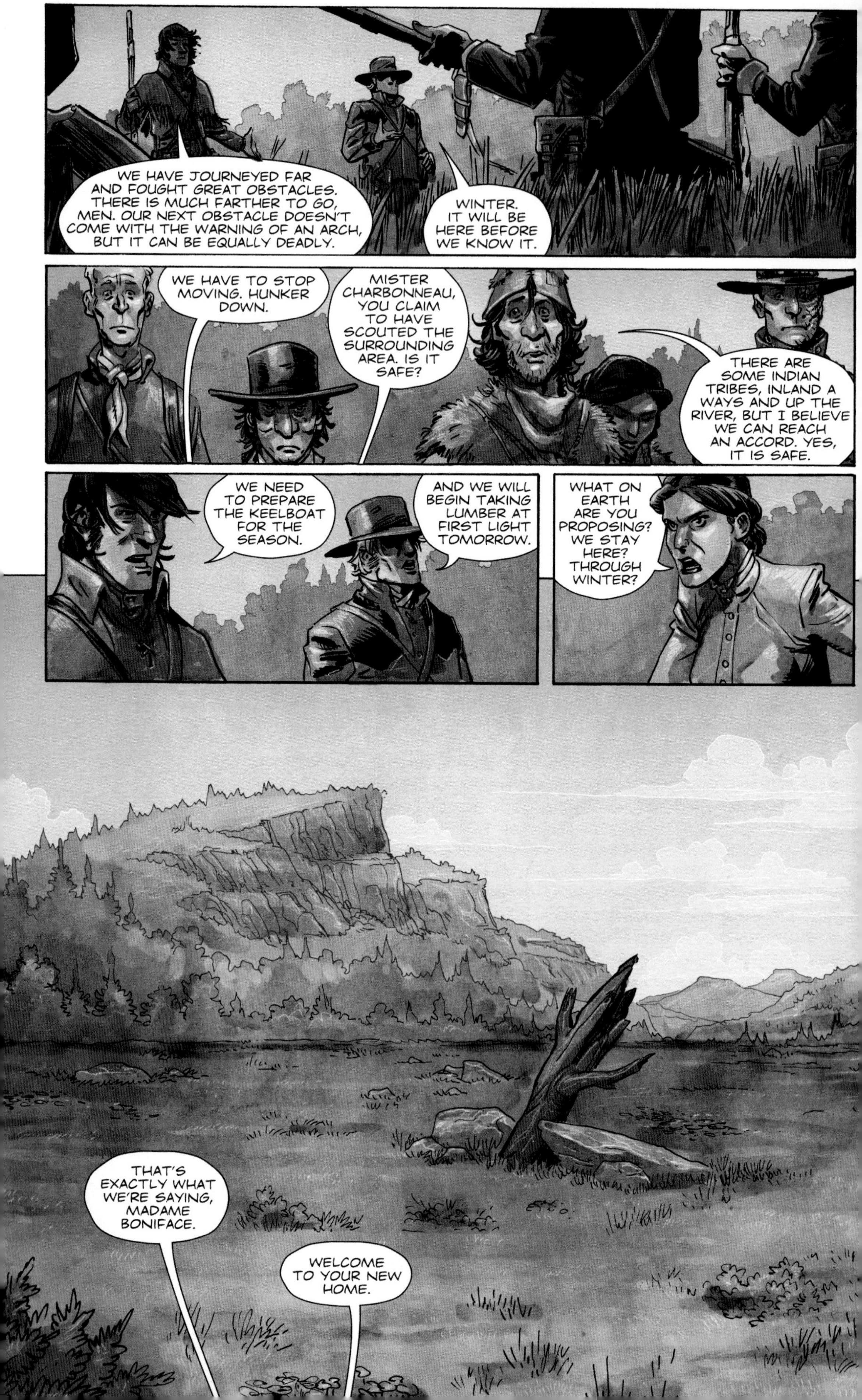

WE HAVE JOURNEYED FAR AND FOUGHT GREAT OBSTACLES. THERE IS MUCH FARTHER TO GO, MEN. OUR NEXT OBSTACLE DOESN'T COME WITH THE WARNING OF AN ARCH, BUT IT CAN BE EQUALLY DEADLY.
WINTER. IT WILL BE HERE BEFORE WE KNOW IT.
WE HAVE TO STOP MOVING. HUNKER DOWN.
MISTER CHARBONNEAU, YOU CLAIM TO HAVE SCOUTED THE SURROUNDING AREA. IS IT SAFE?
THERE ARE SOME INDIAN TRIBES, INLAND A WAYS AND UP THE RIVER, BUT I BELIEVE WE CAN REACH AN ACCORD. YES, IT IS SAFE.
WE NEED TO PREPARE THE KEELBOAT FOR THE SEASON.
AND WE WILL BEGIN TAKING LUMBER AT FIRST LIGHT TOMORROW.
WHAT ON EARTH ARE YOU PROPOSING? WE STAY HERE? THROUGH WINTER?
THAT'S EXACTLY WHAT WE'RE SAYING, MADAME BONIFACE.
WELCOME TO YOUR NEW HOME.

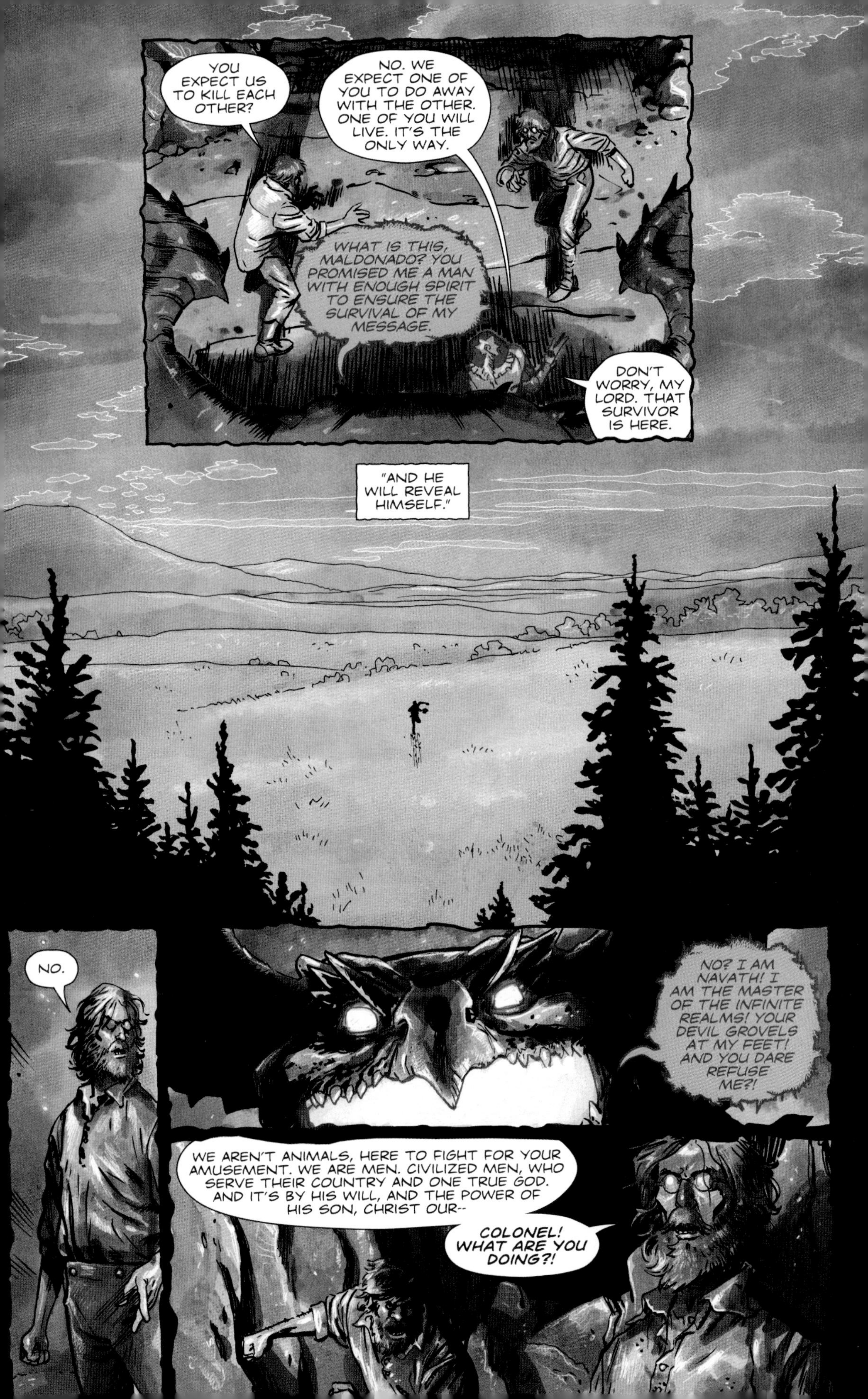
YOU EXPECT US TO KILL EACH OTHER?
NO. WE EXPECT ONE OF YOU TO DO AWAY WITH THE OTHER. ONE OF YOU WILL LIVE. IT'S THE ONLY WAY.
WHAT IS THIS, MALDONADO? YOU PROMISED ME A MAN WITH ENOUGH SPIRIT TO ENSURE THE SURVIVAL OF MY MESSAGE.
DON'T WORRY, MY LORD. THAT SURVIVOR IS HERE.
"AND HE WILL REVEAL HIMSELF."
NO.
NO? I AM NAVATH! I AM THE MASTER OF THE INFINITE REALMS! YOUR DEVIL GROVELS AT MY FEET! AND YOU DARE REFUSE ME?!
WE AREN'T ANIMALS, HERE TO FIGHT FOR YOUR AMUSEMENT. WE ARE MEN. CIVILIZED MEN, WHO SERVE THEIR COUNTRY AND ONE TRUE GOD. AND IT'S BY HIS WILL, AND THE POWER OF HIS SON, CHRIST OUR--
COLONEL! WHAT ARE YOU DOING?!

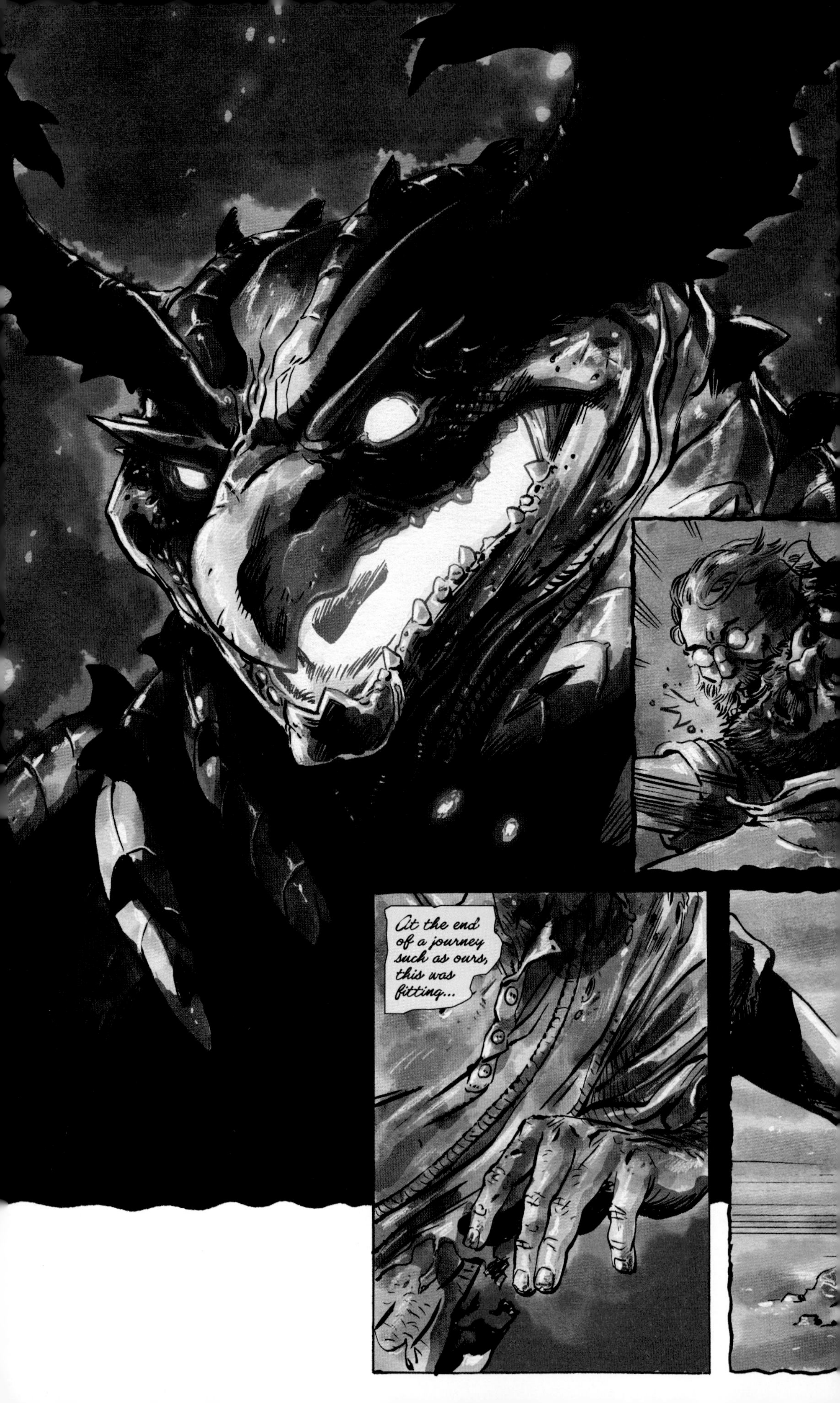
At the end of a journey such as ours, this was fitting...

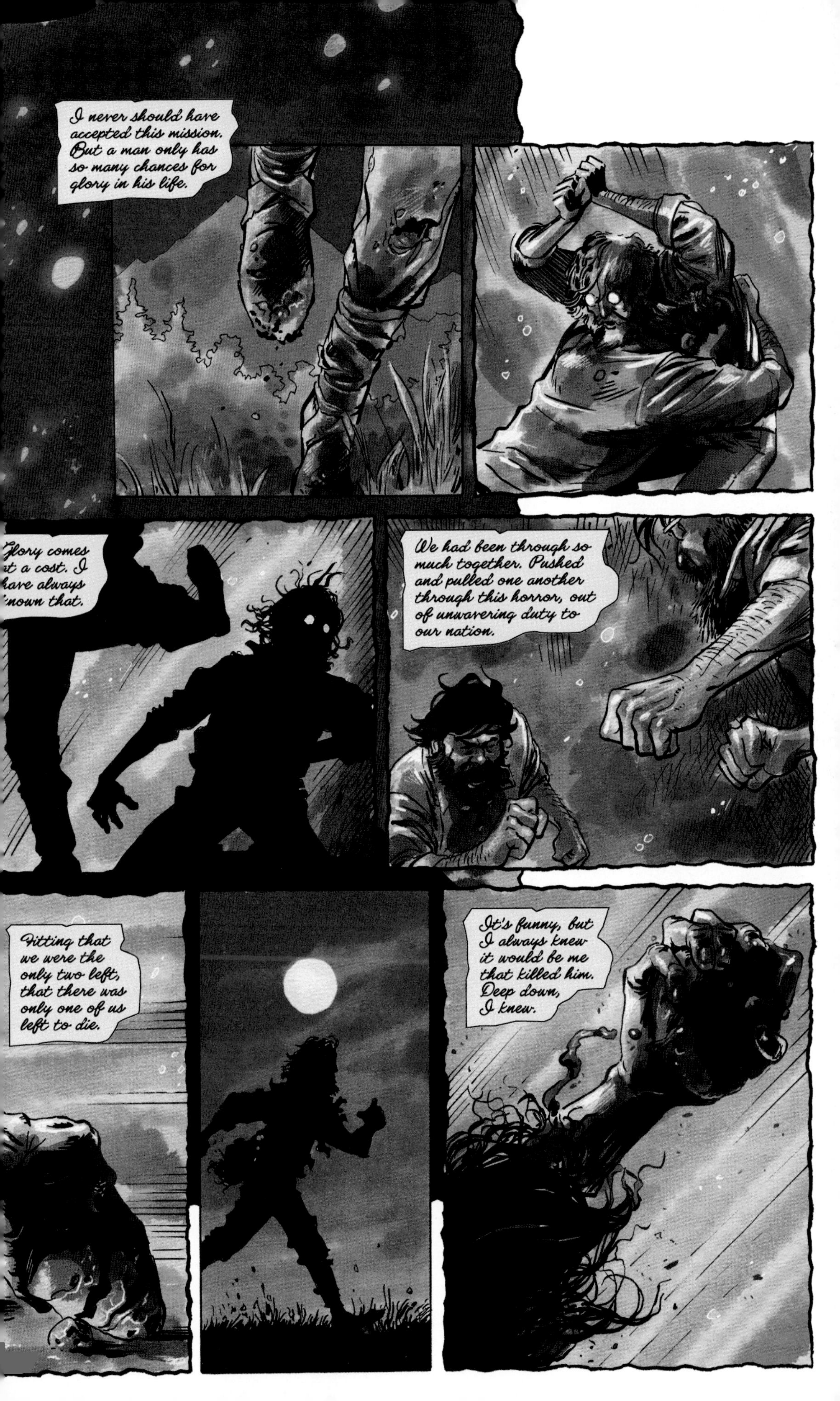
I never should have accepted this mission. But a man only has so many chances for glory in his life.
lory comes t a cost. I have always nown that.
We had been through so much together. Pushed and pulled one another through this horror, out of unwavering duty to our nation.
Fitting that we were the only two left, that there was only one of us left to die.
It's funny, but I always knew it would be me that killed him. Deep down, I knew.

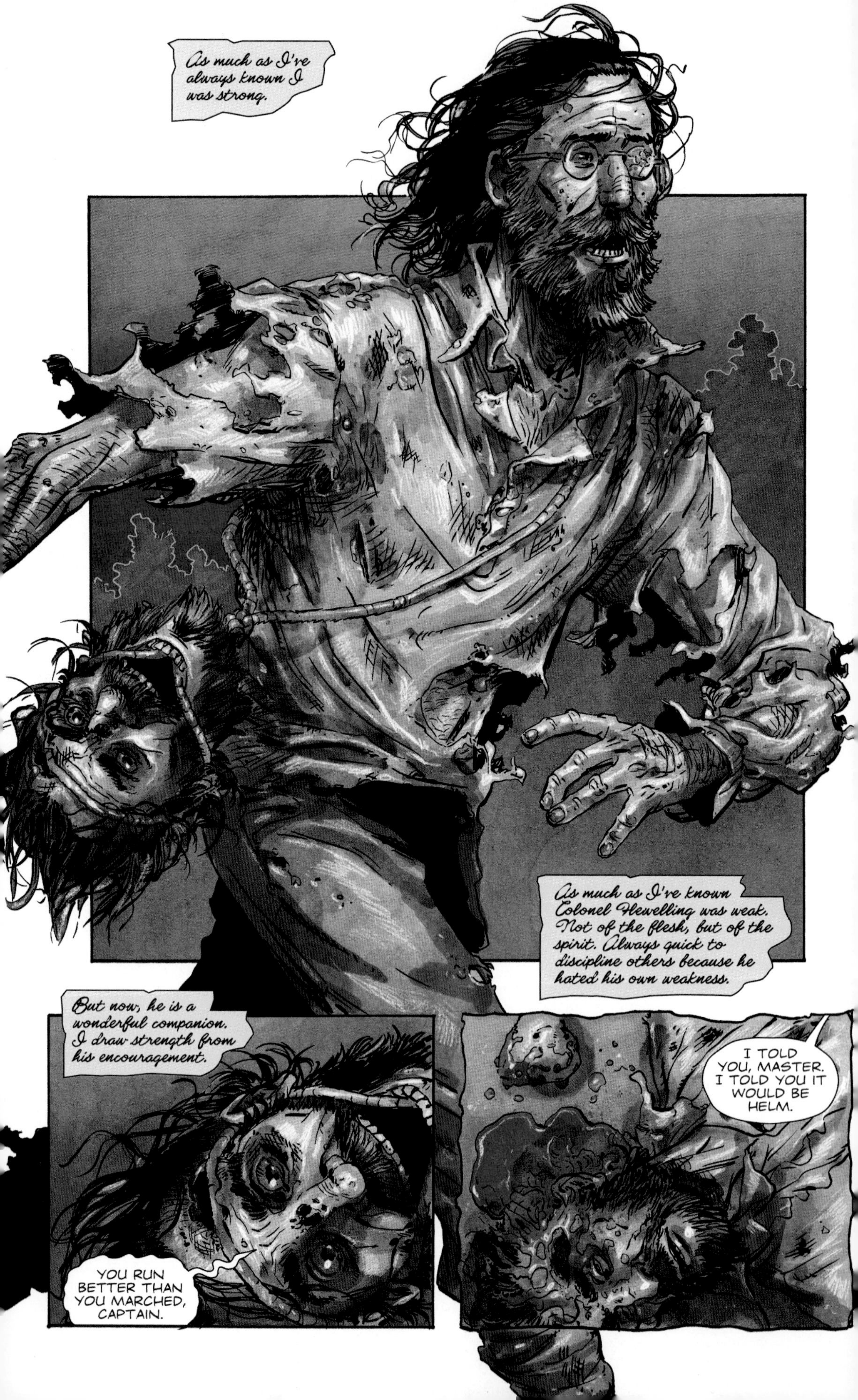
As much as I've always known I was strong.
As much as I've known Colonel Flewelling was weak. Not of the flesh, but of the spirit. Always quick to discipline others because he hated his own weakness.
But now, he is a wonderful companion. I draw strength from his encouragement.
YOU RUN BETTER THAN YOU MARCHED, CAPTAIN.
I TOLD YOU, MASTER. I TOLD YOU IT WOULD BE HELM.

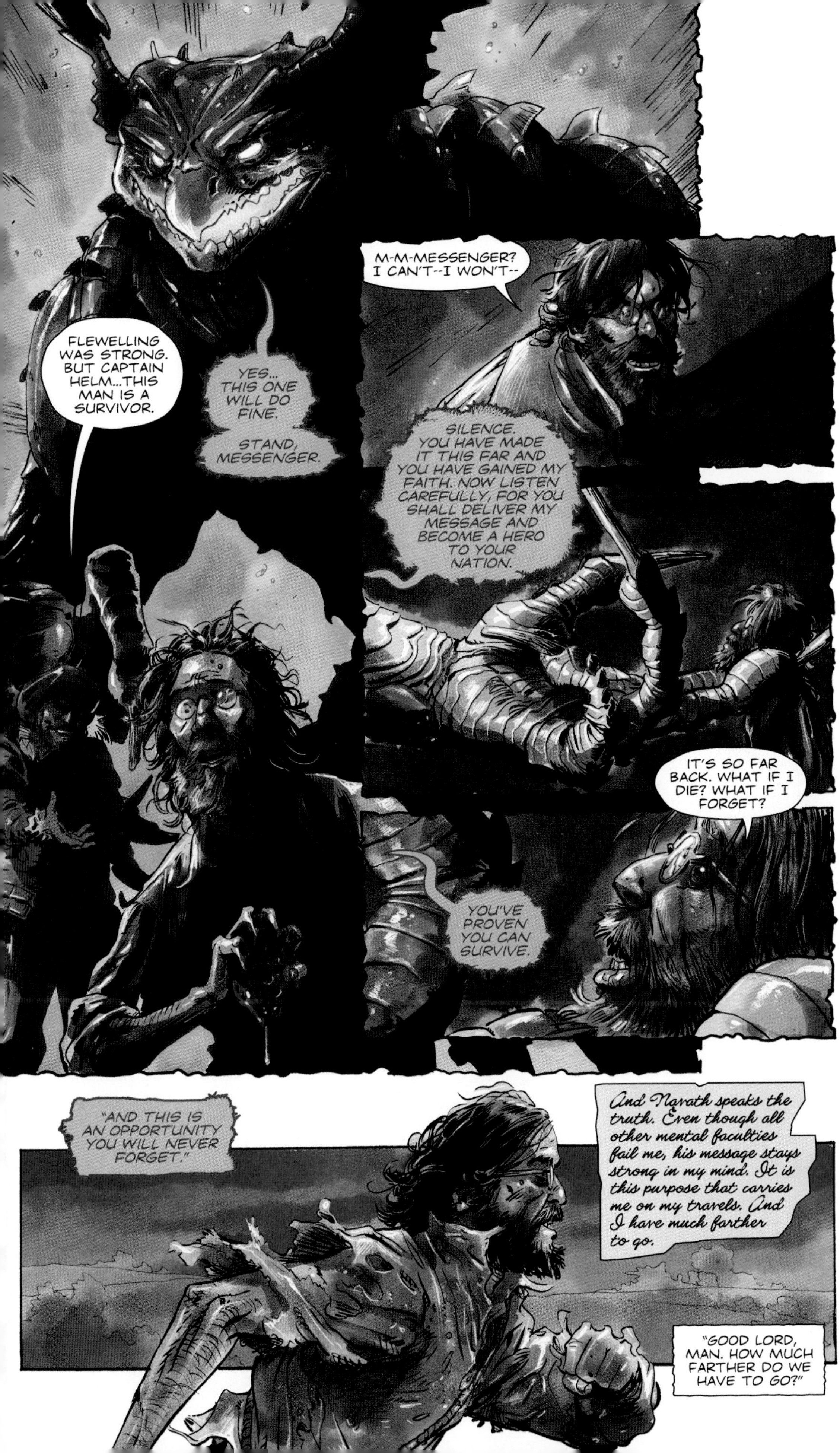
FLEWELLING WAS STRONG. BUT CAPTAIN HELM...THIS MAN IS A SURVIVOR.
YES... THIS ONE WILL DO FINE.
STAND, MESSENGER.
M-M-MESSENGER? I CAN'T--I WON'T--
SILENCE. YOU HAVE MADE IT THIS FAR AND YOU HAVE GAINED MY FAITH. NOW LISTEN CAREFULLY, FOR YOU SHALL DELIVER MY MESSAGE AND BECOME A HERO TO YOUR NATION.
IT'S SO FAR BACK. WHAT IF I DIE? WHAT IF I FORGET?
YOU'VE PROVEN YOU CAN SURVIVE.
"AND THIS IS AN OPPORTUNITY YOU WILL NEVER FORGET."
And Navath speaks the truth. Even though all other mental faculties fail me, his message stays strong in my mind. It is this purpose that carries me on my travels. And I have much farther to go.
"GOOD LORD, MAN. HOW MUCH FARTHER DO WE HAVE TO GO?"

We make our way up the river to meet with the Teton tribe, to parlay and notify them of our intent to build a fort near their hunting grounds. The trip is two days by boat. I don't anticipate much of an obstacle.

IT IS NOT MUCH MORE FARTHER, CAPTAINS.

IS THIS EVEN NECESSARY? WE'RE BUILDING OUR FORT RATHER FAR FROM HERE.

AGREED. WE'RE WASTING TIME THAT COULD BEST BE USED COLLECTING LUMBER AND CLEARING LAND.

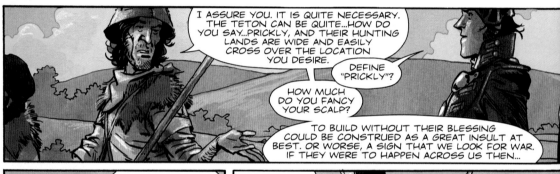

I ASSURE YOU. IT IS QUITE NECESSARY. THE TETON CAN BE QUITE...HOW DO YOU SAY...PRICKLY, AND THEIR HUNTING LANDS ARE WIDE AND EASILY CROSS OVER THE LOCATION YOU DESIRE.

DEFINE "PRICKLY"?

HOW MUCH DO YOU FANCY YOUR SCALP?

TO BUILD WITHOUT THEIR BLESSING COULD BE CONSTRUED AS A GREAT INSULT AT BEST. OR WORSE, A SIGN THAT WE LOOK FOR WAR. IF THEY WERE TO HAPPEN ACROSS US THEN...

IF THEY HAPPEN ACROSS US THEN, AND DISPLAY HOSTILE INTENTIONS, WE WOULD CUT THEM DOWN IN AN INSTANT.

OR WE COULD BREAK BREAD WITH THEM AND COMMIT A MASSACRE WHILE THEY SLEEP.

WHAT'S THAT, COLLINS?

JUST MARVELING AT THIS LAND, CAPTAIN.

SHOULDN'T WE SEND WORD OF OUR VISIT?

I TOLD THEM TO EXPECT US.

THEY HAVE BEEN WATCHING US. THEY KNOW WE ARE COMING.

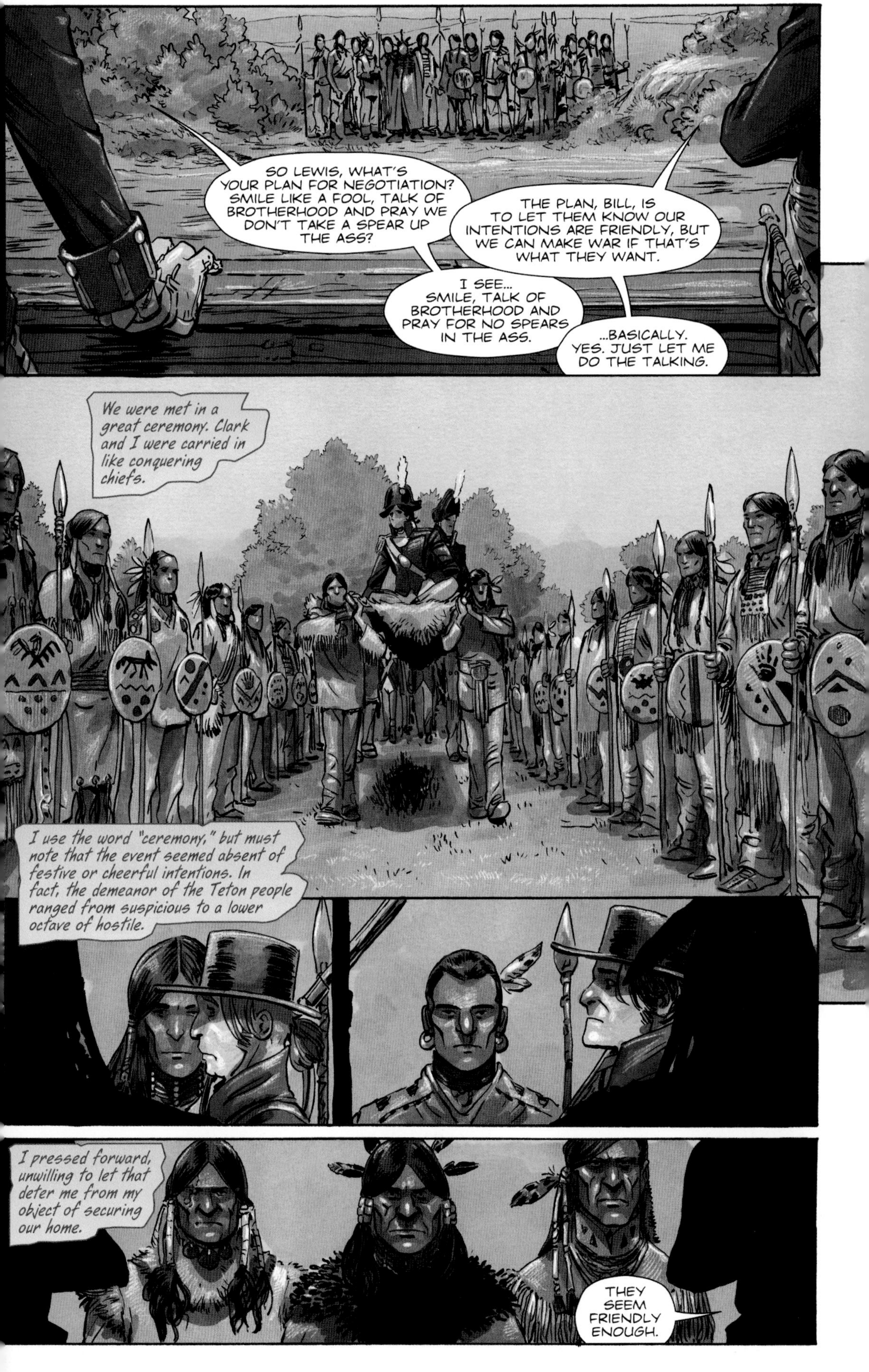
SO LEWIS, WHAT'S YOUR PLAN FOR NEGOTIATION? SMILE LIKE A FOOL, TALK OF BROTHERHOOD AND PRAY WE DON'T TAKE A SPEAR UP THE ASS?
THE PLAN, BILL, IS TO LET THEM KNOW OUR INTENTIONS ARE FRIENDLY, BUT WE CAN MAKE WAR IF THAT'S WHAT THEY WANT.
I SEE... SMILE, TALK OF BROTHERHOOD AND PRAY FOR NO SPEARS IN THE ASS.
...BASICALLY. YES. JUST LET ME DO THE TALKING.
We were met in a great ceremony. Clark and I were carried in like conquering chiefs.
I use the word "ceremony," but must note that the event seemed absent of festive or cheerful intentions. In fact, the demeanor of the Teton people ranged from suspicious to a lower octave of hostile.
I pressed forward, unwilling to let that deter me from my object of securing our home.
THEY SEEM FRIENDLY ENOUGH.

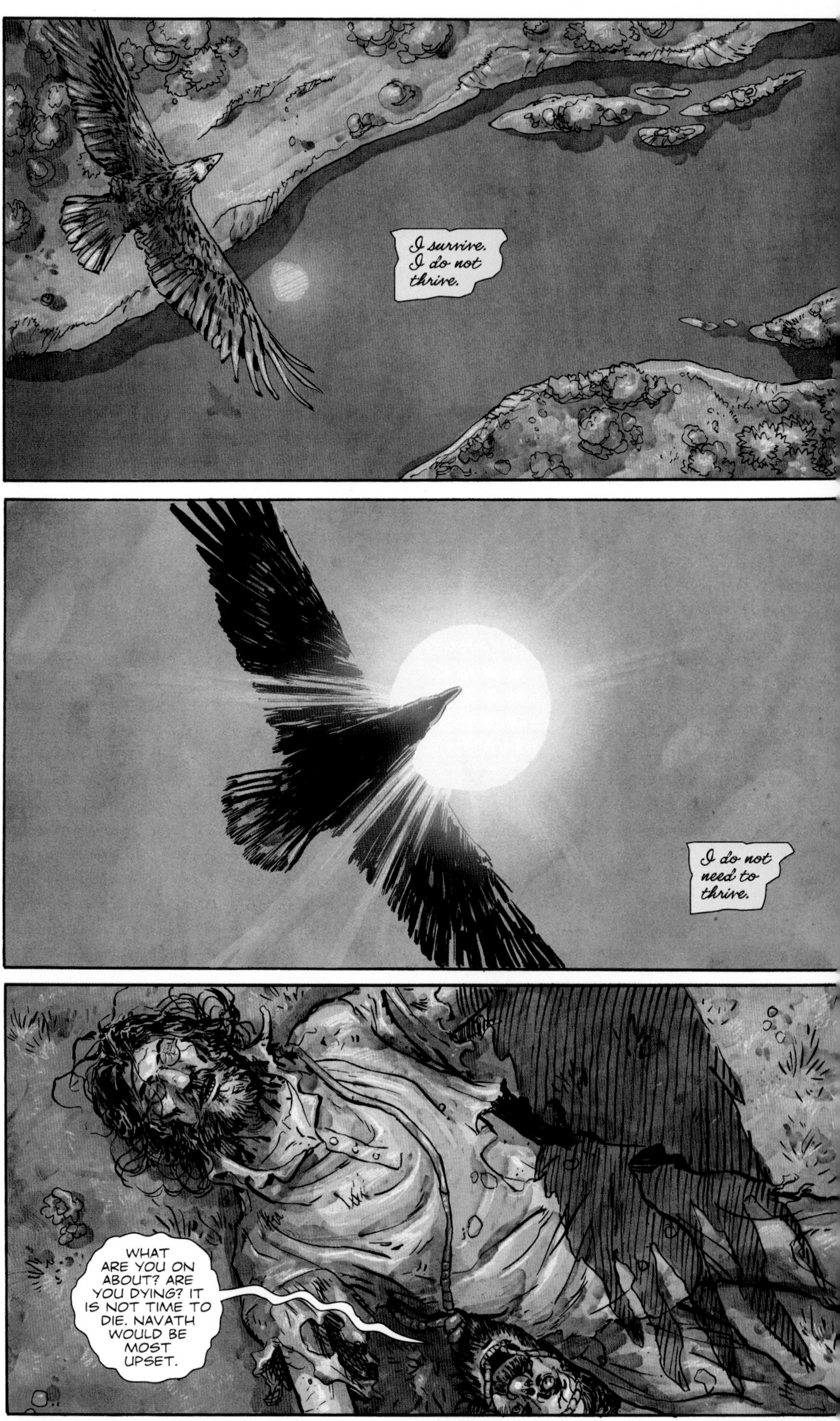
I survive. I do not thrive.
I do not need to thrive.
WHAT ARE YOU ON ABOUT? ARE YOU DYING? IT IS NOT TIME TO DIE. NAVATH WOULD BE MOST UPSET.

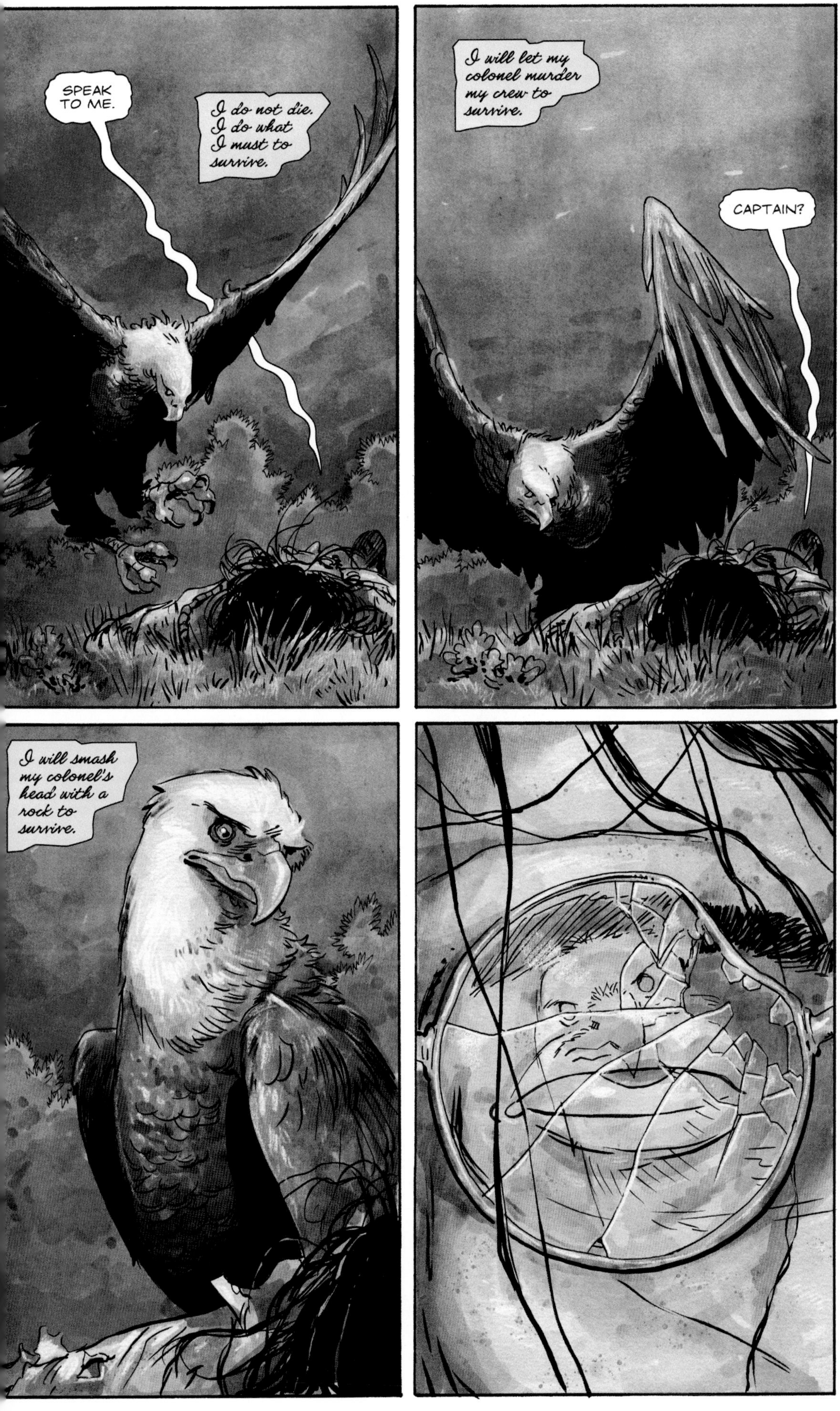
SPEAK TO ME.
I do not die. I do what I must to survive.
I will let my colonel murder my crew to survive.
CAPTAIN?
I will smash my colonel's head with a rock to survive.

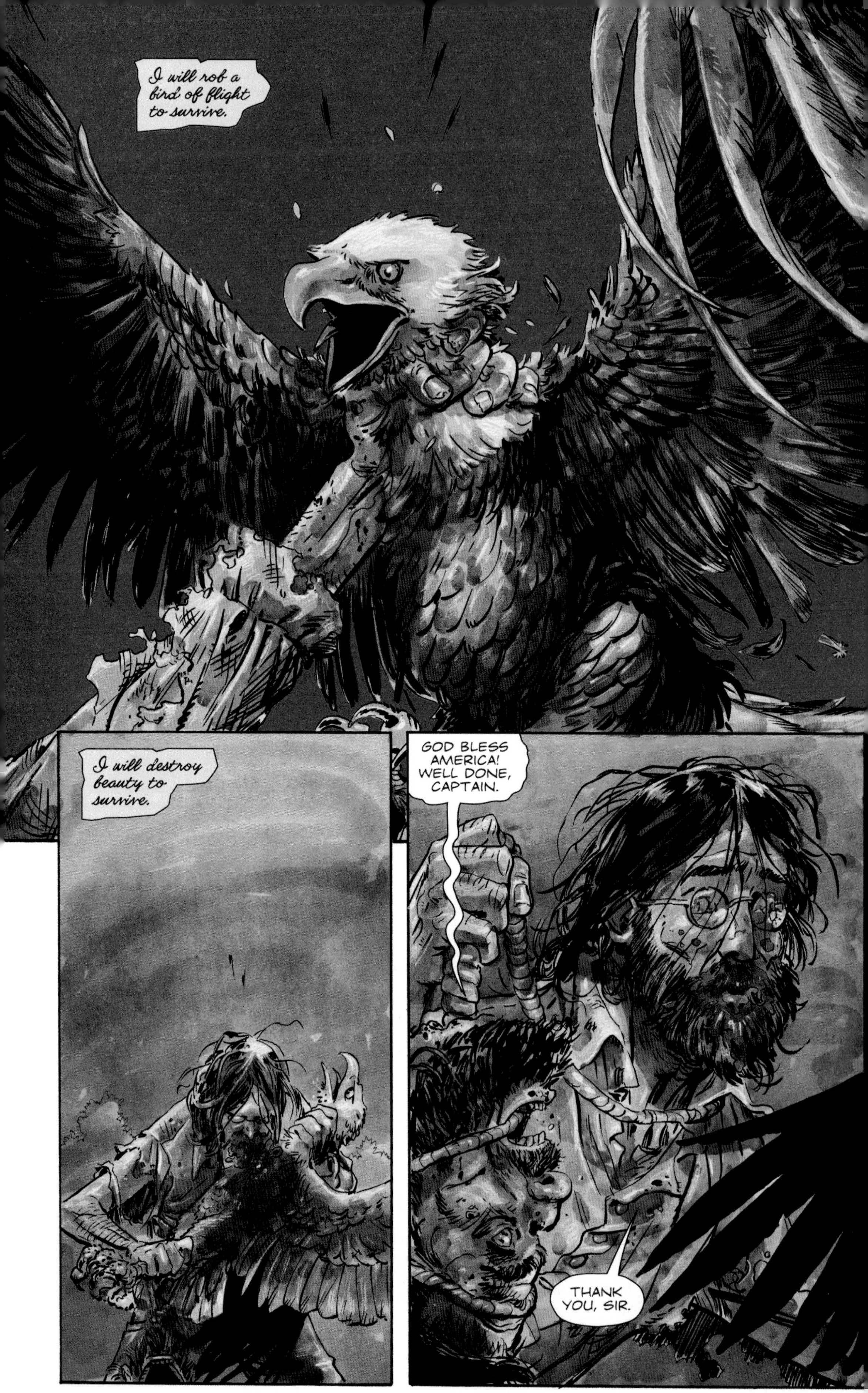
I will rob a bird of flight to survive.
I will destroy beauty to survive.
GOD BLESS AMERICA! WELL DONE, CAPTAIN.
THANK YOU, SIR.

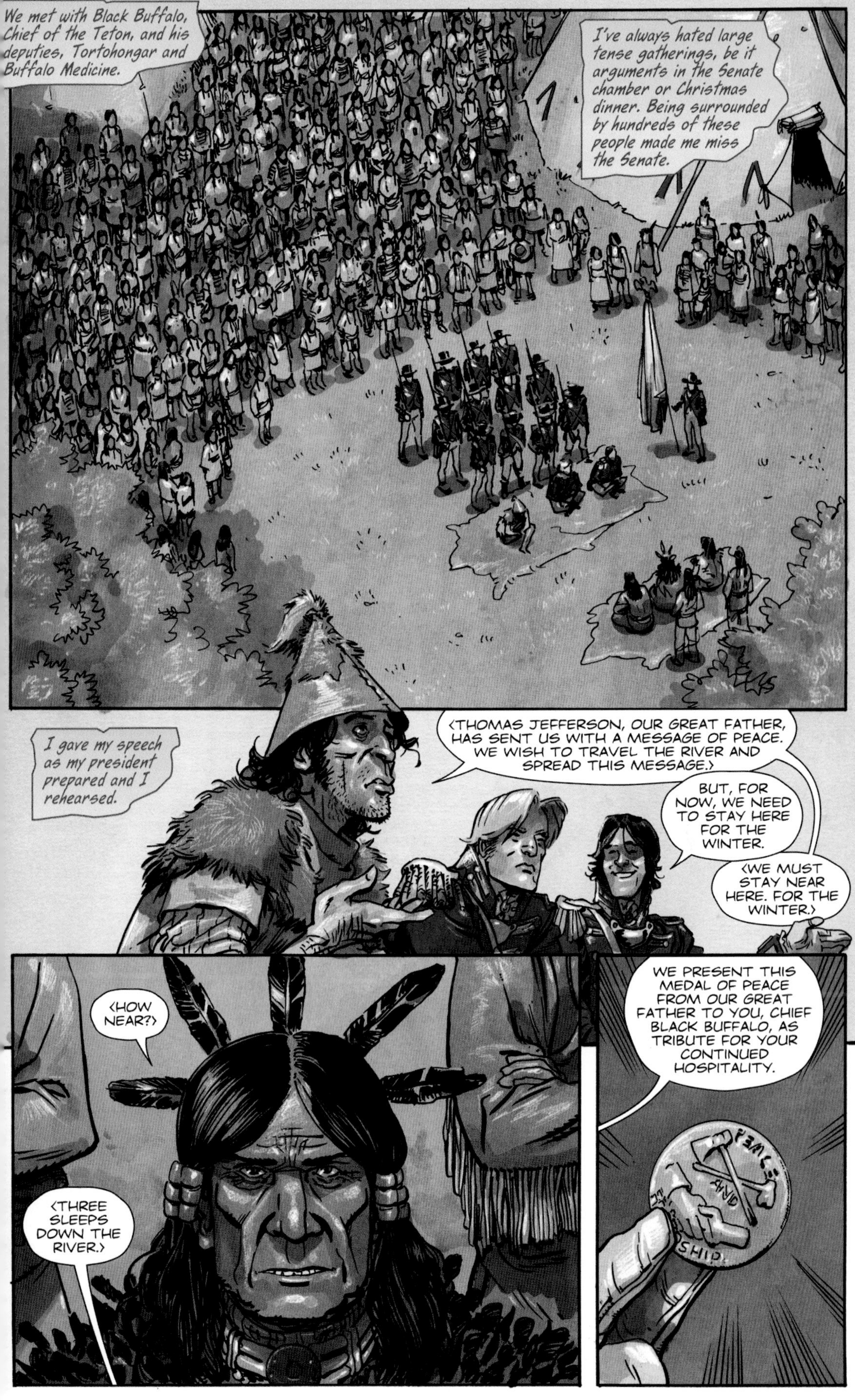
We met with Black Buffalo, Chief of the Teton, and his deputies, Tortohongar and Buffalo Medicine.
I've always hated large tense gatherings, be it arguments in the Senate chamber or Christmas dinner. Being surrounded by hundreds of these people made me miss the Senate.
I gave my speech as my president prepared and I rehearsed.
<THOMAS JEFFERSON, OUR GREAT FATHER, HAS SENT US WITH A MESSAGE OF PEACE. WE WISH TO TRAVEL THE RIVER AND SPREAD THIS MESSAGE.>
BUT, FOR NOW, WE NEED TO STAY HERE FOR THE WINTER.
<WE MUST STAY NEAR HERE. FOR THE WINTER.>
<HOW NEAR?>
<THREE SLEEPS DOWN THE RIVER.>
WE PRESENT THIS MEDAL OF PEACE FROM OUR GREAT FATHER TO YOU, CHIEF BLACK BUFFALO, AS TRIBUTE FOR YOUR CONTINUED HOSPITALITY.

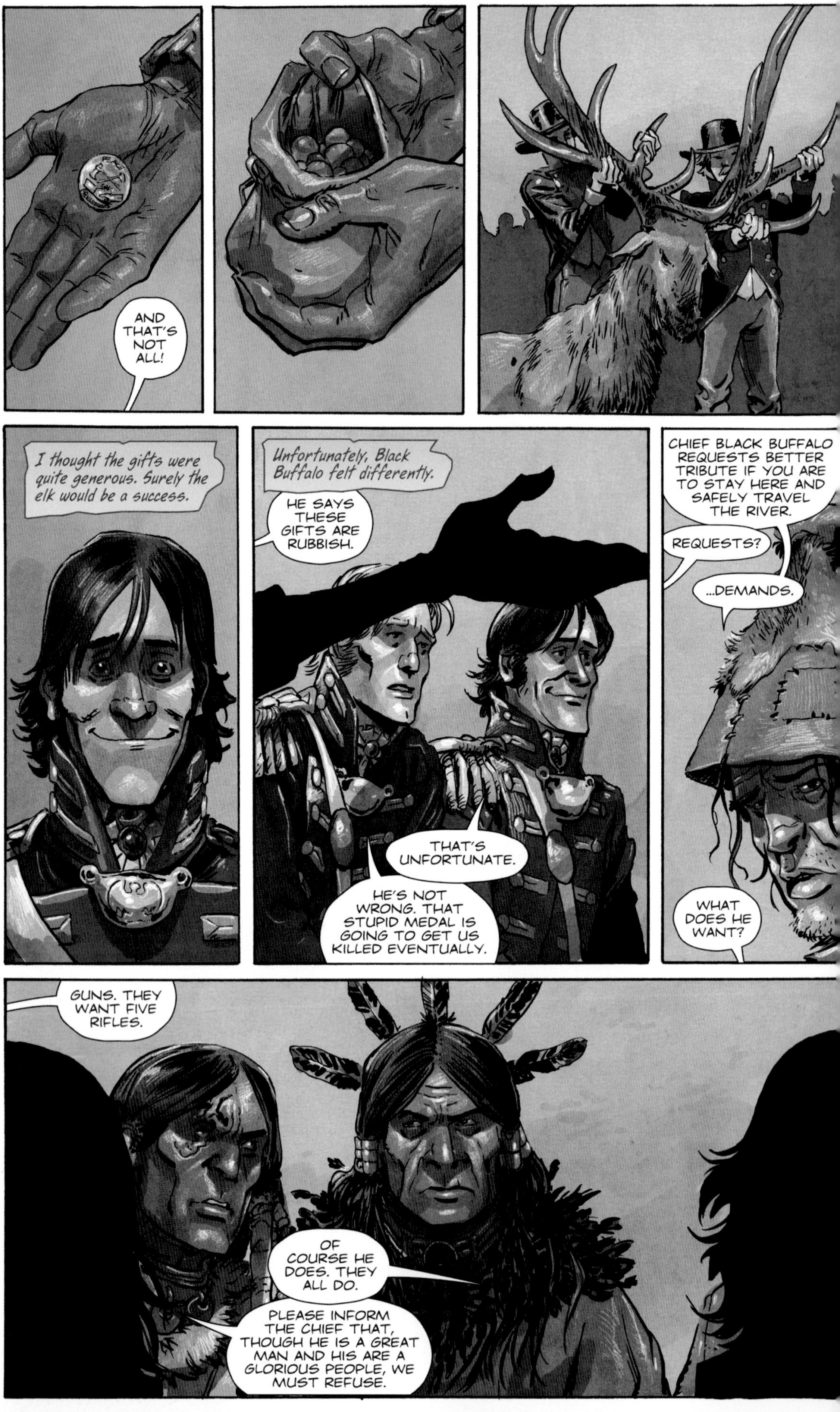
AND THAT'S NOT ALL!
I thought the gifts were quite generous. Surely the elk would be a success.
Unfortunately, Black Buffalo felt differently.
HE SAYS THESE GIFTS ARE RUBBISH.
THAT'S UNFORTUNATE.
HE'S NOT WRONG. THAT STUPID MEDAL IS GOING TO GET US KILLED EVENTUALLY.
CHIEF BLACK BUFFALO REQUESTS BETTER TRIBUTE IF YOU ARE TO STAY HERE AND SAFELY TRAVEL THE RIVER.
REQUESTS?
...DEMANDS.
WHAT DOES HE WANT?
GUNS. THEY WANT FIVE RIFLES.
OF COURSE HE DOES. THEY ALL DO.
PLEASE INFORM THE CHIEF THAT, THOUGH HE IS A GREAT MAN AND HIS ARE A GLORIOUS PEOPLE, WE MUST REFUSE.

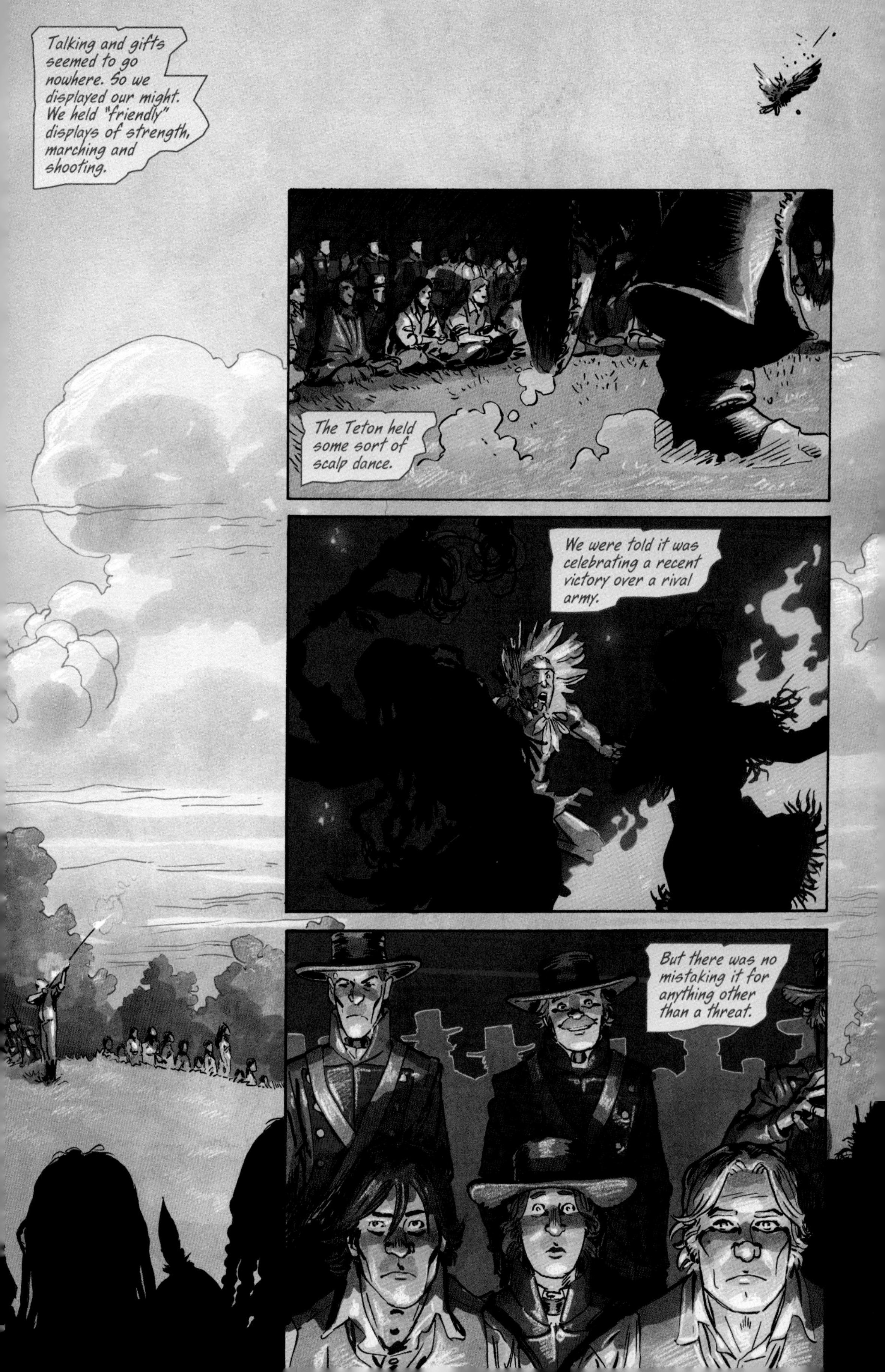
Talking and gifts seemed to go nowhere. So we displayed our might. We held "friendly" displays of strength, marching and shooting.
The Teton held some sort of scalp dance.
We were told it was celebrating a recent victory over a rival army.
But there was no mistaking it for anything other than a threat.

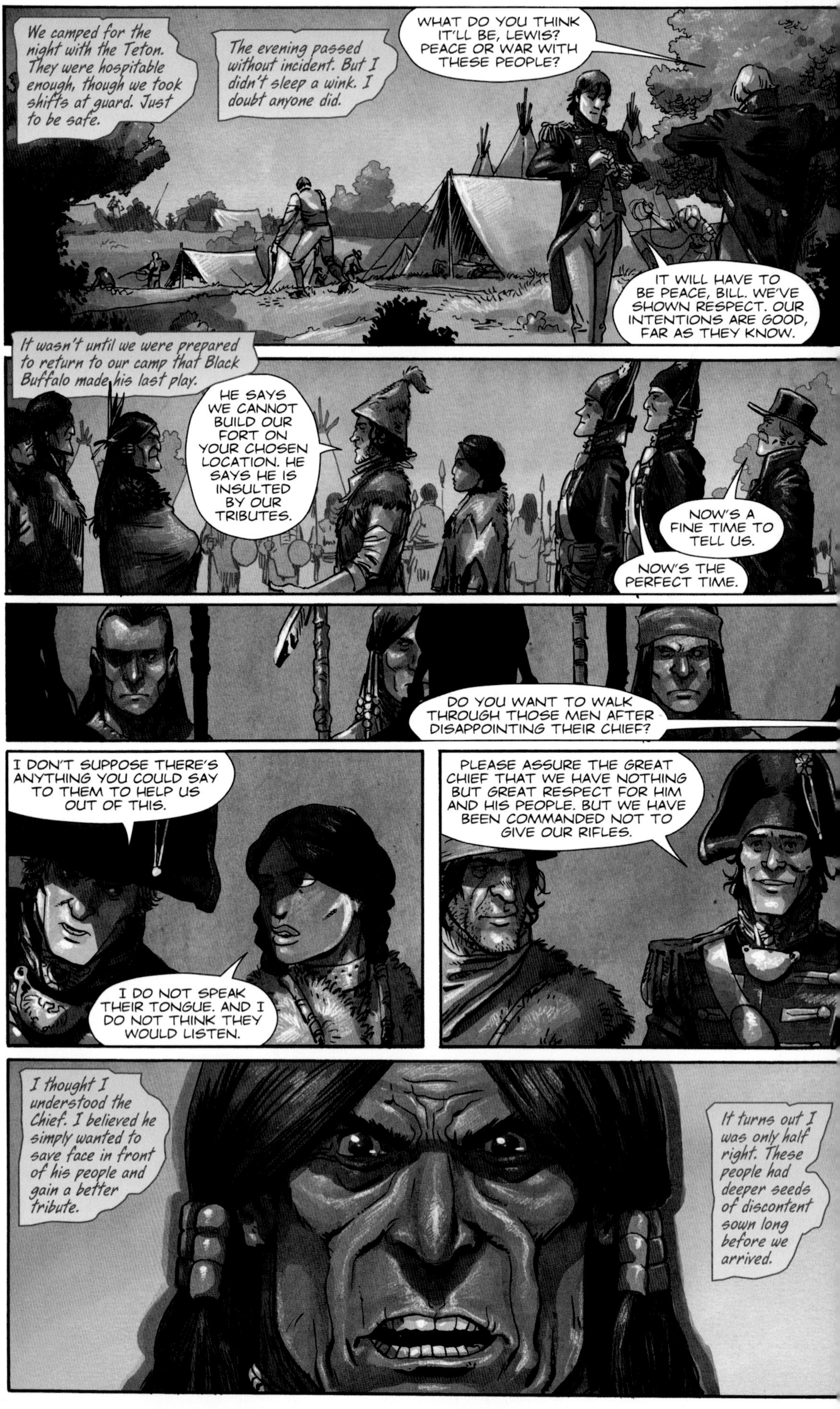
We camped for the night with the Teton. They were hospitable enough, though we took shifts at guard. Just to be safe.
The evening passed without incident. But I didn't sleep a wink. I doubt anyone did.
WHAT DO YOU THINK IT'LL BE, LEWIS? PEACE OR WAR WITH THESE PEOPLE?
IT WILL HAVE TO BE PEACE, BILL. WE'VE SHOWN RESPECT. OUR INTENTIONS ARE GOOD, FAR AS THEY KNOW.
It wasn't until we were prepared to return to our camp that Black Buffalo made his last play.
HE SAYS WE CANNOT BUILD OUR FORT ON YOUR CHOSEN LOCATION. HE SAYS HE IS INSULTED BY OUR TRIBUTES.
NOW'S A FINE TIME TO TELL US.
NOW'S THE PERFECT TIME.
DO YOU WANT TO WALK THROUGH THOSE MEN AFTER DISAPPOINTING THEIR CHIEF?
I DON'T SUPPOSE THERE'S ANYTHING YOU COULD SAY TO THEM TO HELP US OUT OF THIS.
I DO NOT SPEAK THEIR TONGUE. AND I DO NOT THINK THEY WOULD LISTEN.
PLEASE ASSURE THE GREAT CHIEF THAT WE HAVE NOTHING BUT GREAT RESPECT FOR HIM AND HIS PEOPLE. BUT WE HAVE BEEN COMMANDED NOT TO GIVE OUR RIFLES.
I thought I understood the Chief. I believed he simply wanted to save face in front of his people and gain a better tribute.
It turns out I was only half right. These people had deeper seeds of discontent sown long before we arrived.

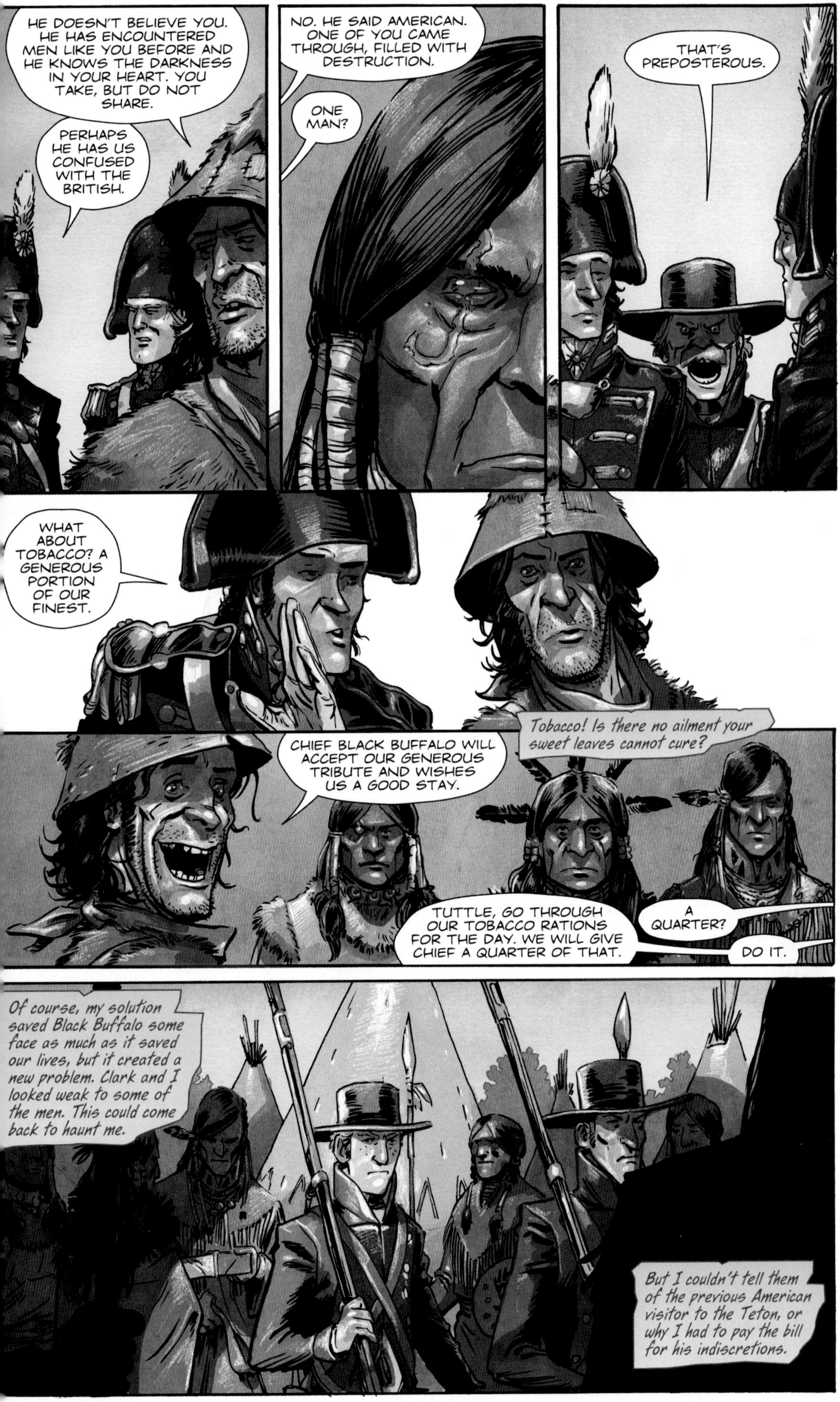

HE DOESN'T BELIEVE YOU. HE HAS ENCOUNTERED MEN LIKE YOU BEFORE AND HE KNOWS THE DARKNESS IN YOUR HEART. YOU TAKE, BUT DO NOT SHARE.
PERHAPS HE HAS US CONFUSED WITH THE BRITISH.
NO. HE SAID AMERICAN. ONE OF YOU CAME THROUGH, FILLED WITH DESTRUCTION.
ONE MAN?
THAT'S PREPOSTEROUS.
WHAT ABOUT TOBACCO? A GENEROUS PORTION OF OUR FINEST.
CHIEF BLACK BUFFALO WILL ACCEPT OUR GENEROUS TRIBUTE AND WISHES US A GOOD STAY.
Tobacco! Is there no ailment your sweet leaves cannot cure?
TUTTLE, GO THROUGH OUR TOBACCO RATIONS FOR THE DAY. WE WILL GIVE CHIEF A QUARTER OF THAT.
A QUARTER?
DO IT.
Of course, my solution saved Black Buffalo some face as much as it saved our lives, but it created a new problem. Clark and I looked weak to some of the men. This could come back to haunt me.
But I couldn't tell them of the previous American visitor to the Teton, or why I had to pay the bill for his indiscretions.

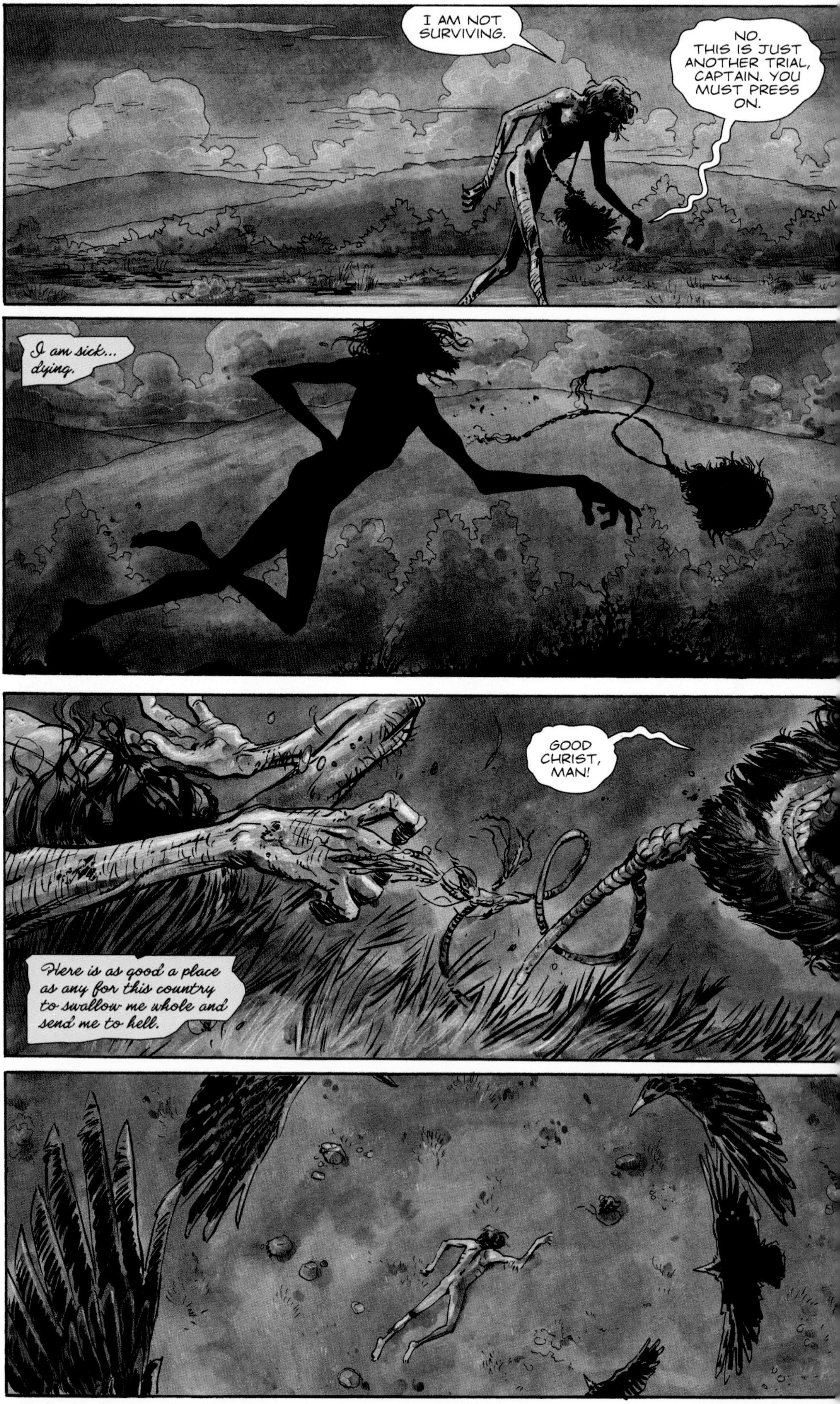
I AM NOT SURVIVING.
NO. THIS IS JUST ANOTHER TRIAL, CAPTAIN. YOU MUST PRESS ON.
I am sick... dying.
GOOD CHRIST, MAN!
Here is as good a place as any for this country to swallow me whole and send me to hell.

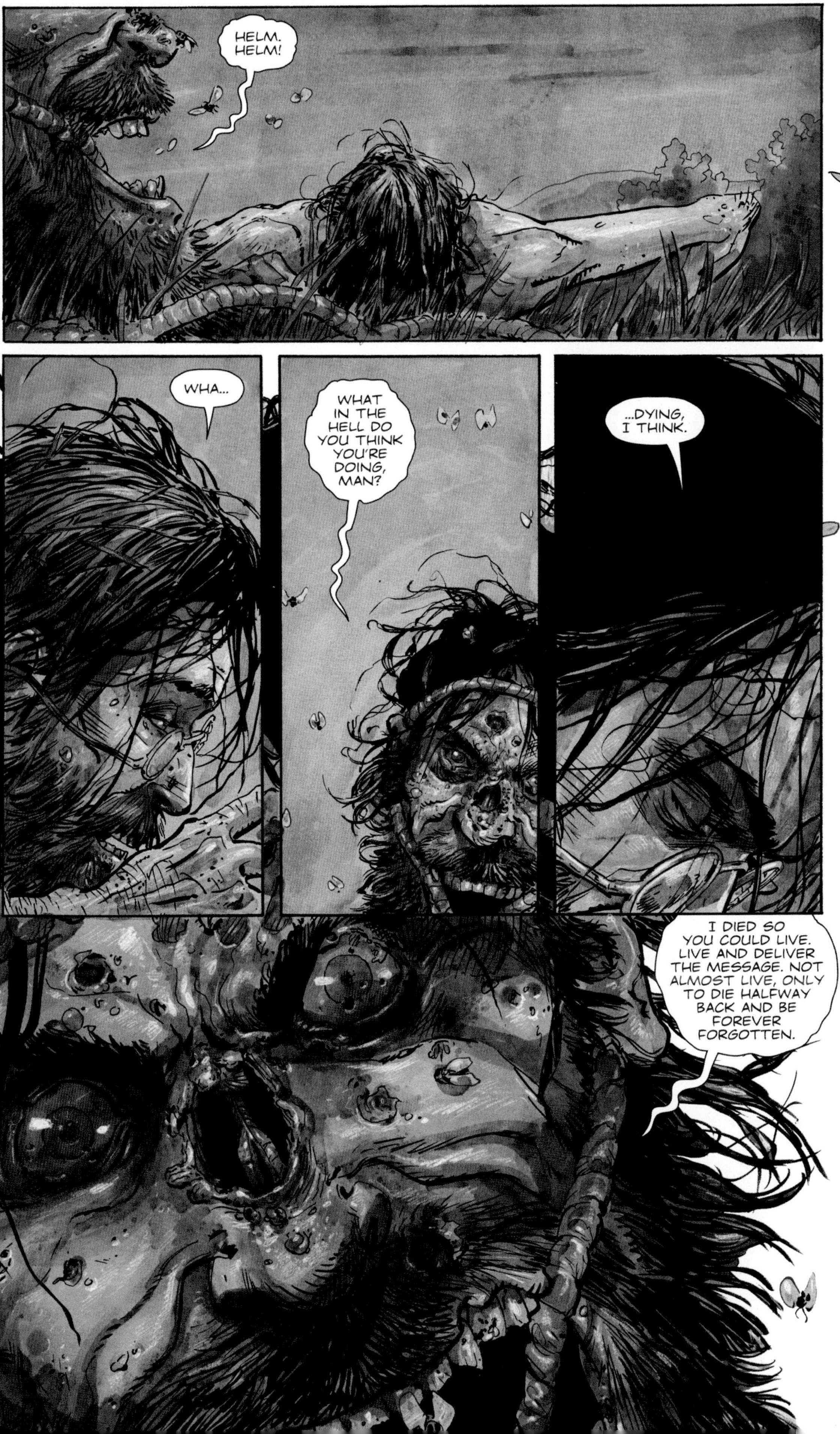
HELM. HELM!
WHA...
WHAT IN THE HELL DO YOU THINK YOU'RE DOING, MAN?
...DYING, I THINK.
I DIED SO YOU COULD LIVE. LIVE AND DELIVER THE MESSAGE. NOT ALMOST LIVE, ONLY TO DIE HALFWAY BACK AND BE FOREVER FORGOTTEN.

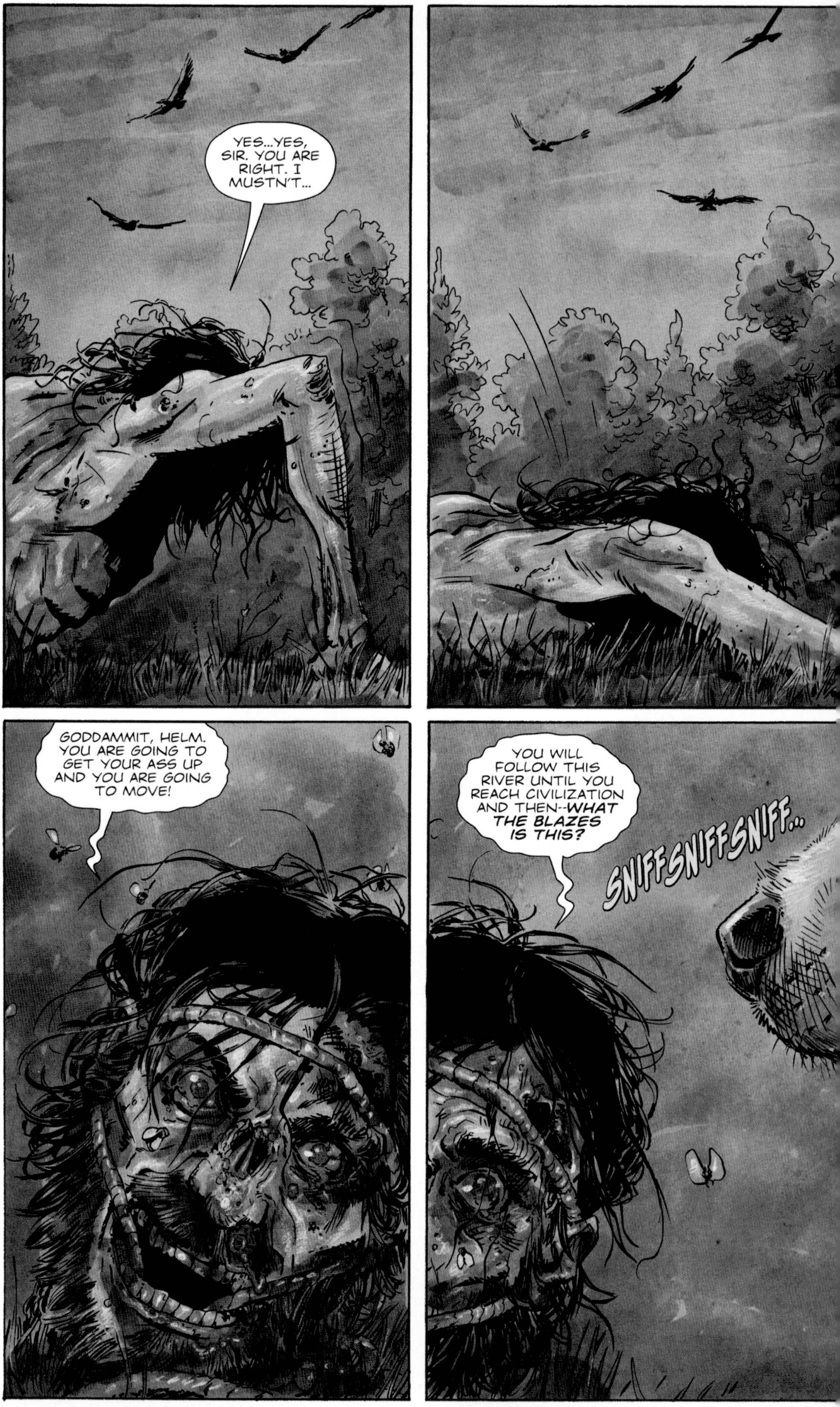
YES...YES, SIR. YOU ARE RIGHT. I MUSTN'T...
GODDAMMIT, HELM. YOU ARE GOING TO GET YOUR ASS UP AND YOU ARE GOING TO MOVE!
YOU WILL FOLLOW THIS RIVER UNTIL YOU REACH CIVILIZATION AND THEN--WHAT THE BLAZES IS THIS?
SNIFFSNIFFSNIFF...

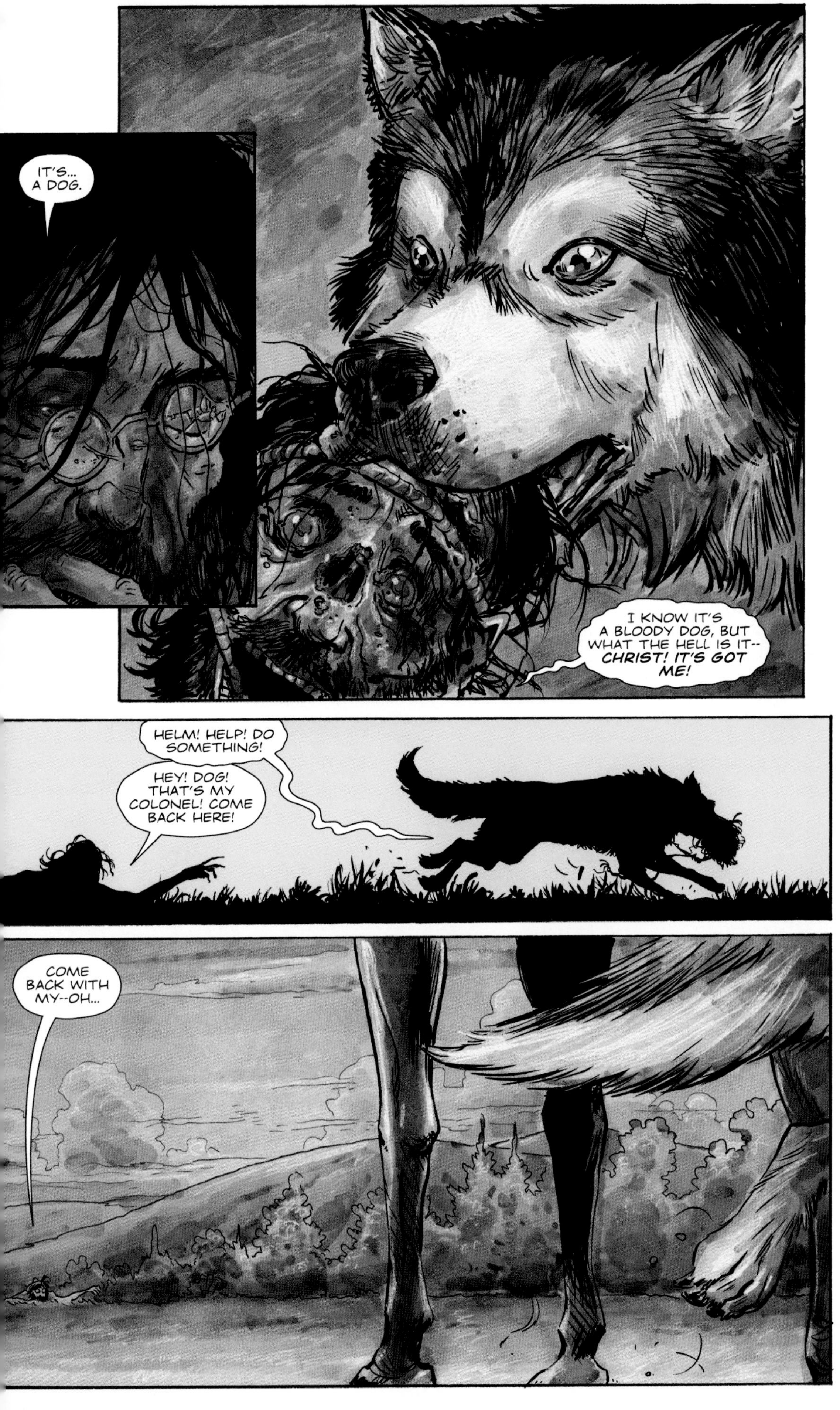
IT'S... A DOG.
I KNOW IT'S A BLOODY DOG, BUT WHAT THE HELL IS IT-- CHRIST! IT'S GOT ME!
HELM! HELP! DO SOMETHING!
HEY! DOG! THAT'S MY COLONEL! COME BACK HERE!
COME BACK WITH MY--OH...

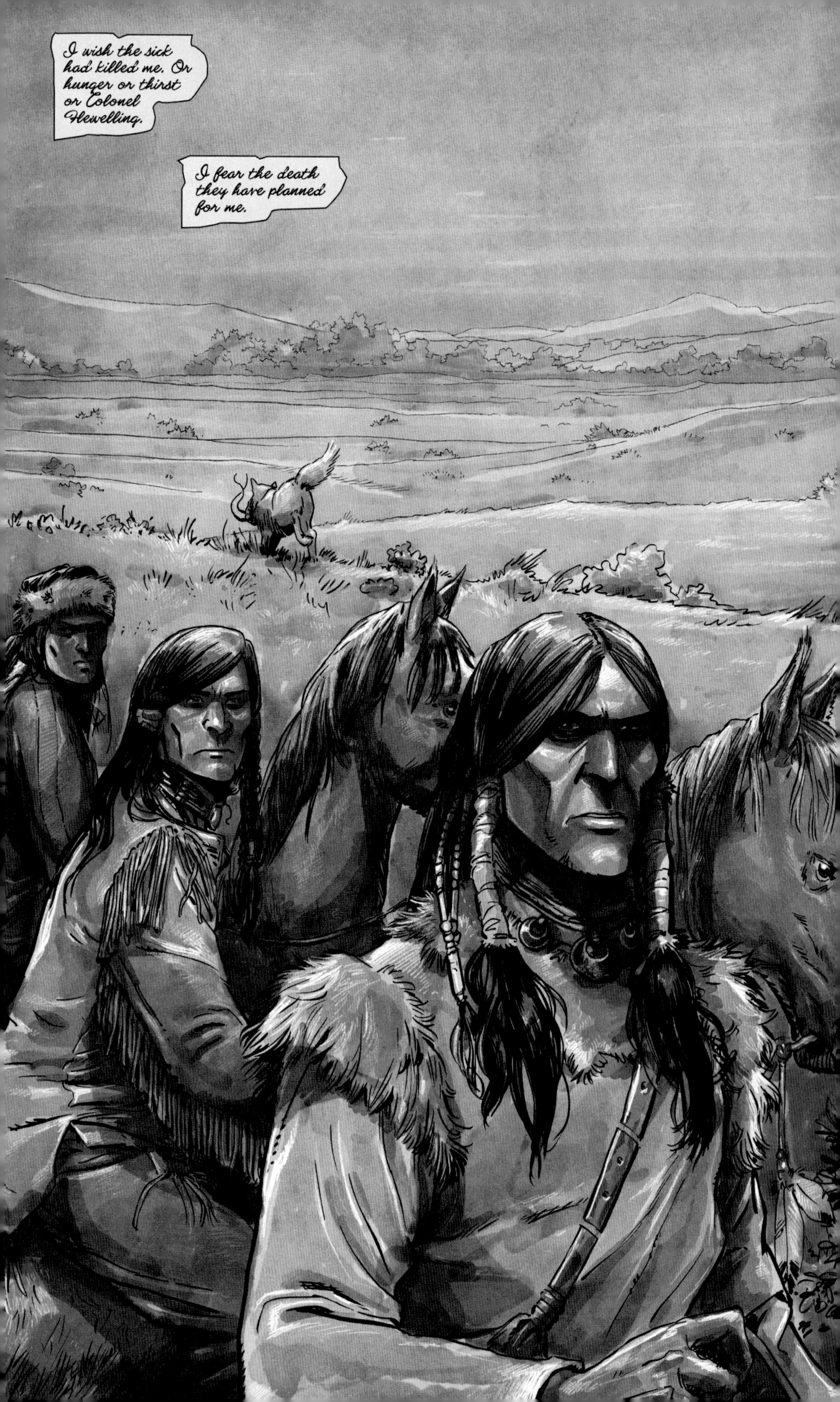
I wish the sick had killed me. Or hunger or thirst or Colonel Flewelling.
I fear the death they have planned for me.

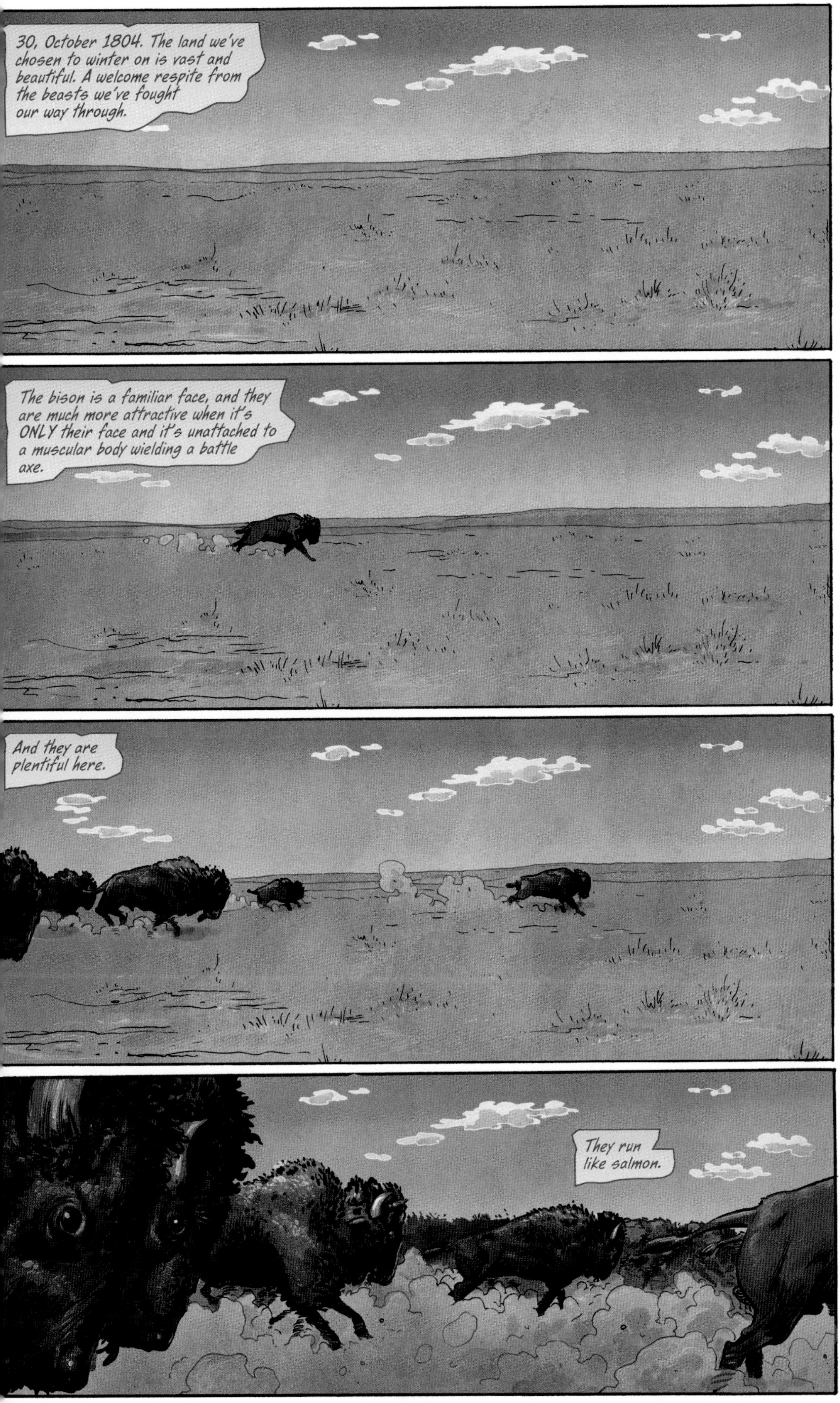

30, October 1804. The land we've chosen to winter on is vast and beautiful. A welcome respite from the beasts we've fought our way through.
The bison is a familiar face, and they are much more attractive when it's ONLY their face and it's unattached to a muscular body wielding a battle axe.
And they are plentiful here.
They run like salmon.

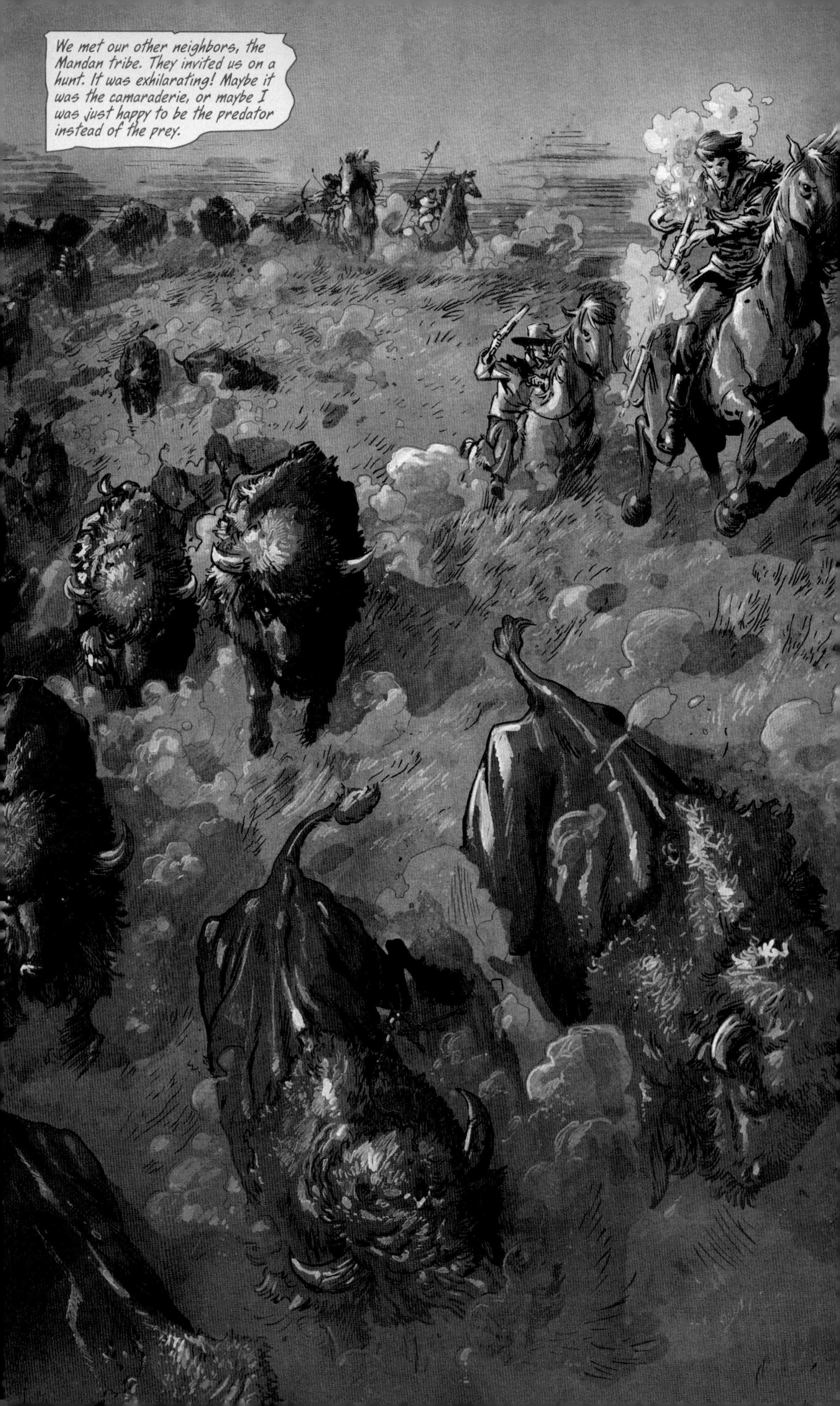
We met our other neighbors, the Mandan tribe. They invited us on a hunt. It was exhilarating! Maybe it was the camaraderie, or maybe I was just happy to be the predator instead of the prey.

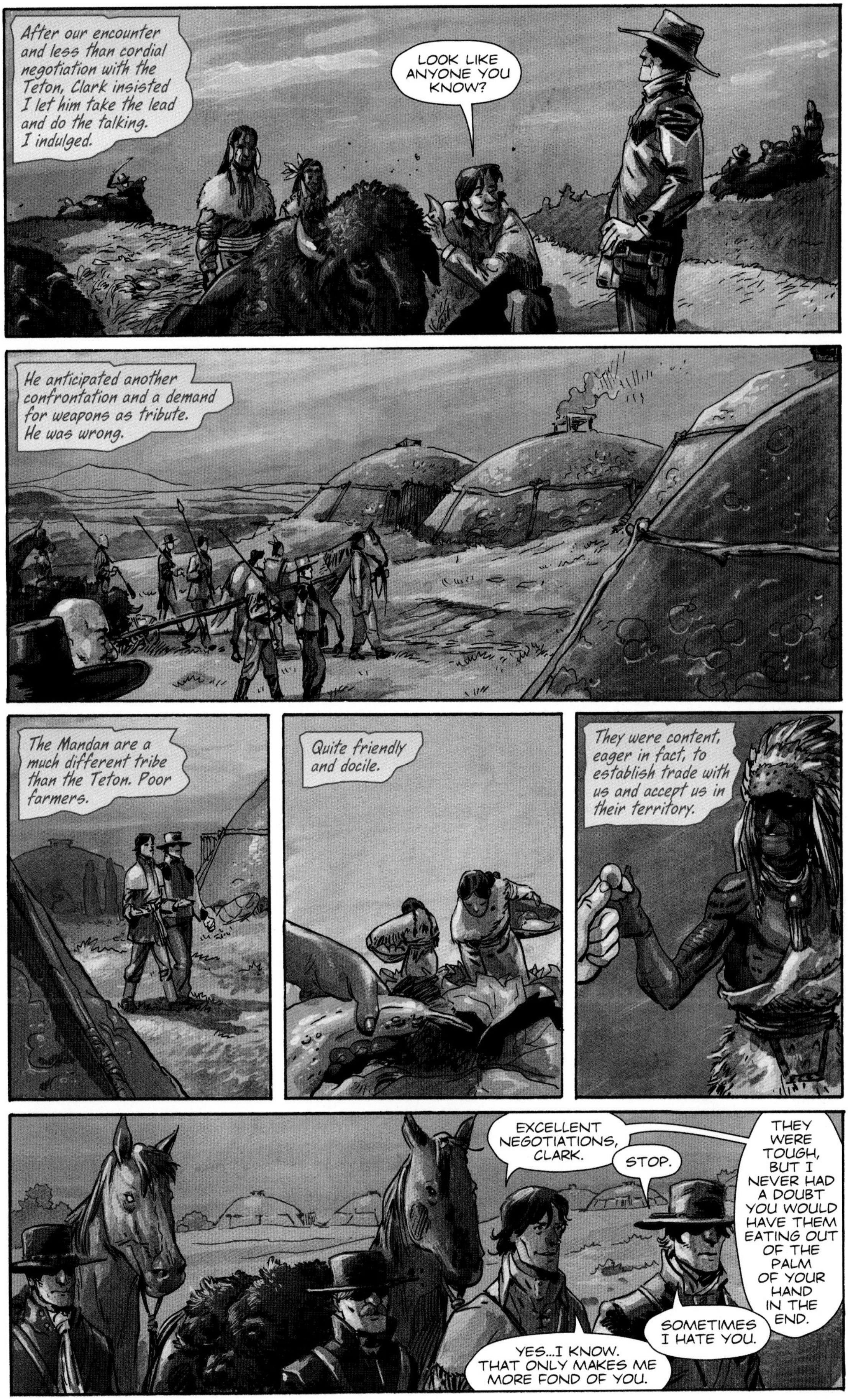
After our encounter and less than cordial negotiation with the Teton, Clark insisted I let him take the lead and do the talking. I indulged.
LOOK LIKE ANYONE YOU KNOW?
He anticipated another confrontation and a demand for weapons as tribute. He was wrong.
The Mandan are a much different tribe than the Teton. Poor farmers.
Quite friendly and docile.
They were content, eager in fact, to establish trade with us and accept us in their territory.
EXCELLENT NEGOTIATIONS, CLARK.
STOP.
THEY WERE TOUGH, BUT I NEVER HAD A DOUBT YOU WOULD HAVE THEM EATING OUT OF THE PALM OF YOUR HAND IN THE END.
SOMETIMES I HATE YOU.
YES...I KNOW. THAT ONLY MAKES ME MORE FOND OF YOU.

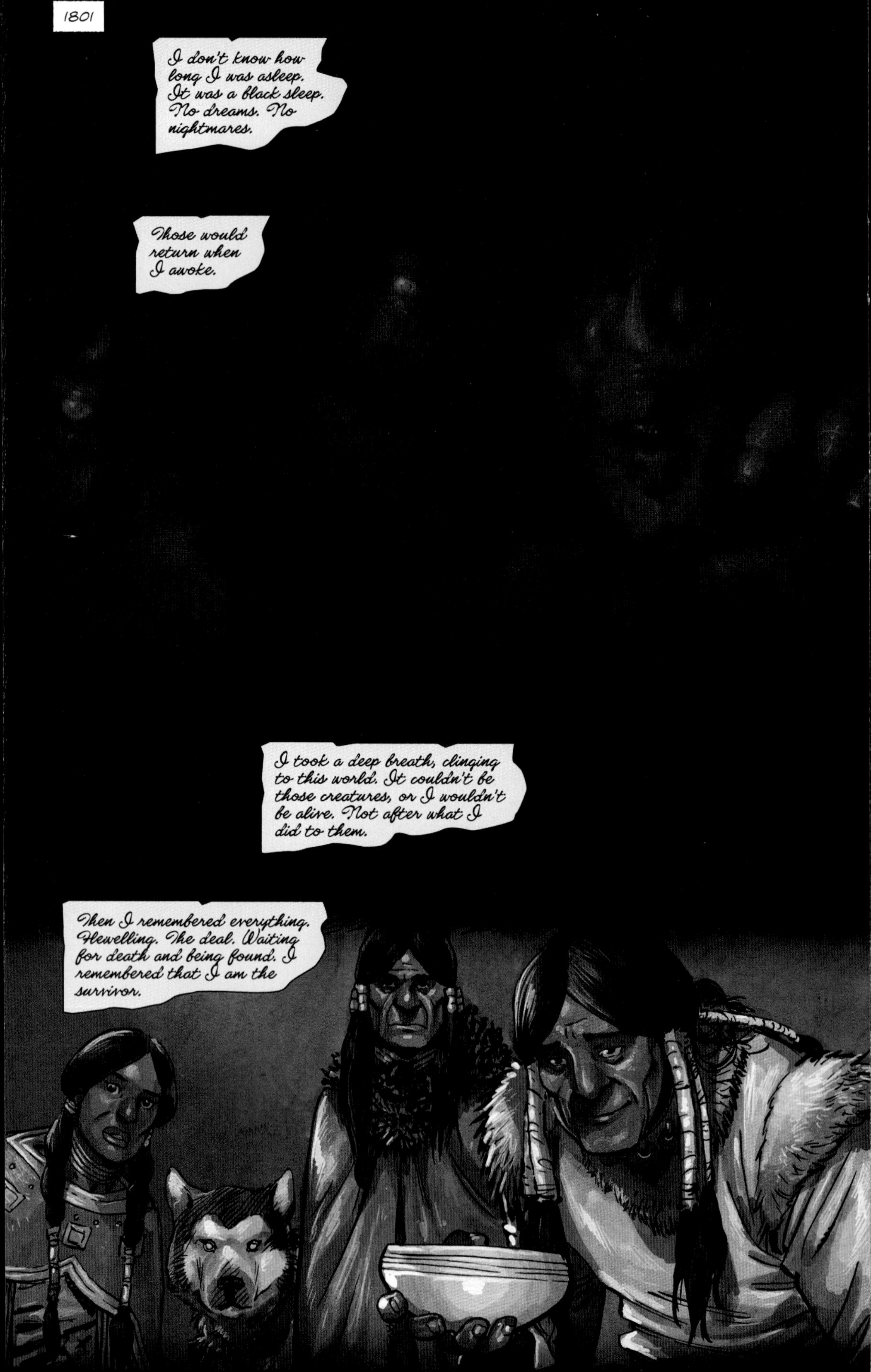
1801
I don't know how long I was asleep. It was a black sleep. No dreams. No nightmares.
Those would return when I awoke.
I took a deep breath, clinging to this world. It couldn't be those creatures, or I wouldn't be alive. Not after what I did to them.
Then I remembered everything. Flewelling. The deal. Waiting for death and being found. I remembered that I am the survivor.

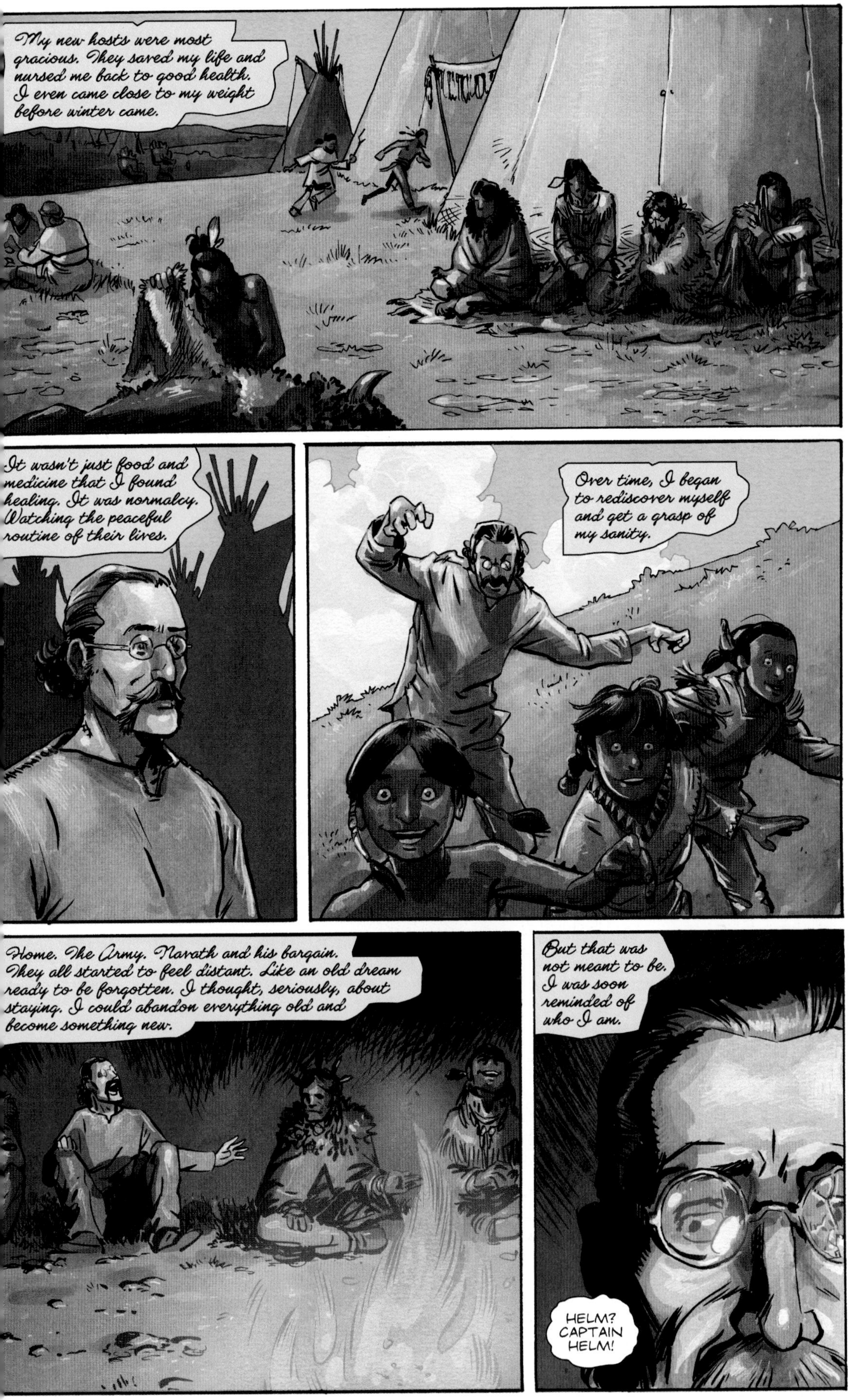
My new hosts were most gracious. They saved my life and nursed me back to good health. I even came close to my weight before winter came.
It wasn't just food and medicine that I found healing. It was normalcy. Watching the peaceful routine of their lives.
Over time, I began to rediscover myself and get a grasp of my sanity.
Home. The Army. Navath and his bargain. They all started to feel distant. Like an old dream ready to be forgotten. I thought, seriously, about staying. I could abandon everything old and become something new.
But that was not meant to be. I was soon reminded of who I am.
HELM? CAPTAIN HELM!

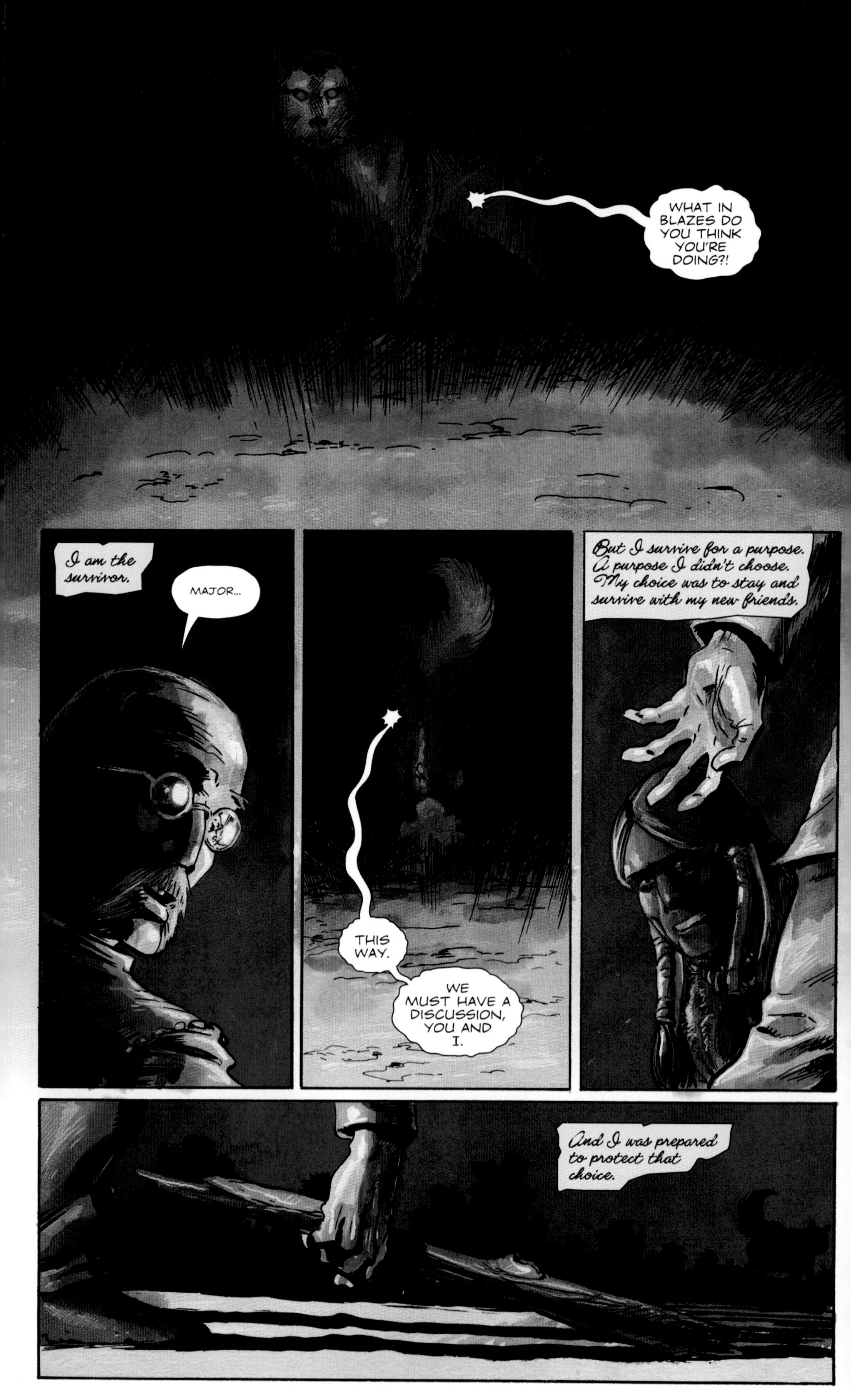
WHAT IN BLAZES DO YOU THINK YOU'RE DOING?!
I am the survivor.
MAJOR...
THIS WAY.
WE MUST HAVE A DISCUSSION, YOU AND I.
But I survive for a purpose. A purpose I didn't choose. My choice was to stay and survive with my new friends.
And I was prepared to protect that choice.

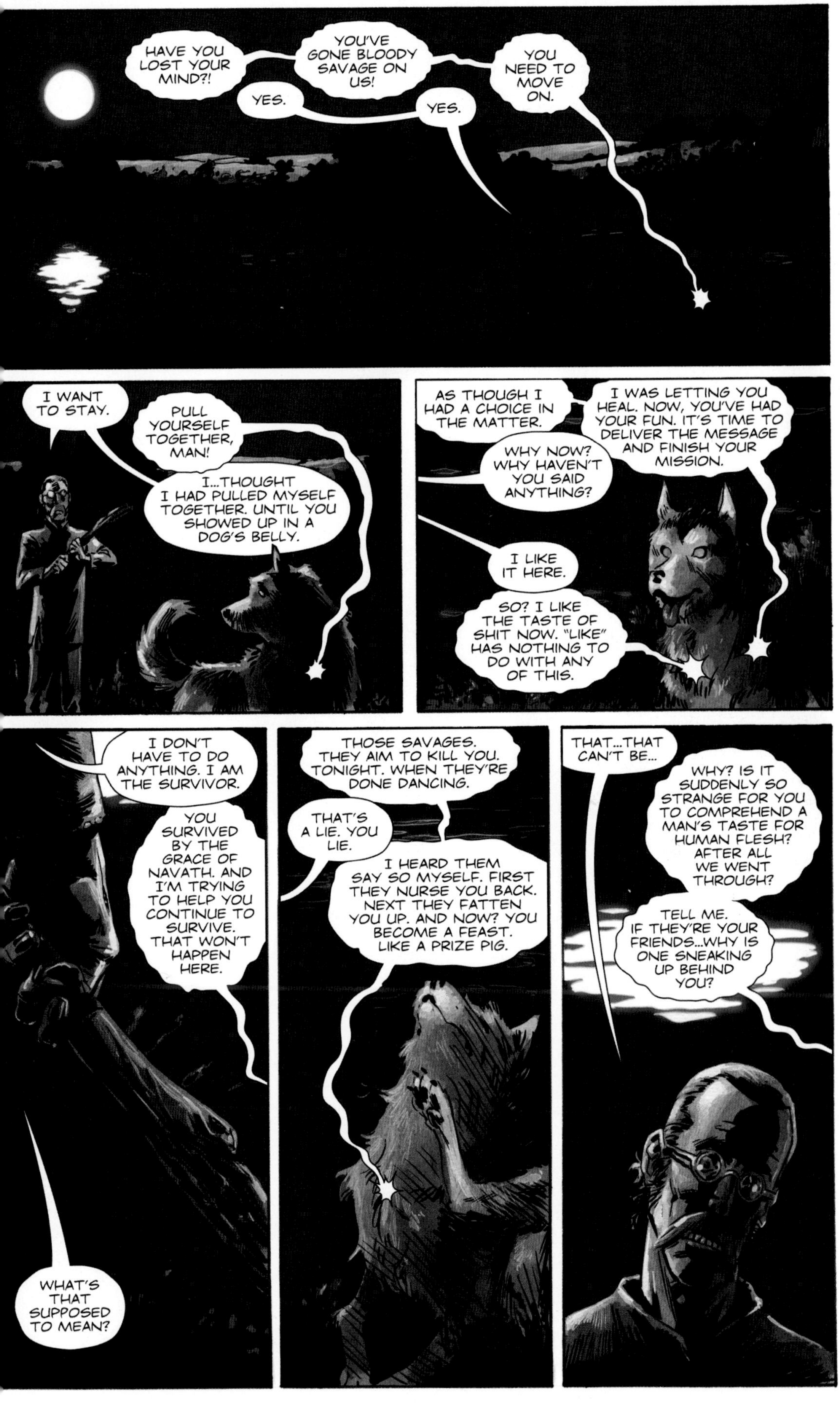
HAVE YOU LOST YOUR MIND?!
YOU'VE GONE BLOODY SAVAGE ON US!
YOU NEED TO MOVE ON.
YES.
YES.
I WANT TO STAY.
PULL YOURSELF TOGETHER, MAN!
I...THOUGHT I HAD PULLED MYSELF TOGETHER. UNTIL YOU SHOWED UP IN A DOG'S BELLY.
AS THOUGH I HAD A CHOICE IN THE MATTER.
I WAS LETTING YOU HEAL. NOW, YOU'VE HAD YOUR FUN. IT'S TIME TO DELIVER THE MESSAGE AND FINISH YOUR MISSION.
WHY NOW? WHY HAVEN'T YOU SAID ANYTHING?
I LIKE IT HERE.
SO? I LIKE THE TASTE OF SHIT NOW. "LIKE" HAS NOTHING TO DO WITH ANY OF THIS.
I DON'T HAVE TO DO ANYTHING. I AM THE SURVIVOR.
YOU SURVIVED BY THE GRACE OF NAVATH. AND I'M TRYING TO HELP YOU CONTINUE TO SURVIVE. THAT WON'T HAPPEN HERE.
WHAT'S THAT SUPPOSED TO MEAN?
THOSE SAVAGES. THEY AIM TO KILL YOU. TONIGHT. WHEN THEY'RE DONE DANCING.
THAT'S A LIE. YOU LIE.
I HEARD THEM SAY SO MYSELF. FIRST THEY NURSE YOU BACK. NEXT THEY FATTEN YOU UP. AND NOW? YOU BECOME A FEAST. LIKE A PRIZE PIG.
THAT...THAT CAN'T BE...
WHY? IS IT SUDDENLY SO STRANGE FOR YOU TO COMPREHEND A MAN'S TASTE FOR HUMAN FLESH? AFTER ALL WE WENT THROUGH?
TELL ME. IF THEY'RE YOUR FRIENDS...WHY IS ONE SNEAKING UP BEHIND YOU?

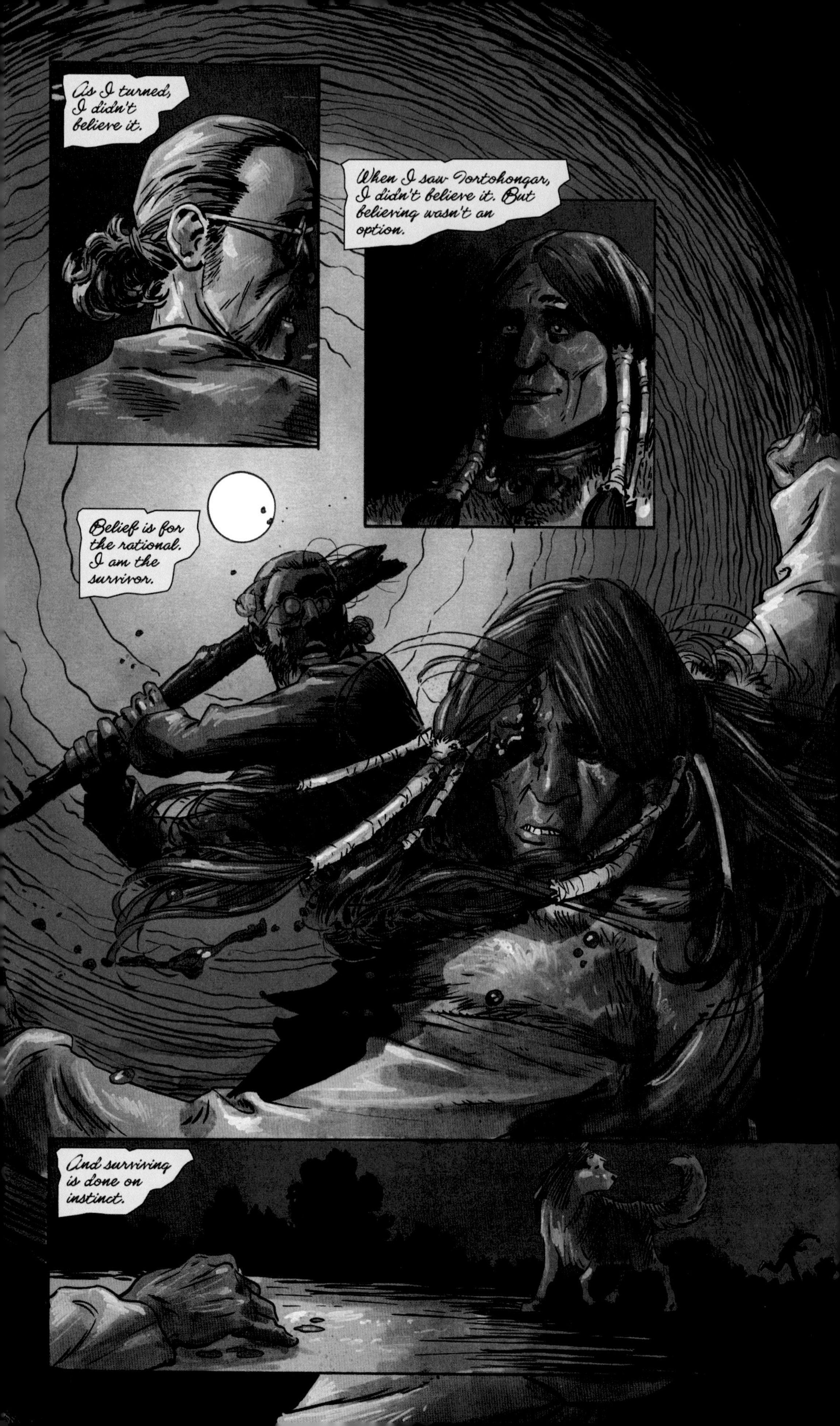
As I turned, I didn't believe it.
When I saw Tortohongar, I didn't believe it. But believing wasn't an option.
Belief is for the rational. I am the survivor.
And surviving is done on instinct.

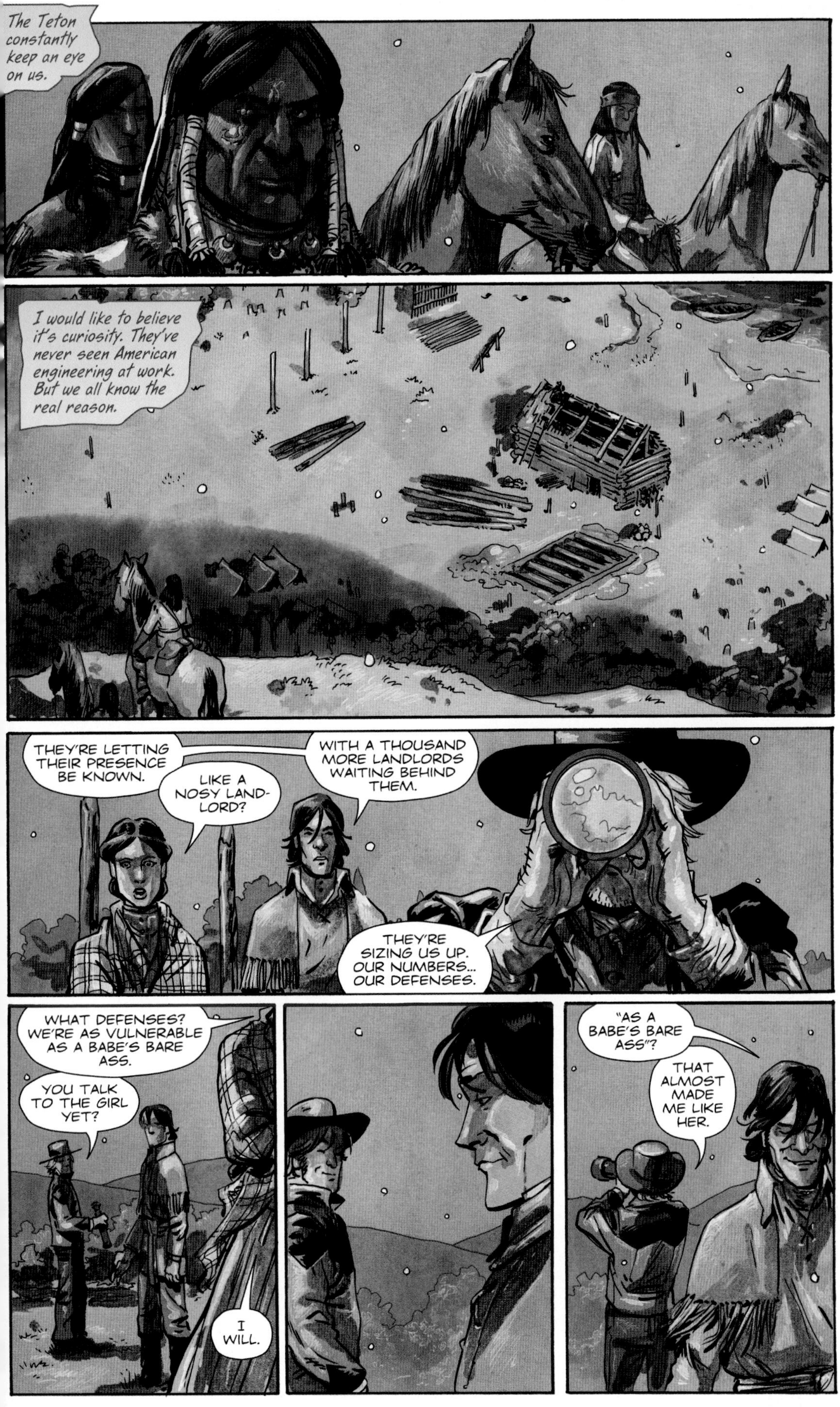
The Teton constantly keep an eye on us.
I would like to believe it's curiosity. They've never seen American engineering at work. But we all know the real reason.
THEY'RE LETTING THEIR PRESENCE BE KNOWN.
LIKE A NOSY LAND-LORD?
WITH A THOUSAND MORE LANDLORDS WAITING BEHIND THEM.
THEY'RE SIZING US UP. OUR NUMBERS... OUR DEFENSES.
WHAT DEFENSES? WE'RE AS VULNERABLE AS A BABE'S BARE ASS.
YOU TALK TO THE GIRL YET?
I WILL.
"AS A BABE'S BARE ASS"?
THAT ALMOST MADE ME LIKE HER.

I have half the mind to thank the Teton. Their presence, while intimidating, helped provide motivation for the men to build their safety.

YESSIR!

WORK FASTER, COLLINS! THIS FORT'LL BE THE ONLY THING BETWEEN US AND THE POINT OF AN ARROW!

YOU REALLY THINK THOSE INDIANS AIM TO KILL US, SERGEANT BURTON?

NAH, BOY. IF THEY WERE GONNA DO US IN, THEY'D BE DOING IT NOW.

Though each man seemed to find his own reason to push forward.

YOU WORK FAST, RANDOLPH! I'M IMPRESSED.

JUST WANNA BUILD A PLACE TO CRAWL IN 'FORE WINTER HITS. I'D ALMOST CHOOSE HAVING MY BALLS RIPPED OFF BY A CYCLOPS THAN FROZEN SOLID BY JACK FROST.

HA!

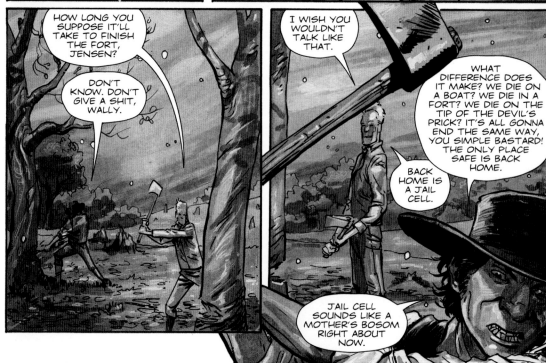

HOW LONG YOU SUPPOSE IT'LL TAKE TO FINISH THE FORT, JENSEN?

DON'T KNOW. DON'T GIVE A SHIT, WALLY.

I WISH YOU WOULDN'T TALK LIKE THAT.

WHAT DIFFERENCE DOES IT MAKE? WE DIE ON A BOAT? WE DIE IN A FORT? WE DIE ON THE TIP OF THE DEVIL'S PRICK? IT'S ALL GONNA END THE SAME WAY, YOU SIMPLE BASTARD! THE ONLY PLACE SAFE IS BACK HOME.

BACK HOME IS A JAIL CELL.

JAIL CELL SOUNDS LIKE A MOTHER'S BOSOM RIGHT ABOUT NOW.

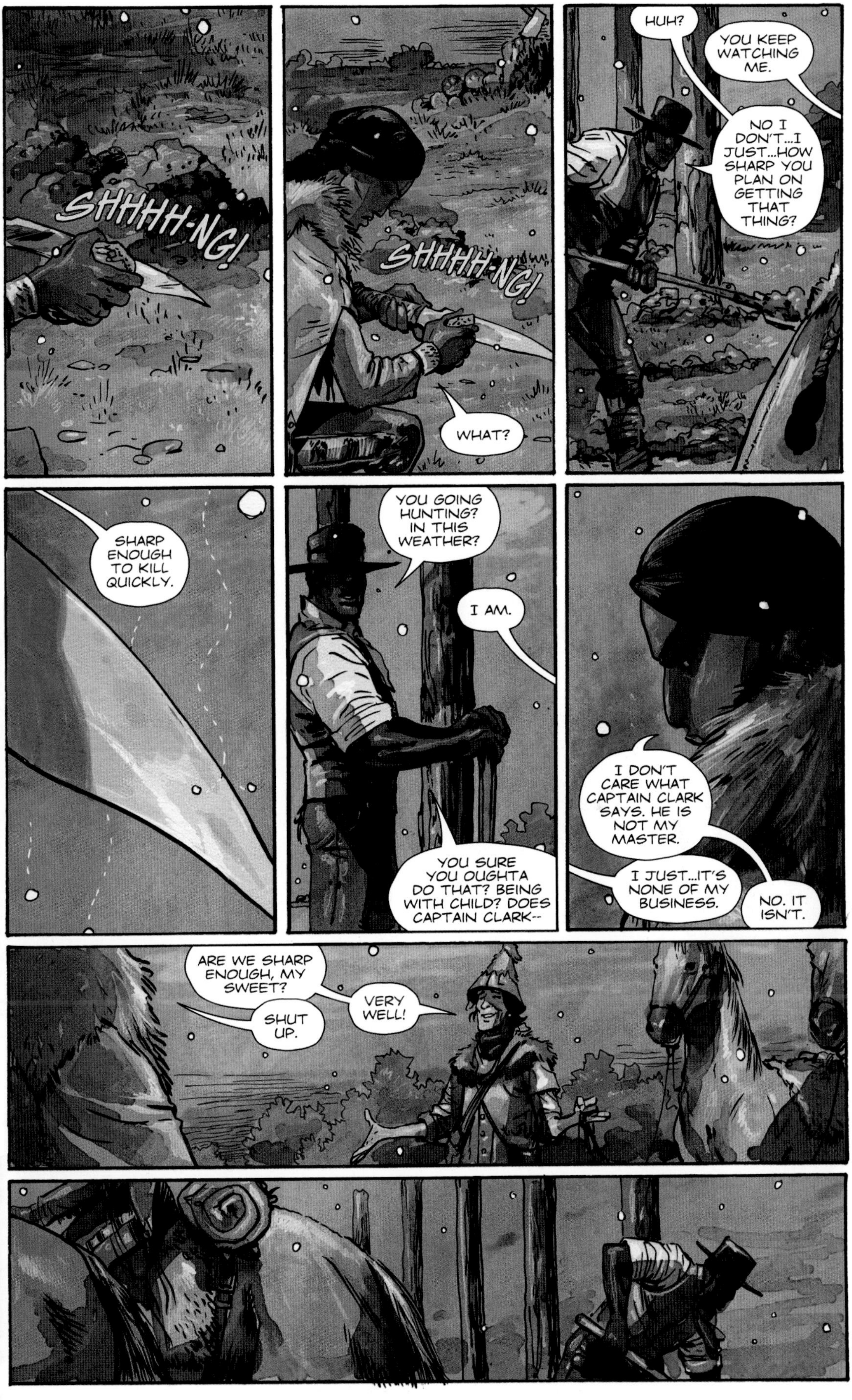
SHHHH-NG!
SHHHH-NG!
WHAT?
HUH?
YOU KEEP WATCHING ME.
NO I DON'T...I JUST...HOW SHARP YOU PLAN ON GETTING THAT THING?
SHARP ENOUGH TO KILL QUICKLY.
YOU GOING HUNTING? IN THIS WEATHER?
I AM.
YOU SURE YOU OUGHTA DO THAT? BEING WITH CHILD? DOES CAPTAIN CLARK--
I DON'T CARE WHAT CAPTAIN CLARK SAYS. HE IS NOT MY MASTER.
I JUST...IT'S NONE OF MY BUSINESS.
NO. IT ISN'T.
ARE WE SHARP ENOUGH, MY SWEET?
VERY WELL!
SHUT UP.

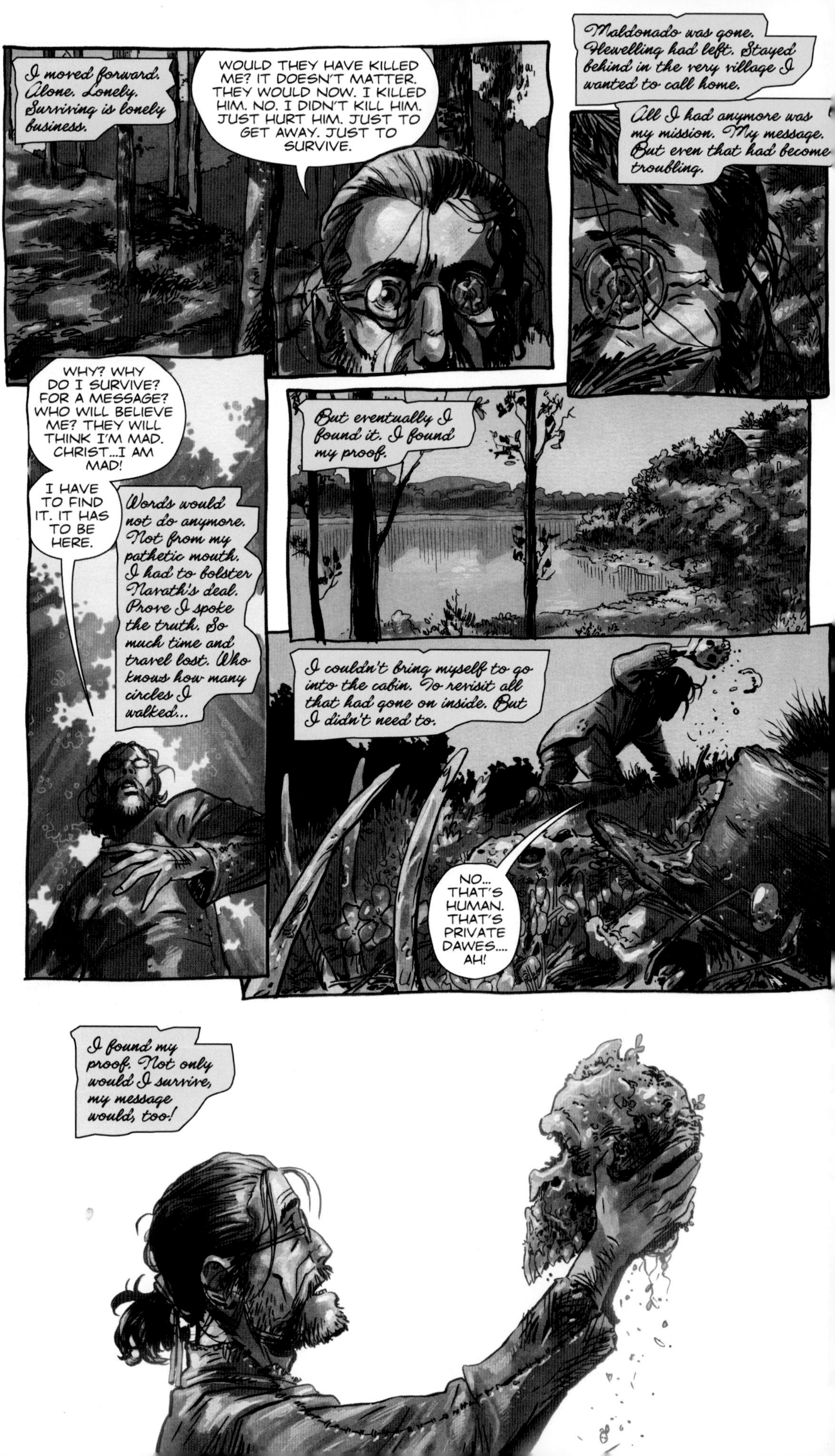
I moved forward. Alone. Lonely. Surviving is lonely business.
WOULD THEY HAVE KILLED ME? IT DOESN'T MATTER. THEY WOULD NOW. I KILLED HIM. NO. I DIDN'T KILL HIM. JUST HURT HIM. JUST TO GET AWAY. JUST TO SURVIVE.
Maldonado was gone. Flewelling had left. Stayed behind in the very village I wanted to call home.
All I had anymore was my mission. My message. But even that had become troubling.
WHY? WHY DO I SURVIVE? FOR A MESSAGE? WHO WILL BELIEVE ME? THEY WILL THINK I'M MAD. CHRIST...I AM MAD!
I HAVE TO FIND IT. IT HAS TO BE HERE.
Words would not do anymore. Not from my pathetic mouth. I had to bolster Narath's deal. Prove I spoke the truth. So much time and travel lost. Who knows how many circles I walked...
But eventually I found it. I found my proof.
I couldn't bring myself to go into the cabin. To revisit all that had gone on inside. But I didn't need to.
NO... THAT'S HUMAN. THAT'S PRIVATE DAWES.... AH!
I found my proof. Not only would I survive, my message would, too!

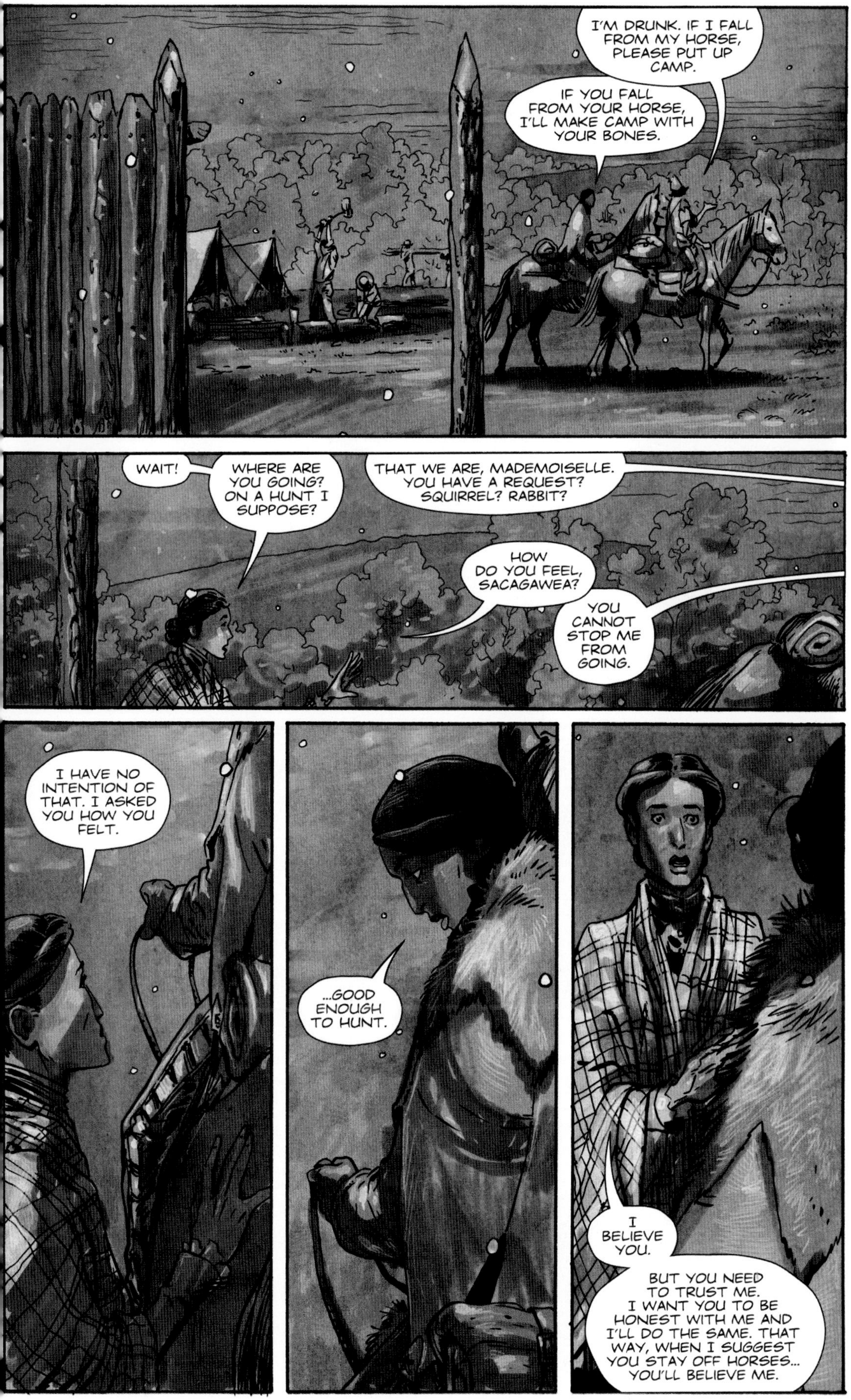
I'M DRUNK. IF I FALL FROM MY HORSE, PLEASE PUT UP CAMP.
IF YOU FALL FROM YOUR HORSE, I'LL MAKE CAMP WITH YOUR BONES.
WAIT!
WHERE ARE YOU GOING? ON A HUNT I SUPPOSE?
THAT WE ARE, MADEMOISELLE. YOU HAVE A REQUEST? SQUIRREL? RABBIT?
HOW DO YOU FEEL, SACAGAWEA?
YOU CANNOT STOP ME FROM GOING.
I HAVE NO INTENTION OF THAT. I ASKED YOU HOW YOU FELT.
...GOOD ENOUGH TO HUNT.
I BELIEVE YOU.
BUT YOU NEED TO TRUST ME. I WANT YOU TO BE HONEST WITH ME AND I'LL DO THE SAME. THAT WAY, WHEN I SUGGEST YOU STAY OFF HORSES... YOU'LL BELIEVE ME.

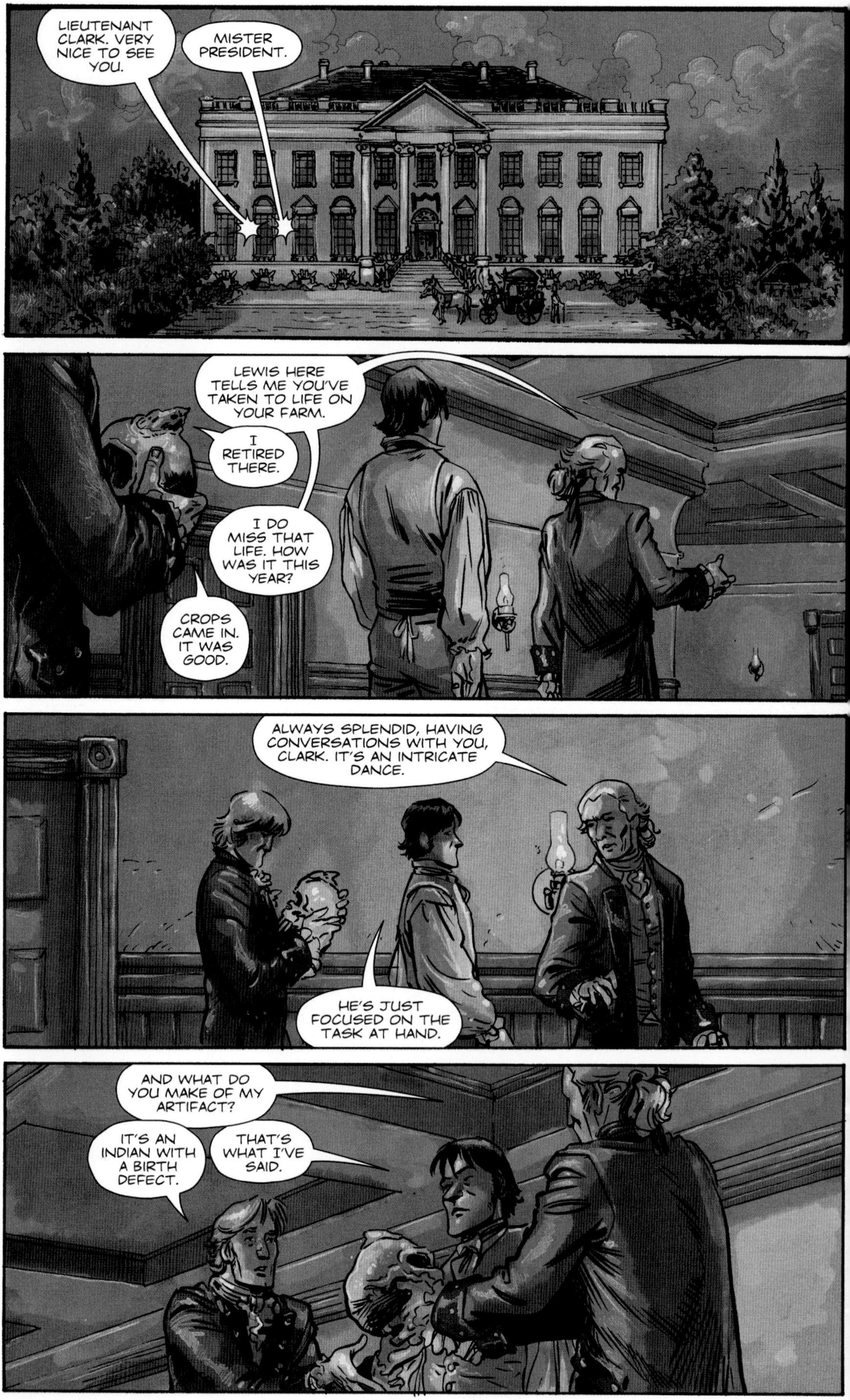
LIEUTENANT CLARK. VERY NICE TO SEE YOU.
MISTER PRESIDENT.
LEWIS HERE TELLS ME YOU'VE TAKEN TO LIFE ON YOUR FARM.
I RETIRED THERE.
I DO MISS THAT LIFE. HOW WAS IT THIS YEAR?
CROPS CAME IN. IT WAS GOOD.
ALWAYS SPLENDID, HAVING CONVERSATIONS WITH YOU, CLARK. IT'S AN INTRICATE DANCE.
HE'S JUST FOCUSED ON THE TASK AT HAND.
AND WHAT DO YOU MAKE OF MY ARTIFACT?
IT'S AN INDIAN WITH A BIRTH DEFECT.
THAT'S WHAT I'VE SAID.

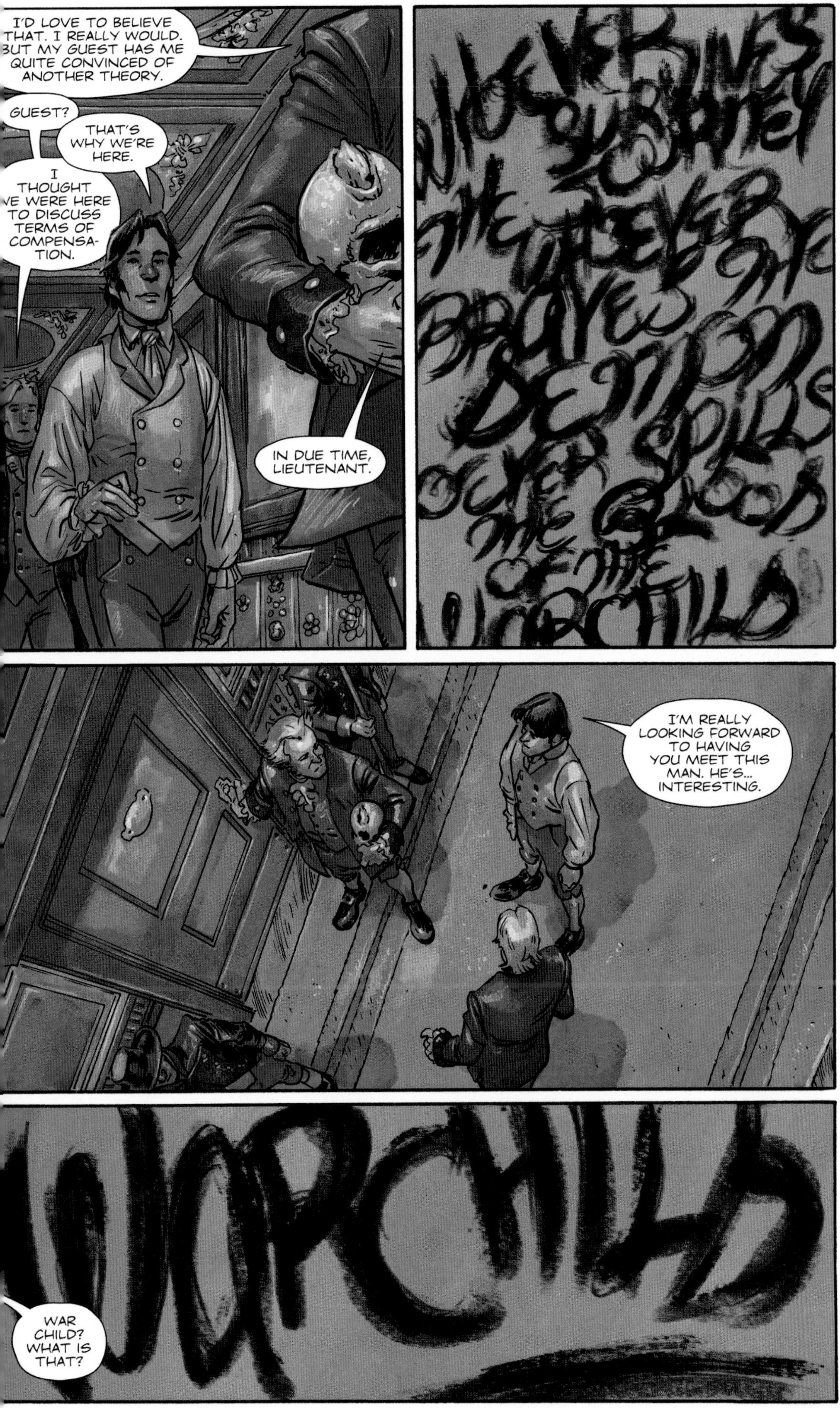
I'D LOVE TO BELIEVE THAT. I REALLY WOULD. BUT MY GUEST HAS ME QUITE CONVINCED OF ANOTHER THEORY.
GUEST?
THAT'S WHY WE'RE HERE.
I THOUGHT WE WERE HERE TO DISCUSS TERMS OF COMPENSATION.
IN DUE TIME, LIEUTENANT.
I'M REALLY LOOKING FORWARD TO HAVING YOU MEET THIS MAN. HE'S... INTERESTING.
WAR CHILD? WHAT IS THAT?

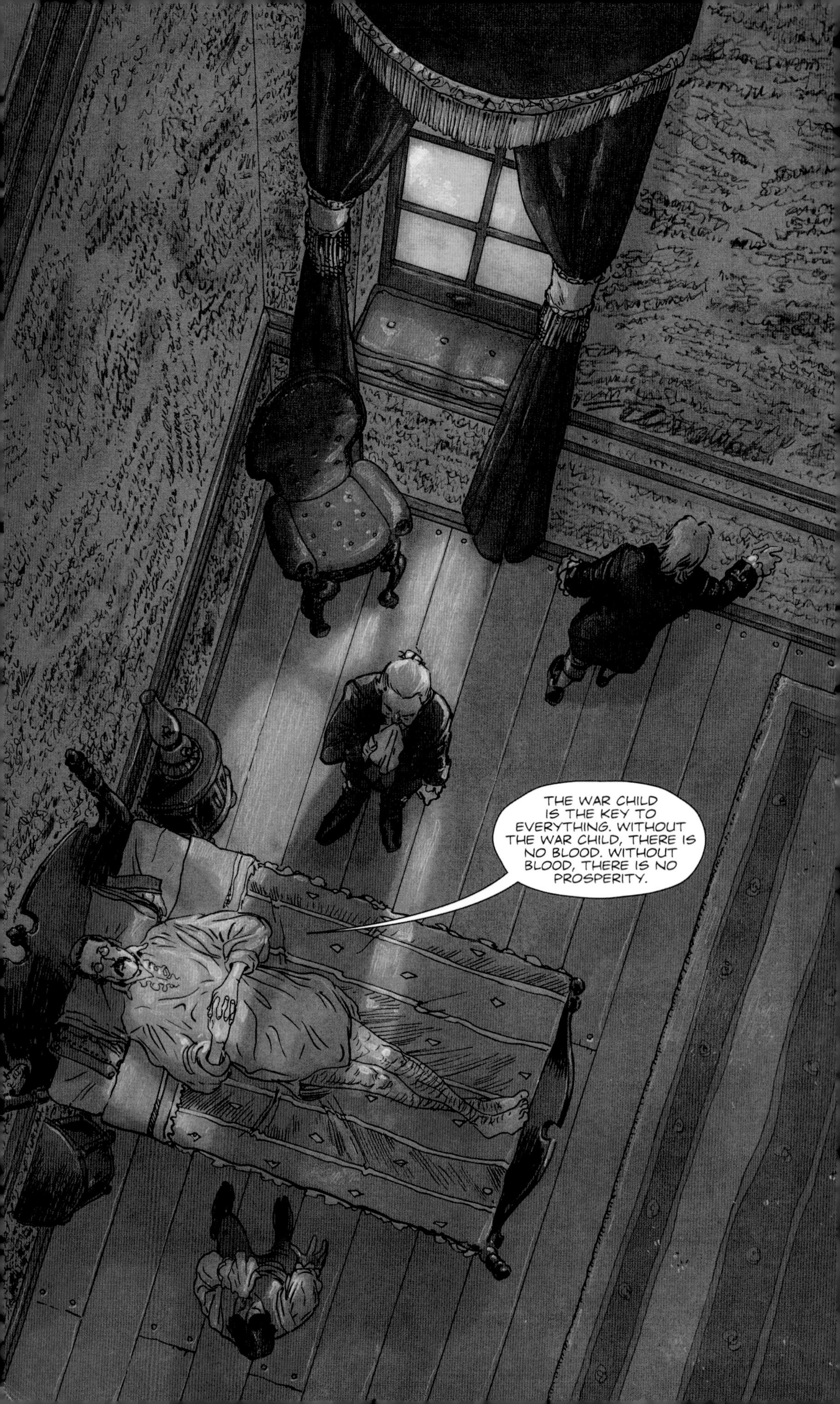
THE WAR CHILD IS THE KEY TO EVERYTHING. WITHOUT THE WAR CHILD, THERE IS NO BLOOD. WITHOUT BLOOD, THERE IS NO PROSPERITY.

I SEE. BUT WHY DID YOU STOP WRITING AFTER THAT WORD?

THEY TOOK AWAY MY PENCIL.

YOUR PENCIL WAS EXCREMENT.

THAT EXPLAINS THE SMELL.

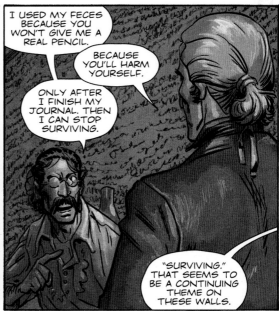

I USED MY FECES BECAUSE YOU WON'T GIVE ME A REAL PENCIL.

BECAUSE YOU'LL HARM YOURSELF.

ONLY AFTER I FINISH MY JOURNAL. THEN I CAN STOP SURVIVING.

"SURVIVING." THAT SEEMS TO BE A CONTINUING THEME ON THESE WALLS.

CAPTAIN HELM. YOU DON'T HAVE TO WRITE ANYMORE. YOU CAN JUST TELL US. TELL LIEUTENANT CLARK ABOUT YOUR DEMON.

NAVATH?

YES. TELL HIM ABOUT NAVATH.

THEN I CAN DIE?

MAYBE. IF YOU WISH.

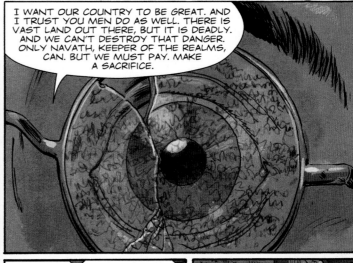

I WANT OUR COUNTRY TO BE GREAT. AND I TRUST YOU MEN DO AS WELL. THERE IS VAST LAND OUT THERE, BUT IT IS DEADLY. AND WE CAN'T DESTROY THAT DANGER. ONLY NAVATH, KEEPER OF THE REALMS, CAN. BUT WE MUST PAY. MAKE A SACRIFICE.

AND WHAT KIND OF SACRIFICE IS THAT?

THE BLOOD OF THE WAR CHILD. WHICHEVER ANTAGONIST SPILLS THE BLOOD OF THE WAR CHILD SHALL WIN THE WAR AND RULE THE LAND.

WHICHEVER SIDE? WAR? WE AREN'T AT WAR.

COME NOW, LIEUTENANT...

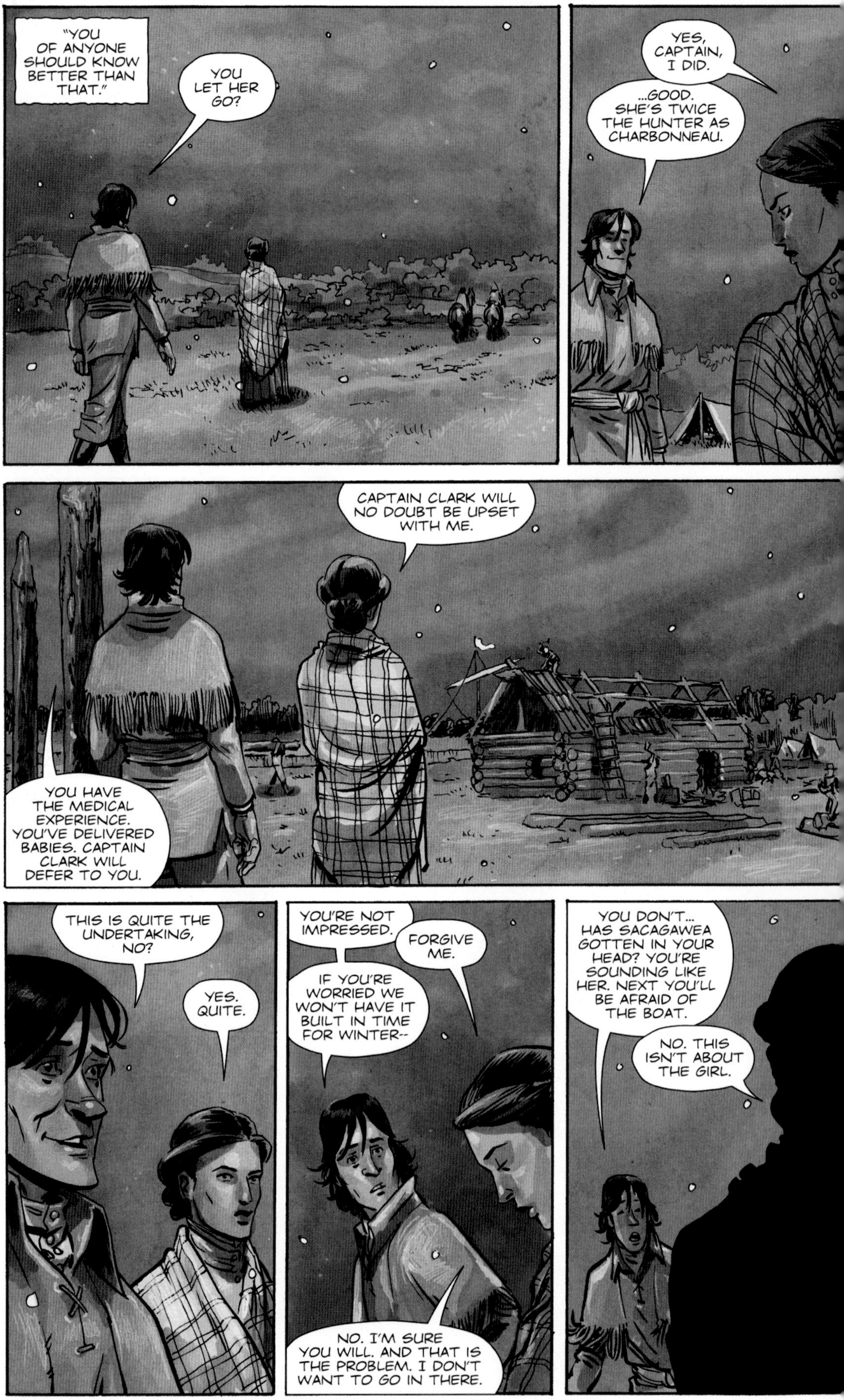
"YOU OF ANYONE SHOULD KNOW BETTER THAN THAT."
YOU LET HER GO?
YES, CAPTAIN, I DID.
...GOOD. SHE'S TWICE THE HUNTER AS CHARBONNEAU.
CAPTAIN CLARK WILL NO DOUBT BE UPSET WITH ME.
YOU HAVE THE MEDICAL EXPERIENCE. YOU'VE DELIVERED BABIES. CAPTAIN CLARK WILL DEFER TO YOU.
THIS IS QUITE THE UNDERTAKING, NO?
YES. QUITE.
YOU'RE NOT IMPRESSED.
FORGIVE ME.
IF YOU'RE WORRIED WE WON'T HAVE IT BUILT IN TIME FOR WINTER--
NO. I'M SURE YOU WILL. AND THAT IS THE PROBLEM. I DON'T WANT TO GO IN THERE.
YOU DON'T... HAS SACAGAWEA GOTTEN IN YOUR HEAD? YOU'RE SOUNDING LIKE HER. NEXT YOU'LL BE AFRAID OF THE BOAT.
NO. THIS ISN'T ABOUT THE GIRL.

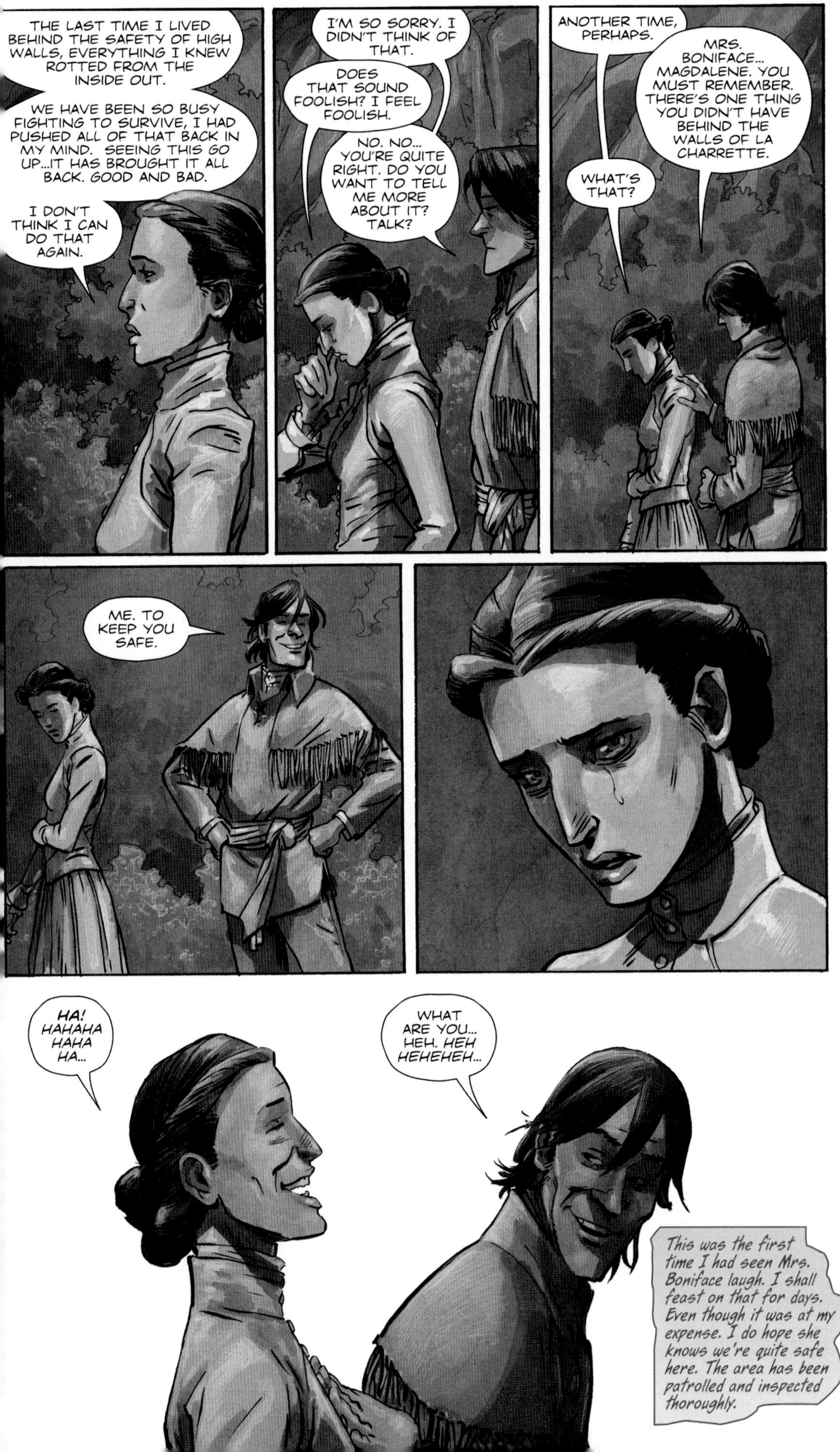
THE LAST TIME I LIVED BEHIND THE SAFETY OF HIGH WALLS, EVERYTHING I KNEW ROTTED FROM THE INSIDE OUT.
WE HAVE BEEN SO BUSY FIGHTING TO SURVIVE, I HAD PUSHED ALL OF THAT BACK IN MY MIND. SEEING THIS GO UP...IT HAS BROUGHT IT ALL BACK. GOOD AND BAD.
I DON'T THINK I CAN DO THAT AGAIN.
I'M SO SORRY. I DIDN'T THINK OF THAT.
DOES THAT SOUND FOOLISH? I FEEL FOOLISH.
NO. NO... YOU'RE QUITE RIGHT. DO YOU WANT TO TELL ME MORE ABOUT IT? TALK?
ANOTHER TIME, PERHAPS.
MRS. BONIFACE... MAGDALENE. YOU MUST REMEMBER. THERE'S ONE THING YOU DIDN'T HAVE BEHIND THE WALLS OF LA CHARRETTE.
WHAT'S THAT?
ME. TO KEEP YOU SAFE.
HA! HAHAHA HAHA HA...
WHAT ARE YOU... HEH. HEH HEHEHEH...
This was the first time I had seen Mrs. Boniface laugh. I shall feast on that for days. Even though it was at my expense. I do hope she knows we're quite safe here. The area has been patrolled and inspected thoroughly.

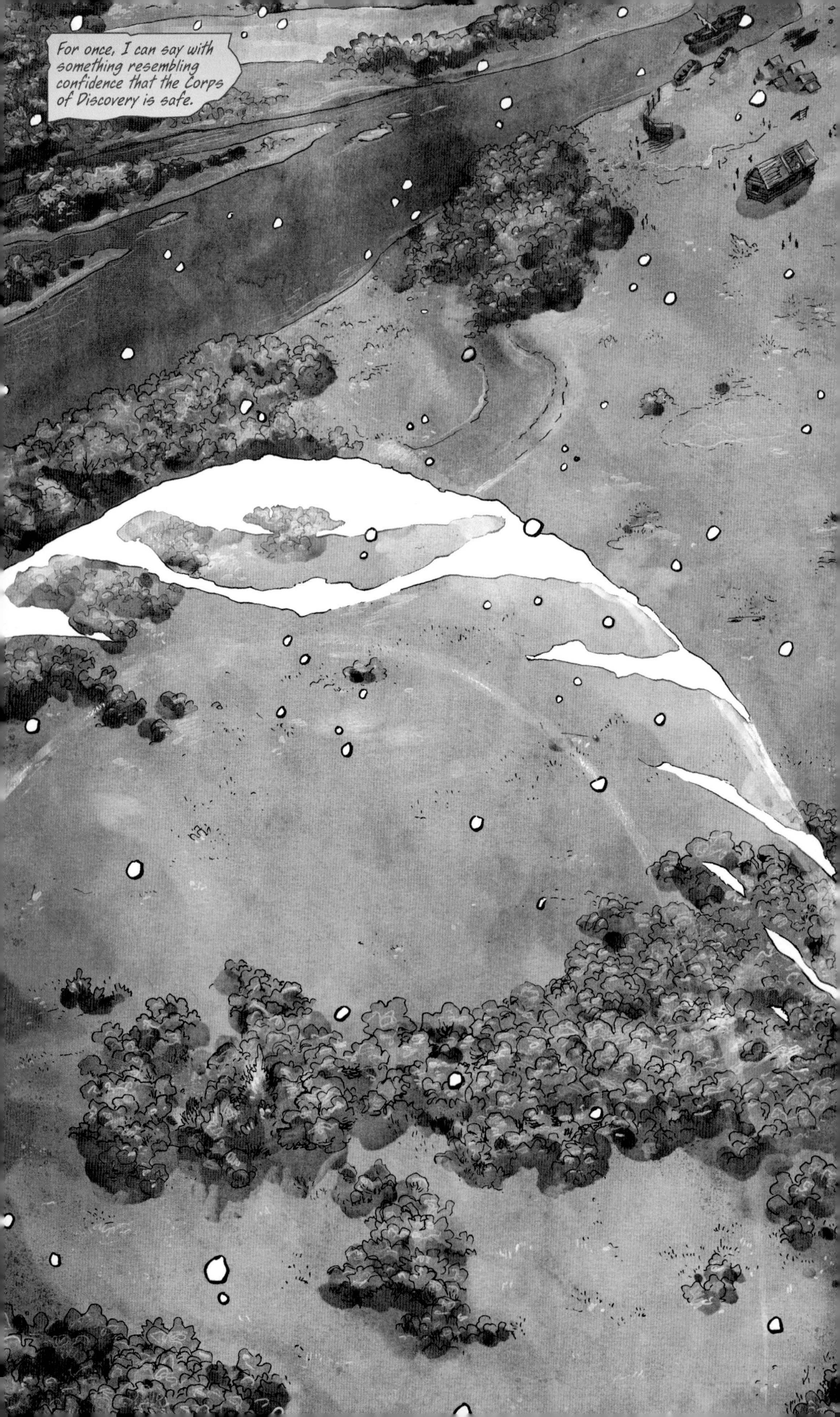
For once, I can say with something resembling confidence that the Corps of Discovery is safe.

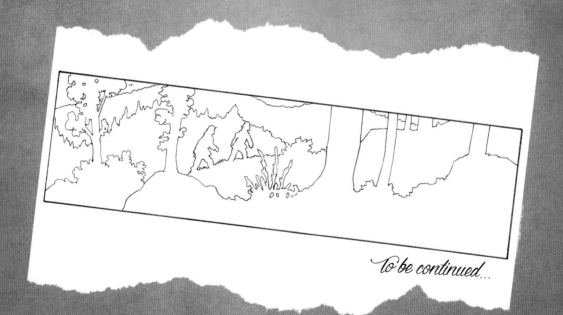

To be continued...

For more tales from Robert Kirkman and Skybound

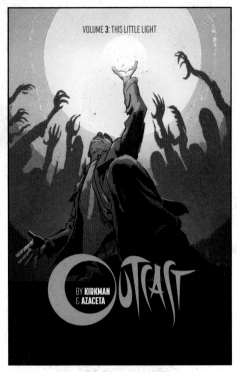

VOLUME 3: THIS LITTLE LIGHT
OUTCAST
BY KIRKMAN & AZACETA

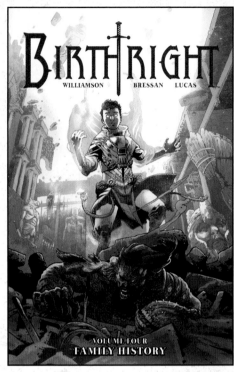

BIRTHRIGHT
WILLIAMSON BRESSAN LUCAS
VOLUME FOUR
FAMILY HISTORY

VOL. 1: A DARKNESS SURROUNDS HIM TP
ISBN: 978-1-63215-053-0
$9.99

VOL. 2: A VAST AND UNENDING RUIN TP
ISBN: 978-1-63215-448-4
$14.99

VOL. 3: THIS LITTLE LIGHT TP
ISBN: 978-1-63215-693-8
$14.99

VOL. 1: HOMECOMING TP
ISBN: 978-1-63215-231-2
$9.99

VOL. 2: CALL TO ADVENTURE TP
ISBN: 978-1-63215-446-0
$12.99

VOL. 3: ALLIES AND ENEMIES TP
ISBN: 978-1-63215-683-9
$12.99

VOL. 4: FAMILY HISTORY TP
ISBN: 978-1-63215-871-0
$12.99

CLONE
VOLUME 4
FOURTH GENERATION

WILLIAMSON · LACI · RYP · MRVA
GHOSTED
VOLUME FOUR · GHOST TOWN

BRANDON SEIFERT
LUKAS KETNER
ANDY TROY

THIEF OF THIEVES
VOLUME 5
"TAKE ME."

VOL. 1: FIRST GENERATION TP
ISBN: 978-1-60706-683-5
$12.99

VOL. 2: SECOND GENERATION TP
ISBN: 978-1-60706-830-3
$12.99

VOL. 3: THIRD GENERATION TP
ISBN: 978-1-60706-939-3
$12.99

VOL. 4: FOURTH GENERATION TP
ISBN: 978-1-63215-036-3
$12.99

VOL. 1: HAUNTED HEIST TP
ISBN: 978-1-60706-836-5
$9.99

VOL. 2: BOOKS OF THE DEAD TP
ISBN: 978-1-63215-046-2
$12.99

VOL. 3: DEATH WISH TP
ISBN: 978-1-63215-051-6
$12.99

VOL. 4: GHOST TOWN TP
ISBN: 978-1-63215-317-3
$12.99

VOL. 1: FLORA & FAUNA TP
ISBN: 978-1-60706-982-9
$9.99

VOL. 2: AMPHIBIA & INSECTA TP
ISBN: 978-1-63215-052-3
$14.99

VOL. 3: CHIROPTERA & CARNIFORMAVES TP
ISBN: 978-1-63215-397-5
$14.99

VOL. 1: "I QUIT."
ISBN: 978-1-60706-592-0
$14.99

VOL. 2: "HELP ME."
ISBN: 978-1-60706-676-7
$14.99

VOL. 3: "VENICE."
ISBN: 978-1-60706-844-0
$14.99

VOL. 4: "THE HIT LIST."
ISBN: 978-1-63215-037-0
$14.99

VOL. 5: "TAKE ME."
ISBN: 978-1-63215-401-9
$14.99

FOR MORE OF THE WALKING DEAD

TRADE PAPERBACKS

VOL. 1: DAYS GONE BYE TP
ISBN: 978-1-58240-672-5
$14.99
VOL. 2: MILES BEHIND US TP
ISBN: 978-1-58240-775-3
$14.99
VOL. 3: SAFETY BEHIND BARS TP
ISBN: 978-1-58240-805-7
$14.99
VOL. 4: THE HEART'S DESIRE TP
ISBN: 978-1-58240-530-8
$14.99
VOL. 5: THE BEST DEFENSE TP
ISBN: 978-1-58240-612-1
$14.99
VOL. 6: THIS SORROWFUL LIFE TP
ISBN: 978-1-58240-684-8
$14.99
VOL. 7: THE CALM BEFORE TP
ISBN: 978-1-58240-828-6
$14.99
VOL. 8: MADE TO SUFFER TP
ISBN: 978-1-58240-883-5
$14.99
VOL. 9: HERE WE REMAIN TP
ISBN: 978-1-60706-022-2
$14.99
VOL. 10: WHAT WE BECOME TP
ISBN: 978-1-60706-075-8
$14.99
VOL. 11: FEAR THE HUNTERS TP
ISBN: 978-1-60706-181-6
$14.99
VOL. 12: LIFE AMONG THEM TP
ISBN: 978-1-60706-254-7
$14.99
VOL. 13: TOO FAR GONE TP
ISBN: 978-1-60706-329-2
$14.99
VOL. 14: NO WAY OUT TP
ISBN: 978-1-60706-392-6
$14.99
VOL. 15: WE FIND OURSELVES TP
ISBN: 978-1-60706-440-4
$14.99
VOL. 16: A LARGER WORLD TP
ISBN: 978-1-60706-559-3
$14.99
VOL. 17: SOMETHING TO FEAR TP
ISBN: 978-1-60706-615-6
$14.99
VOL. 18: WHAT COMES AFTER TP
ISBN: 978-1-60706-687-3
$14.99
VOL. 19: MARCH TO WAR TP
ISBN: 978-1-60706-818-1
$14.99
VOL. 20: ALL OUT WAR PART ONE TP
ISBN: 978-1-60706-882-2
$14.99
VOL. 21: ALL OUT WAR PART TWO TP
ISBN: 978-1-63215-030-1
$14.99
VOL. 22: A NEW BEGINNING TP
ISBN: 978-1-63215-041-7
$14.99
VOL. 23: WHISPERS INTO SCREAMS TP
ISBN: 978-1-63215-258-9
$14.99
VOL. 24: LIFE AND DEATH TP
ISBN: 978-1-63215-402-6
$14.99
VOL. 25: NO TURNING BACK TP
ISBN: 978-1-63215-612-9
$14.99
VOL. 26: CALL TO ARMS TP
ISBN: 978-1-63215-917-5
$14.99
VOL. 1: SPANISH EDITION TP
ISBN: 978-1-60706-797-9
$14.99
VOL. 2: SPANISH EDITION TP
ISBN: 978-1-60706-845-7
$14.99
VOL. 3: SPANISH EDITION TP
ISBN: 978-1-60706-883-9
$14.99
VOL. 4: SPANISH EDITION TP
ISBN: 978-1-63215-035-6
$14.99

HARDCOVERS

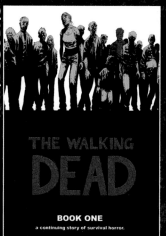

BOOK ONE HC
ISBN: 978-1-58240-619-0
$34.99
BOOK TWO HC
ISBN: 978-1-58240-698-5
$34.99
BOOK THREE HC
ISBN: 978-1-58240-825-5
$34.99
BOOK FOUR HC
ISBN: 978-1-60706-000-0
$34.99
BOOK FIVE HC
ISBN: 978-1-60706-171-7
$34.99
BOOK SIX HC
ISBN: 978-1-60706-327-8
$34.99
BOOK SEVEN HC
ISBN: 978-1-60706-439-8
$34.99
BOOK EIGHT HC
ISBN: 978-1-60706-593-7
$34.99
BOOK NINE HC
ISBN: 978-1-60706-798-6
$34.99
BOOK TEN HC
ISBN: 978-1-63215-034-9
$34.99
BOOK ELEVEN HC
ISBN: 978-1-63215-271-8
$34.99
BOOK TWELVE HC
ISBN: 978-1-63215-451-4
$34.99
BOOK THIRTEEN HC
ISBN: 978-1-63215-916-8
$34.99

COMPENDIUMS

COMPENDIUM TP, VOL. 1
ISBN: 978-1-60706-076-5
$59.99
COMPENDIUM TP, VOL. 2
ISBN: 978-1-60706-596-8
$59.99
COMPENDIUM TP, VOL. 3
ISBN: 978-1-63215-456-9
$59.99

SPECIALTY BOOKS

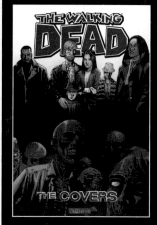

THE WALKING DEAD: THE COVERS, VOL. 1 HC
ISBN: 978-1-60706-002-4
$24.99
THE WALKING DEAD: ALL OUT WAR HC
ISBN: 978-1-63215-038-7
$34.99
THE WALKING DEAD COLORING BOOK
ISBN: 978-1-63215-774-4
$14.99
THE WALKING DEAD RICK GRIMES COLORING BOOK
ISBN: 978-1-5343-0003-3
$14.99

OMNIBUS

OMNIBUS, VOL. 1
ISBN: 978-1-60706-503-6
$100.00
OMNIBUS, VOL. 2
ISBN: 978-1-60706-515-9
$100.00
OMNIBUS, VOL. 3
ISBN: 978-1-60706-330-8
$100.00
OMNIBUS, VOL. 4
ISBN: 978-1-60706-616-3
$100.00
OMNIBUS, VOL. 5
ISBN: 978-1-63215-042-4
$100.00
OMNIBUS, VOL. 6
ISBN: 978-1-63215-521-4
$100.00

FOR MORE OF INVINCIBLE

TRADEPAPERBACKS

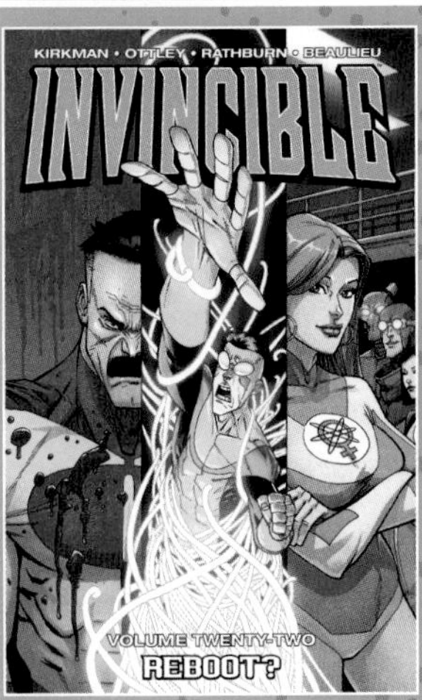
KIRKMAN • OTTLEY • RATHBURN • BEAULIEU
INVINCIBLE
VOLUME TWENTY-TWO
REBOOT?

VOL. 1: FAMILY MATTERS TP
ISBN: 978-1-58240-711-1
$12.99
VOL. 2: EIGHT IS ENOUGH TP
ISBN: 978-1-58240-347-2
$12.99
VOL. 3: PERFECT STRANGERS TP
ISBN: 978-1-58240-793-7
$12.99
VOL. 4: HEAD OF THE CLASS TP
ISBN: 978-1-58240-778-4
$14.99
VOL. 5: THE FACTS OF LIFE TP
ISBN: 978-1-58240-554-4
$14.99
VOL. 6: A DIFFERENT WORLD TP
ISBN: 978-1-58240-579-7
$14.99
VOL. 7: THREE'S COMPANY TP
ISBN: 978-1-58240-656-5
$14.99
VOL. 8: MY FAVORITE MARTIAN TP
ISBN: 978-1-58240-683-1
$16.99
VOL. 9: OUT OF THIS WORLD TP
ISBN: 978-1-58240-827-9
$14.99

VOL. 10: WHO'S THE BOSS TP
ISBN: 978-1-60706-013-0
$16.99
VOL. 11: HAPPY DAYS TP
ISBN: 978-1-60706-062-8
$16.99
VOL. 12: STILL STANDING TP
ISBN: 978-1-60706-166-3
$16.99
VOL. 13: GROWING PAINS TP
ISBN: 978-1-60706-251-6
$16.99
VOL. 14: THE VILTRUMITE WAR TP
ISBN: 978-1-60706-367-4
$19.99
VOL. 15: GET SMART TP
ISBN: 978-1-60706-498-5
$16.99
VOL. 16: FAMILY TIES TP
ISBN: 978-1-60706-579-1
$16.99
VOL. 17: WHAT'S HAPPENING TP
ISBN: 978-1-60706-662-0
$16.99
VOL. 18: DEATH OF EVERYONE TP
ISBN: 978-1-60706-762-7
$16.99

VOL. 19: THE WAR AT HOME TP
ISBN: 978-1-60706-856-3
$16.99
VOL. 20: FRIENDS TP
ISBN: 978-1-63215-043-1
$16.99
VOL. 21: MODERN FAMILY TP
ISBN: 978-1-63215-318-0
$16.99
VOL. 22: REBOOT? TP
ISBN: 978-1-63215-626-6
$16.99

THE OFFICIAL HANDBOOK OF
THE INVINCIBLE UNIVERSE TP
ISBN: 978-1-58240-831-6
$12.99
INVINCIBLE PRESENTS,
VOL. 1: ATOM EVE & REX SPLODE TP
ISBN: 978-1-60706-255-4
$14.99

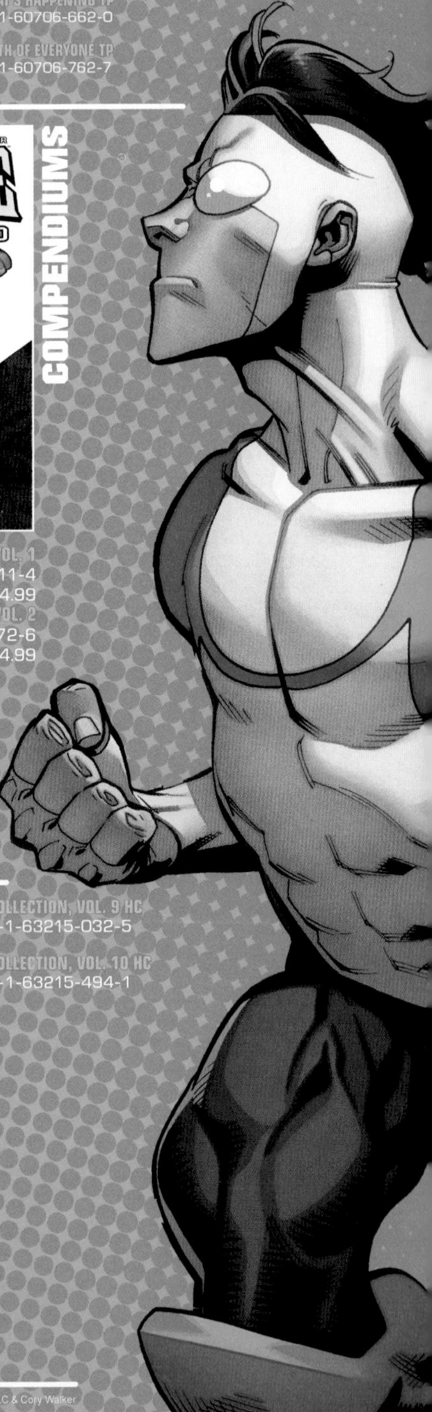

COMPLETE LIBRARY

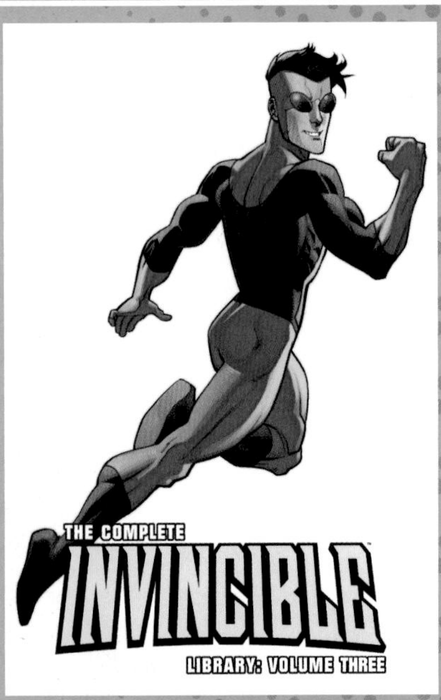
THE COMPLETE
INVINCIBLE
LIBRARY: VOLUME THREE

THE COMPLETE INVINCIBLE LIBRARY, VOL. 2 HC
ISBN: 978-1-60706-112-0
$125.00
THE COMPLETE INVINCIBLE LIBRARY, VOL. 3 HC
ISBN: 978-1-60706-421-3
$125.00

COMPENDIUMS

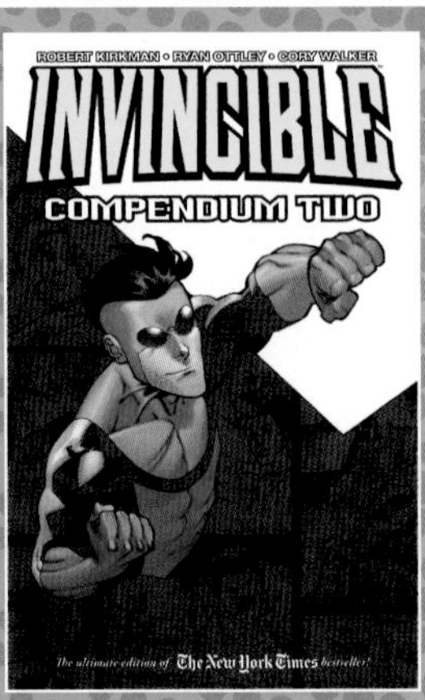
ROBERT KIRKMAN • RYAN OTTLEY • CORY WALKER
INVINCIBLE
COMPENDIUM TWO

COMPENDIUM VOL. 1
ISBN: 978-1-60706-411-4
$64.99
COMPENDIUM VOL. 2
ISBN: 978-1-60706-772-6
$64.99

ULTIMATE COLLECTIONS

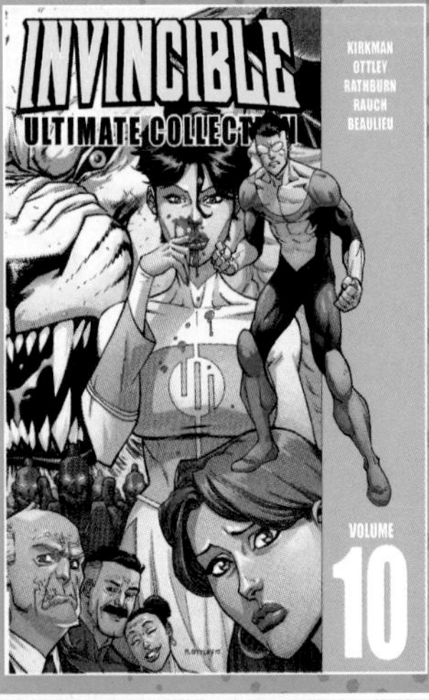
INVINCIBLE
ULTIMATE COLLECTION
KIRKMAN
OTTLEY
RATHBURN
RAUCH
BEAULIEU
VOLUME
10

ULTIMATE COLLECTION, VOL. 1 HC
ISBN 978-1-58240-500-1
$34.99
ULTIMATE COLLECTION, VOL. 2 HC
ISBN: 978-1-58240-594-0
$34.99
ULTIMATE COLLECTION, VOL. 3 HC
ISBN: 978-1-58240-763-0
$34.99
ULTIMATE COLLECTION, VOL. 4 HC
ISBN: 978-1-58240-989-4
$34.99
ULTIMATE COLLECTION, VOL. 5 HC
ISBN: 978-1-60706-116-8
$34.99
ULTIMATE COLLECTION, VOL. 6 HC
ISBN: 978-1-60706-360-5
$34.99
ULTIMATE COLLECTION, VOL. 7 HC
ISBN: 978-1-60706-509-8
$39.99
ULTIMATE COLLECTION, VOL. 8 HC
ISBN: 978-1-60706-680-4
$39.99

ULTIMATE COLLECTION, VOL. 9 HC
ISBN: 978-1-63215-032-5
$39.99
ULTIMATE COLLECTION, VOL. 10 HC
ISBN: 978-1-63215-494-1
$39.99

SKYBOUND INSIDER

Join the **Skybound Insider** program and get updates on all of Skybound's great content including **The Walking Dead**.

- Get a **monthly** newsletter
- **Invites** to members-only events
- **Sneak peeks** of new comics
- **Discounts** on merchandise at the Skybound and Walking Dead online stores.

Membership is **free** and it only takes a minute to sign up.

BECOME A SKYBOUND INSIDER TODAY!
insider.skybound.com

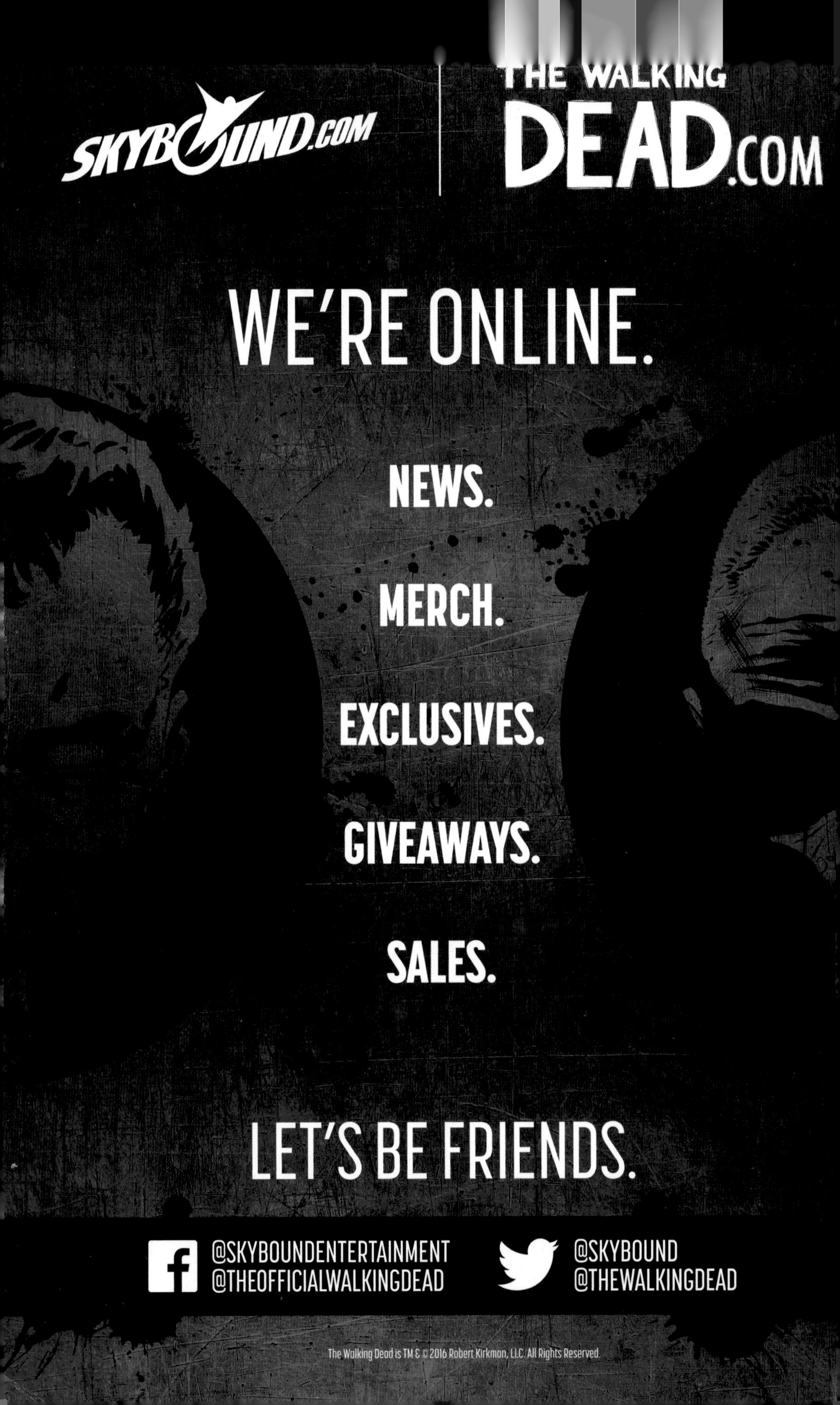
SKYBOUND.COM
THE WALKING DEAD.COM
WE'RE ONLINE.
NEWS.
MERCH.
EXCLUSIVES.
GIVEAWAYS.
SALES.
LET'S BE FRIENDS.
@SKYBOUNDENTERTAINMENT
@THEOFFICIALWALKINGDEAD
@SKYBOUND
@THEWALKINGDEAD
The Walking Dead is TM & © 2016 Robert Kirkman, LLC. All Rights Reserved.